POTTAGES

POT

MIDDLESBROUGH

TOWN AND COMMUNITY 1830–1950

MIDDLESBROUGH

TOWN AND COMMUNITY 1830–1950

Edited by A.J. POLLARD

FOREWORD BY **ASA BRIGGS**

SUTTON PUBLISHING

MIDDLESBROUGH BOROUGH COUNCIL

THE UNIVERSITY OF TEESSIDE

First published in the United Kingdom in 1996 by
Sutton Publishing Ltd · Phoenix Mill
Thrupp · Stroud · Gloucestershire · GL5 2BU
in association with
Middlesbrough Borough Council and The University of Teesside

British Library Cataloguing in Publication Data
A catalogue record for this book is available from the British Library.

ISBN 0-7509-1270-7

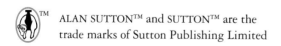 ALAN SUTTON™ and SUTTON™ are the
trade marks of Sutton Publishing Limited

Typeset in 11/12½ Garamond.
Typesetting and origination by
Sutton Publishing Limited.
Printed in Great Britain by
Hartnolls, Bodmin, Cornwall.

CONTENTS

LIST OF ILLUSTRATIONS

Abbreviations used
AJP – Tony Pollard
CA – Cleveland Archives
MCL – Middlesbrough Central Library
JJT – Jim Turner
LP – Linda Polley
RL – Richard Lewis

With thanks to the Ordnance Survey, on whose 1904 (published 1907) map the plans on pp. xiii and xiv are based.

FOREWORD

I am glad to have the opportunity of writing the foreword to this interesting, well-timed volume. With the latest changes in local government areas and structures, it is a good time to look both backwards and forwards in the knowledge that whatever the areas and structures Middlesbrough has retained the sense of a distinctive community. The writers of the different chapters in this volume, approaching their subjects in different ways, are aware of the community interconnections and interactions that link them all. They have all been involved too in the pursuit of local history in the University of Teesside, one community institution which no one foresaw in the nineteenth century when Middlesbrough found its place on the national and international map. The attractive possibility of initiating and fostering studies of local history within an international context has inspired them all, as it has inspired the vice-chancellor of the university who has himself made an important and distinctive contribution to this field of genuinely interdisciplinary study.

When in the early 1960s I wrote my own essay on Middlesbrough, which is reprinted unchanged in this volume, serious urban studies were still in their infancy. I included Middlesbrough in *Victorian Cities*, which presented a series of profiles of different nineteenth-century communities, not only on the grounds of its distinctiveness but also because the story of its rise and the economic and social vicissitudes that it underwent then and subsequently is interesting in itself. I was aware, of course, that all cities, not least Victorian cities, conform to general patterns as well as reveal unique features; and I was aware also that unless both the unique and general influences associated with nineteenth-century urbanization are conjointly taken into account, any version of Victorian history is incomplete.

The scholarly study of both urban history and Victorian history has been transformed since *Victorian Cities* appeared at least as much as the structures and areas of local government. In 1963 there were small groups of urban historians in Britain and in the United States, and I had learnt something from them both, but I had published my *History of Birmingham* in 1952 at a time when there were no such groups. My own personal history as a historian is intimately interwoven with the future of urban history as a field of study. I examined the thesis of H.J. Dyos, who was to pioneer the organization of urban studies in this country from a firm base in Leicester until his death in 1978, and I met Blake McKelvey, American city historian of Rochester (the first such full-time post) in 1953, one year before he joined with my friend Bayrd Still of New York in creating an Urban History Group at an American Historical Association gathering in Chicago. When I wrote of

Middlesborough in *Victorian Cities* I had both Birmingham and Chicago in view. Knowing how important international and intercultural comparisons are I also looked to Melbourne and Ballarat.

Urban historians are now scattered throughout the world, and there is much traffic between them. Strategic developments have shaped demography, and the related history of such subjects as housing has opened up. Like the writers in this volume, urban historians do not follow one single approach. Nor do they share a common purpose. This is a point made by S.J. Mandelbaum in 1985, and it remains as true now as it was then. Fortunately it has never held back the cultivation of the field, but it would be as sad now as it was in the 1970s and 1980s for workers in the field to spend more time arguing with each other about terminology and methodology than in cultivation and communication. No field of study benefits more from joint enterprises between historians and geographers or sociologists. No field lends itself more to communication between professional and 'amateur' historians. This volume draws on such joint work.

Victorian studies benefit too from such modes of communication, and we are now more sophisticated (if not necessarily more knowledgeable) than we were a generation ago in distinguishing between 'fact' and 'rhetoric' in nineteenth-century social and cultural history, and between 'image' and 'reality'. The fashion now is to focus neither on economic nor social history but on cultural history, but just as economic and social history benefited from being bracketed together, so cultural history benefits from a broader convergence of disciplines, including the arts.

I am happy that the Borough of Middlesbrough is directly associated with the university in this venture in unofficial history. I owe a great deal myself to the City of Birmingham, and I am sure that this volume, which is in no sense final, will be followed by other monographs and by other collective volumes. There is never any final version of history, even local history. There is always more to find out and more still to reinterpret. This volume is the start of a journey, therefore, not a journey's end.

Asa Briggs
May 1996

PREFACE

This collection of essays, sponsored jointly by the University of Teesside and the Borough of Middlesbrough, has been brought together to mark the formation of the new unitary authority in 1996. When the old Borough of Middlesbrough was absorbed into the short-lived County Borough of Teesside in 1968, and subsequently the county of Cleveland, few believed that the infant Hercules would ever be reborn. It is fitting, therefore, to mark his rebirth with a reminder of his former life.

The studies in this volume are, with one exception, written by members of staff, former members of staff and former graduate students of the University, all of whom have been associated with an MA in Local History run by the University since 1979. The exception, of course, is Asa Briggs, who, although an honorary doctor of philosophy of the University, is better known for his pioneering essay on the Victorian town first published in 1963. He has kindly given his consent for this essay to be reprinted and additionally written a foreword to the new volume.

The Middlesbrough at the centre of these essays was never a fixed entity. The small coal port of 1830, the incorporated town of 1853 and the Middlesbrough surveyed by Max Lock at the end of the Second World War, while they shared the same name and a dependency on iron and steel-making, were in many other respects quite different communities. The maps on pages xiii and xiv show the extending borough boundaries as expansion south of the railway and towards Newport, then the development of the suburb of Linthorpe and ultimately the planned rehousing of the interwar period took place. Until 1913, however, North Ormesby, a separate new town planted in the mid-nineteenth century, although as close to the original Middlesbrough as Newport, remained in the North Riding. Yet the first parliamentary constituency of Middlesbrough, formed in 1868, included not only North Ormesby but also the expanding industrial settlements of Cargo Fleet, South Bank and Grangetown downstream to the east. The constituency was divided in 1918 to reflect the growth of the town over fifty years. The two new constituencies of Middlesbrough East and Middlesbrough West were brought into line with the borough boundary established in 1913. This meant that Cargo Fleet, South Bank and Grangetown were now excluded from Middlesbrough East. Although the borough boundary was extended further south to Ladgate Lane in 1939, the parliamentary constituencies were not altered again until 1948. Thus, to say nothing of the equally illogical, if largely accidental, pattern of parochial, poor law and quarter session boundaries, the 'Middlesbrough' of this collection differs according to time and context. There may now be a unitary authority, but there was no unitary past.

Finally the editor would like to acknowledge many debts of gratitude: to Professor Fraser and Derek Elsey of the University; to Neil Bennett of Middlesbrough Borough Council; to David Tyrell of Cleveland Archives; to Jenny Parker and Richard Pears of Cleveland, now once again Middlesbrough Central Library; to Hilary Wade at the Dorman Museum; to Roger Thorp, Jane Crompton and Anne Bennett of Sutton Publishing; and to all the authors who strove might and main successfully to deliver their typescripts on schedule.

A.J. Pollard
August 1996

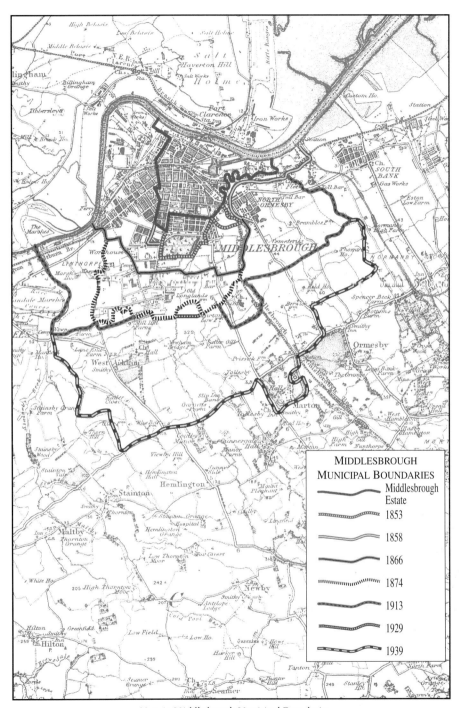

MIDDLESBROUGH
MUNICIPAL BOUNDARIES

	Middlesbrough Estate
	1853
	1858
	1866
	1874
	1913
	1929
	1939

Map 1: Middlesbrough Municipal Boundaries

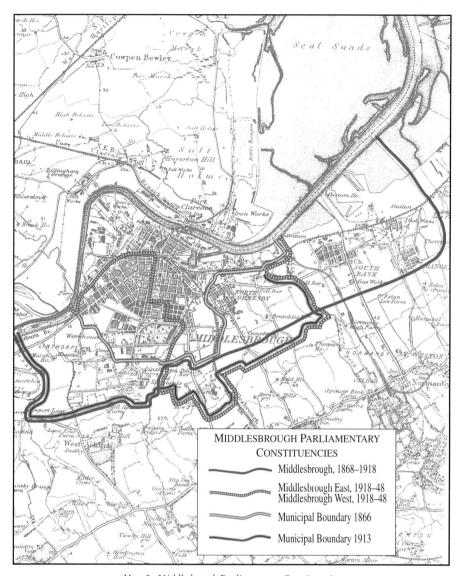

MIDDLESBROUGH PARLIAMENTARY
CONSTITUENCIES

Middlesbrough, 1868–1918

Middlesbrough East, 1918–48
Middlesbrough West, 1918–48

Municipal Boundary 1866

Municipal Boundary 1913

Map 2: Middlesbrough Parliamentary Constituencies

CHAPTER 1

MIDDLESBROUGH: THE GROWTH OF A NEW COMMUNITY

Asa Briggs

This remarkable place, THE YOUNGEST CHILD OF ENGLAND'S
ENTERPRISE. . . . It is an infant, gentlemen, but it is an infant Hercules.
W.E. GLADSTONE on his visit to
Middlesbrough (October 1862)

1

During Joseph Chamberlain's mayoralty, the rateable value of Birmingham
was £1,229,844; that of Middlesbrough at the same date was £130,255. The
population of the two communities was around 344,000 and 40,000. Yet it
was Middlesbrough which Gladstone compared with Hercules, an infant
Hercules, no doubt, but 'an Hercules all the same'.

Within the reign of Queen Victoria itself Middlesbrough grew from a very
tiny rural community to a very large town of over 100,000 people. There
were cities outside Britain, in the United States or Australia, which grew
from nothing even faster during the nineteenth century, but there was no
other English town. By comparison, Birmingham was old, old enough to
have been called 'the toyshop of Europe' by Edmund Burke, reputed to be old
enough in the boast of William Hutton, its first historian, to have
manufactured the wheels for Queen Boadicea's chariot. The great engineer,
Thomas Telford, had described it long before Queen Victoria came to the
throne as 'famous for its buttons and its locks, its ignorance and its
barbarism'.

Middlesbrough was a town 'which had won a name without history, an
importance without antiquity'. The other new English communities of the
nineteenth century, the railway town of Crewe, for example, or Barrow-in-
Furness, with which Middlesbrough had much in common, were smaller than
Middlesbrough and, despite many claims to continuing interest, left a less
vivid impression on contemporaries. 'The outcome of present century
enterprise and discovery', the Victorians called Middlesbrough, and went on
to claim that it occupied 'an unique position in the annals of our native land'.
It was known throughout the world, too. 'The iron it supplies furnishes

1

railways to Europe; it runs by Neapolitan and Papal dungeons; it startles the bandit in his haunts in Cilicia; it streaks the prairies of America; it stretches over the plains of India; it surprises the Belochees; it pursues the peggunus of Gangotri. It has crept out of the Cleveland Hills, where it has slept since the Roman days, and now, like a strong and invincible serpent, coils itself round the world.'

This romantic language demonstrates how the 'magic of industry' fascinated the Victorians. It did not, however, inhibit them from being didactic too. The story of Middlesbrough, like all good Victorian stories, had a moral. 'Middlesbrough, the delineation of whose growth and development forms the subject-matter of the following pages', a historian of the town began in 1899, 'must ever present to the mind of the thoughtful a most striking illustration of England's enormous industrial progress during the nineteenth century.' Another writer spoke proudly of 'a modern progressive spirit working upon old materials'. Middlesbrough was felt to be 'unparalleled in its proofs of rapid and genuine progress', a creation both of individual enterprise and of the powerful 'associative principle', the supremely practical product of 'a beautiful system of interwoven interests and mutual dependence'. 'In towns such as this, you see the secret workings of that indefatigable machine of spirited and patriotic industry, which goes on forcing this tight little island steadily ahead, and far ahead, of all competitors.'

The origins of Middlesbrough can be traced back before Queen Victoria's reign. Yet it contained only four houses and twenty-five inhabitants in 1801, and only forty inhabitants in 1829. At the census of 1831 the number had risen to 154, and in 1841 to 5,463. The ten years from 1831 to 1841 saw the planned development of the community by the 'Middlesbrough [or Middlesburgh] Owners' as a port for the shipment of coals at the terminus of the famous Stockton and Darlington Railway. The railway, opened in September 1825, had been sponsored by a little group of 'Quaker gentlemen' in Darlington and the surrounding countryside, and it was nicknamed in consequence 'the Quakers' line'. They were anxious to export local supplies of coal from the River Tees to London and other markets, and it was with this end in view that they extended the line to Middlesbrough, six miles nearer the sea where the river was deeper. Stockton, an older town, was difficult to navigate, and Middlesbrough, which at that time consisted of 500 acres of bleak salt marshes, was developed instead. It says much for the quality of vision of the leading personality in the enterprise, Joseph Pease, not to speak of his initiative, that in 1828 after he had looked at the one farmhouse which then constituted 'Middlesbrough', he wrote in his diary that 'imagination here has very ample scope in fancying a coming day when the bare fields . . . will be covered with a busy multitude and numerous vessels crowding to these banks denote the busy seaport.'

Four houses and twenty-five inhabitants: rural Middlesbrough in the early eighteenth century (CA)

Otley's impression of the planned coal drops, showing considerable licence over the landscape, which in 1830–1 handled 150,000 tons of coal (CA)

Pease and his associates, Thomas Richardson, a relative, Henry Birbeck, Simon Martin, and Francis Gibson, all of them Quakers, bought the Middlesbrough estate for £30,000 in 1829, and they set out resolutely to develop it as a rival to large and well-established ports, like Sunderland and even Newcastle. They talked eloquently of 'taking the lead of both Tyne and Wear'. There was also a pronounced local rivalry of a more immediate kind with Stockton, a quiet country town which boasted of a roll of mayors covering a period of nearly 400 years; good feelings were scarcely improved by the fact that Middlesbrough's mail arrived for several years at the Stockton post office addressed 'Middlesbrough, near Stockton-on-Tees'.

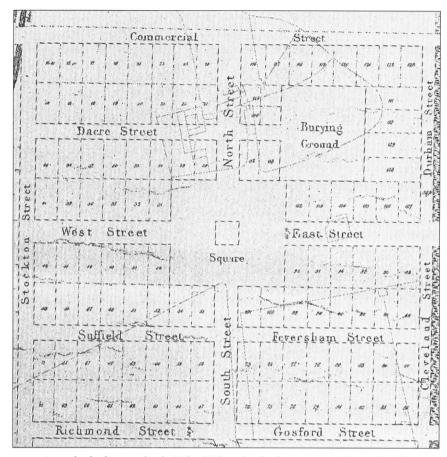

A port for the shipment of coals. Richard Otley's plan for the new town, 1830, detail (CA)

In 1826 Pease had made the modest estimate that 10,000 tons of coal could be exported each year from Teesside. The actual figure in 1830–1, the first year after the Stockton and Darlington Railway had been extended to Middlesbrough, was over 150,000 tons. The first load of coal included one immense block of 'black diamonds' which it was calculated would make, when broken, two London chaldrons. By 1840 the total of coal exports had risen to over 1.5 million tons. The early prosperity of Middlesbrough was thus guaranteed. The building of superior shipping staiths was followed by the making of a new cut in the Tees and the construction of docks, and with the staiths and the docks came the first local industry. A Middlesbrough pottery was started in 1834, and the first order shipped to Gibraltar in the same year. In 1840, the year that the first public market was opened (on the site of the old farm pond) and the first church consecrated, John Harris, one of Pease's colleagues in the management of the Stockton and Darlington Railway Company, persuaded two iron-founders, Henry Bolckow and John Vaughan, to settle in Middlesbrough and open a foundry and rolling mill.

It was this early growth, continuing through the 1840s, which inspired J.W. Ord, the first historian of the Cleveland district, to describe Middlesbrough in 1846 as 'one of the commercial prodigies of the nineteenth century'. Anticipating the lyrical language of the later century, he added that, to the stranger visiting Middlesbrough after the lapse of a few years, 'this proud array of ships, docks, warehouses, churches, foundries, wharves, etc., would seem like some enchanted spectacle, some Arabian Nights' vision, "such stuff as dreams are made of"'. The 'etc.' is hardly such stuff as dreams are made of, but it is very easy to see what Ord meant when he referred to Middlesbrough's population in 1841 as an 'amazing number'. He usually preferred to dwell not on the statistics set out in the census returns of the nineteenth century, but on the evidence of Domesday Book: Middlesbrough was impressive enough to shift the focus of his attention. It was also impressive enough for its first royal visitor, the Duke of Sussex, who was taken to see Middlesbrough by the Lord Lieutenant of the North Riding in 1838, to congratulate the inhabitants on the 'spirit of progress' they displayed. William Fallows, agent of the Stockton and Darlington Railway Company and later, among his many other duties, first postmaster of Middlesbrough, Justice of the Peace, and mayor, replied appropriately to the duke that though the town could not boast of 'the ancient and valuable institutions' which might be seen in the older towns around them, 'yet we have far greater pleasure in seeing those institutions rising up in the midst of us, by our own industry and exertions, growing with our growth and strengthening with our strength'.

The Middlesbrough Owners were interested, somewhat paternalistically, like the Railway Company at Crewe or at Barrow-in-Furness, in the creation of social institutions. They set out some of their plans in a deed of covenant entered into in February 1831. In order to 'produce some uniformity and respectability in the houses to be built', they laid out a 'new town' behind the wharves on a strictly symmetrical plan with a central square from which four main streets – North Street, South Street, East Street, and West Street – each moved out at right-angles. It is a tragedy that in an age of deliberate 'new town' building this fascinating example of nineteenth-century town planning has been almost destroyed in recent years.

Church and market were at the centre of a planned community, which, as Middlesbrough grew, ceased to be the effective centre of the Victorian city. The planning was concerned with spiritual welfare as well as with material well-being. The Quaker owners did not hesitate, to the delight of the Bishop of Durham, to give high priority to the building of the parish church of St Hilda. They provided land: £500 was provided by the Church Building

Society and £1,200 was raised by a grand bazaar and lottery. That care for spiritual welfare was needed in Middlesbrough was suggested by the high incidence of drunkenness among the new population. 'A large part of the inhabitants', one Middlesbrough veteran reminisced later in the century, 'was given up to intemperance.'

Middlesbrough was on a turbulent urban frontier, despite its Quaker inspiration. It is said that in the very early days one publican did a roaring trade with no other seats for his customers than a few planks supported on beer barrels. 'Seafaring men – living next door to each other in what was soon to form a street, but separated by a few unoccupied building sites – used to talk to one another from their own doors, when at home, through their speaking trumpets, same as they did at sea, because they could not travel between the two houses without sinking up to the calves of their legs in mire.' In a letter of January 1838, Thomas Richardson was told: 'Very lately a person was relating to us what a rough set you were in Middlesbrough, *not one gentleman in the place*, but correcting himself, "Yes, there was one gentleman, Mr Holmes."' (J.G. Holmes, a shipbuilder, was a well-known teetotaller, who had helped to found the first temperance society in 1837.) The letter writer added, 'You must not place yourself too high, mind, when he is thought to be the only *gentleman* among you.'

During the 1840s Middlesbrough acquired its first complex of urban institutions. A Centenary Wesleyan Methodist Chapel was opened in 1840, and Richmond Street Primitive Methodist Chapel in 1841. A Mechanics' Institute was founded in 1840, and a separate Oddfellows' District was carved out in 1842. Friendly societies had been active in the town from the start. In 1843 the first new school buildings were erected by the British and Foreign School Society; there had been schools in existence in the 1830s, although it had proved difficult 'to prevail or to compel the attendance of the children'.

The government of the town passed in 1841 to twelve Improvement Commissioners, who by an Improvement Act of that year were given power to deal with watch, paving, lighting, cleansing and drainage. Hitherto government had been by annual general meeting; now the twelve commissioners included Fallows, Holmes, Otley, a proprietor of the pottery, William Blenkinsop, an innkeeper, Isaac Sharp, the local agent of the Middlesbrough Owners, and Henry Bolckow. They were empowered to levy a rate not exceeding two shillings in the pound (the same as the Birmingham figure) or two shillings and sixpence with the consent of a majority of ratepayers at a town meeting, and they could borrow up to £5,000. They took their work most conscientiously and by 1843 had set up a sanitary committee as one of their five standing committees. It was a sign of their energy that they were soon involved in disputes with the local gas company, formed in 1838; these disputes led to its early municipalization.

Government in general was tough but cheap, as it passed from a paternalistic to a representative phase. The clerk to the commissioners was a

A very unpretentious pile; looking up South Street to the first town hall built in 1846 (MCL)

local solicitor, and R. Ord held the combined posts of chief of police, surveyor, and collector of rates and tolls at a salary of £60 a year. When in 1846 a town hall was built in the central square of the 'new town', it was 'a very unpretentious pile . . . designed evidently with an eye to utility rather than to ornament'. Later in the century it was used as a branch police station and for market offices; in the late 1840s a fire engine was kept there. The engine had been bought for £15 from another local authority.

2

Middlesbrough was incorporated in 1853, and by then a big leap forward in its economic life had further guaranteed its future prosperity. Middlesbrough could hardly have captured the inspiration of men like Gladstone had it simply been a coal-exporting centre; indeed, its coal trade declined sharply in the mid-Victorian years. Ironically the completion of the national railway network hastened the decline, for it became more profitable to move coal by rail than by sea. What coastal trade was left passed back into the hands of

Newcastle or to nearby Hartlepool. This decline, which might have reduced Middlesbrough to a ghost town, was completely overshadowed, however, by the growth of the local iron industry, so much so that the first modest phases of Middlesbrough's urban life before 1850 were almost forgotten in the light of what came afterwards. A population of 7,431 at the census of 1851, living in 1,262 houses, had risen in 1861 to a population of 19,416, living in 3,203 houses. In 1871 there was a further rise to 39,563, in 1881 to 55,934, in 1891 to 75,532, and in 1901 to 91,302.

People were attracted to Middlesbrough from all parts of the country in the same way as they were attracted to Liverpool and Birkenhead. In 1861 73.2 per cent of its population was born in Yorkshire, but by 1871 both ironworkers from Durham, South Wales, Staffordshire, and Scotland and labourers from Ireland had flocked to the town in such numbers that the native county element had sunk to 50.1 per cent. During the next decade immigration continued but at a diminished rate. There were even immigrants from the British Colonies, the East Indies, and the United States, with 551 people being described as coming from 'foreign parts' at the census of 1871. Middlesbrough had a very different demographic pattern from that of most English towns, with West Bromwich, Norwich, Ipswich, Leicester, and Northampton the most 'intensely English towns', as Ravenstein called them, at the other end of the scale. Indeed, in his view, Middlesbrough's 'rapid growth, the heterogeneous composition of its population, and the preponderance of the male sex, recall features generally credited only to towns of the American West'. The 'preponderance of the male sex', so long a feature of Australian demographic history, deserves as much attention as the mixture of origins, for certainly it left its mark on the ways of life of the growing town. The only other British towns which proved more attractive to male than to female immigrants were West Ham, St Helens, Airdrie, Hamilton, Greenock, Hawick and, an interesting overlap, West Bromwich. Whereas female immigrants, seeking jobs in domestic service, were prominent in most Victorian cities, they were far less prominent in essentially working-class Middlesbrough.

The religious mix was interesting also. It was a sign of the times that a Jewish Synagogue was opened in 1874. The Roman Catholics had built their first church in 1838. Before that they had worshipped in a room later taken over by the Unitarians, the first of Middlesbrough's religious groups to have a meeting room – as early as 1833. The Catholics built up a huge congregation, largely Irish, during the sixteen years of Father Burns's priesthood from 1854 to 1870, and in 1878 Middlesbrough became the centre of a Roman Catholic bishopric with a new cathedral church described as 'the handsomest and largest ecclesiastical edifice in the town'.

The preponderance of males and the variety of religions were two signs only that Middlesbrough had many of the features of a 'melting-pot' community. Bradford woolcombers, sent to Middlesbrough in the 1850s, praised their 'marsters' and acknowledged that the workmen were 'very civel to us'; at the same time, they warned their comrades back in Bradford that 'if you send men hear in Large Numbers and the Marsters begin to turn the irish of[f] it will very likely lead to a disturbance'.

Against this background it was appropriate that Henry Bolckow, who transformed both the economic and social life of Middlesbrough, and thereby made possible the great leap ahead of population, was himself a Mecklenberger, who had arrived in Newcastle in 1827 at the age of twenty-one. He worked for a time as accountant, foreign correspondent and commission agent. He settled in Middlesbrough in 1841 with a capital of £50,000 to invest. His partner, John Vaughan, was also an outsider, a man who looked at several places before he settled in Middlesbrough. Born at Worcester in 1799, he had been employed at the famous Dowlais ironworks in Wales before becoming a manager first at Carlisle and then at Newcastle. He was a remarkable man, a perfect hero of self help of the type extolled by Samuel Smiles. The two men formed an impressive partnership. 'For a number of years they were nearly as much part and parcel of each other as the Siamese twins. They had one objection in common; they lived not together, but next door to each other; they were continually in each other's company, consulting, controlling, planning, advising for the same ends.' The site of their future ironworks was a piece of waste land by the riverside; at low tide, part of it was a dreary waste of mud on which sailors had discharged their ballast.

From 1841 until 1850 Bolckow and Vaughan were engaged in an arduous and small-scale enterprise in Middlesbrough, looking laboriously to places miles outside Middlesbrough for the ironstone they needed. Ore might be collected from Whitby, for example, carried by sea to Middlesbrough, taken by rail to blastfurnaces 25 miles away at Witton Park near Bishop Auckland on the South Durham coalfields, converted into pig-iron, and brought back by rail to the Middlesbrough foundry. This complicated economic chain was broken by what has usually been called 'a great stroke of luck' in the year 1850. Vaughan is said to have discovered a magnificent supply of workable ironstone in the nearby Cleveland Hills at Eston. The local ores, the existence of which had been known for centuries, had generally been thought to be of poor quality and had been dismissed by J.W. Ord as 'of little value except as ballast, and scarcely of sufficient importance to encourage speculation'. Vaughan, who was advised by John Marley, a competent mining engineer, proved Ord and a number of distinguished geologists to be completely wrong. He did not, however, stumble over a block of ironstone while out shooting on the Cleveland Hills. This legend, which he always denied, concealed the care that was taken to find good sites for ironworks.

Extremely advantageous leases were acquired from the owner of the land, a trial quarry was begun in August 1850, a temporary tramway was laid down in September, and the first lot of seven tons of iron transported within three weeks after discovery. It is said that Vaughan, excited as he was, had as little sense of the ultimate quantitative significance of his discovery as Pease and his colleague had had of the volume of coal exports when they first built Middlesbrough. He talked of a thousand tons of ironstone being taken from Eston each week: in fact, that quantity was exceeded in a few months, and before very long three times the amount was extracted daily.

This story has an American or an Australian ring to it, for it was about this time that gold was discovered first in California (1849) and next in Victoria (1851). Whole new communities came into being with a rough but vigorous life of their own. Middlesbrough was, in a sense, the British Ballarat. Certainly, despite the inferior popular appeal of iron to gold, the Cleveland statistics were felt to be breathtaking by all the writers on the British economy in newspapers and periodicals. Production of pig-iron increased tenfold in the five years after 1851, by 1861 had leapt to half a million tons, and by 1867 to nearly a million tons. By 1873 the North-Eastern ironfield, with Middlesbrough as its capital, was producing over five and a half million tons of ore and making over two million tons of pig-iron, about one third of the total British output. A great wave of mid-Victorian prosperity pushed the price of iron to unprecedented heights.

The region was completely transformed in appearance as a result of these economic advances. In 1851, the year of the Great Exhibition, the first blastfurnace in Middlesbrough was blown in; before ten years had elapsed there were over forty furnaces in Cleveland and Teesside. In 1862 there were fifteen at Eston alone. Changes in technique were as exciting and important as these spectacular quantitative changes. Both the height and capacity of the furnaces were raised dramatically, waste was reduced, and daily output increased to as much as 5,000 tons a day. The lavish praise bestowed on Middlesbrough's 'progressive enterprise' was deserved: techniques were greatly ahead of those of other places.

Bolckow and Vaughan had led the way; other ironmasters, some of whom very quickly became powerful men in the life of the town, followed quickly. The first were Edgar Gilkes and C.A. Leatham, both Quakers, the former an engineer with the Stockton and Darlington Railway Company, the latter the son-in-law of Joseph Pease. Their 'Tees Furnaces' passed later into the hands of Wilson, Pease & Company, again a Quaker concern. Isaac Wilson, who had settled in Middlesbrough in 1841 and had been one of the owners of the pottery, was also connected by marriage with the Pease family. Joseph Pease died in 1903, but there were four distinct local businesses directed by members of the Pease family during the later nineteenth century – Joseph Pease and Partners dealing in coal; J.W. Pease & Company in ironstone and

By 1860, when this print of an ironworks was made, there were over forty blastfurnaces in the area
(MCL)

limestone; J. and J.W. Pease in banking; and Henry Pease & Company in manufacturing. This remarkable concentration of economic power in the hands of one family was converted into social power locally in the nineteenth century and nationally in the twentieth, when members of the Pease family acquired a bundle of titles. An aristocracy was in the making. Such extended influence somewhat disturbed Edward Pease, the aged head of the family, who lived from 1767 to 1858 and was known as 'the father of the railways' for his work in connection with the opening of the Stockton and Darlington. In his diary for November 1851 he wrote that 'now there are prospects of great advantages from the discovery of iron ore in the Cleveland range of hills, I feel a great anxiety that none of my beloved family may be caught in its enticings; they have quite enough of this world's engagements.'

Distinct from the Peases were Isaac Lowthian Bell and his two brothers, the sons of Thomas Bell, an ironmaster of Newcastle, yet in this case also there was an odd link with Vaughan, who had been superintendent at the Bells' Newcastle works. The Bells leased ironstone deposits at Normanby in 1853 and built the Port Clarence furnaces on the north side of the Tees opposite Middlesbrough. They used not the Stockton and Darlington Railway but the West Hartlepool Railway, in which the lease owner was financially interested. This provided an additional element of rivalry in the local situation. The Bells progressed, however, and built up a huge enterprise by efficient, up-to-date methods. Lowthian Bell had had an exceptionally good scientific education for a nineteenth-century British businessman and throughout his life he was keenly interested in science; he was also interested in the economic and social statistics of his industry. He became the acknowledged spokesman of the north-east as he built up his business power.

The other local pioneers included William Hopkins and Thomas Snowden, two men who were associated with the Stockton and Darlington Railway interest and opened the Tees-side Iron Works in 1853; the Cochranes, a family of ironmasters from Staffordshire, who built their first furnace at Ormsby in 1854; and Bernhard Samuelson, son of a Liverpool merchant and head of an agricultural engineering works at Banbury, who after building furnaces at South Bank in 1854 leased a 10-acre field there at a rent of £5 an acre and set about creating yet another new community of his own.

In Middlesbrough itself Henry Bolckow was an outstanding figure in this dynamic phase of the community's history. When the town was incorporated in 1853, with a population which was still less than 10,000, Bolckow became the first mayor. He was also the first President of the Chamber of Commerce when the Chamber was formed in 1863 and the first Member of Parliament for Middlesbrough – returned unopposed – when it became a parliamentary constituency in 1868. He had to have a special Act of Parliament passed to qualify him as British subject. His rugged Liberalism was a by-product of his business career, and he is remembered more by his deeds than by his speeches.

Disraeli understood the type better than Gladstone. 'They say we all have our hobbies,' he made his Mr Trafford say, 'and it was mine to improve the conditions of my workpeople, to see what good tenements, and good schools, and just wages paid in a fair manner, and the encouragement of civilizing pursuits would do to elevate their character. I should find an ample reward in the moral tone and material happiness of this community; but really, viewing it in a pecuniary point of view, the investment of capital has been one of the most profitable I ever made.' Certainly Bolckow had much in common with other businessmen who founded new communities and almost automatically took their place in Parliament. John Laird, the Conservative shipbuilder, who became first Member of Parliament for Birkenhead in 1861, and Ralph Ward-Jackson in nearby West Hartlepool were similar types. There was something of the same strain also in Sir Titus Salt.

Bolckow talked like a benevolent proprietor when he gave Middlesbrough its first public park in 1868 and in the same year new schools capable of providing for 900 children. He headed local subscription lists for every good cause while he lived, and left generous benefactions when he died. He talked the language too, of 'pride in his order'. He was chairman of the Middlesbrough Exchange Company, which was as much a symbol of business pride in Middlesbrough as the town hall was of civic enthusiasm in Leeds. He laid the foundation stone of the Exchange in 1866, Middlesbrough's most ambitious building to that date: it cost £28,000 and was deemed, without undue boasting, to constitute 'a pile of buildings which would do credit to any town'. The architect was a Stockton man, C.J. Adams, but this did not seem to matter.

A statue of Bolckow, unveiled by Lord Frederick Cavendish in 1881, depicts him handing over to the people the charter of incorporation of Middlesbrough. It had always seemed to be in his gift to offer, for as Prince Arthur said in opening the park Bolckow gave to the town, he had stood by the side of the iron cradle in which Middlesbrough was rocked and had watched over the child with care as it grew. 'He knows what it wants, and what its interests are.' Bolckow may well have chosen Middlesbrough's motto, *Erimus*, which may be compared with Robert Bruce's *Fuimus*. It seemed particularly appropriate to Gladstone. When Bolckow died, the *North Eastern Gazette* appeared with wide black borders around its columns.

The influence of other ironmasters was strong also in the life of Middlesbrough. When Bolckow was mayor in 1853, Isaac Wilson and John Vaughan were two of the four aldermen. Wilson succeeded Bolckow as mayor (and later as Member of Parliament) and he was succeeded the following year by Vaughan. William Fallows, Edgar Gilkes, William Hopkins got their chance during the next twelve years. Thomas Hugh Bell got his in 1874. The constitution of the town council changed – it was elected on a ward basis from 1858 and was increased in size after a new Improvement Act in 1866 – but effective power continued to reside in a small group of men, who controlled the local economy. They were mostly Liberal in politics – Hopkins and Cochrane were exceptions – and they formed a Liberal Reform Association in 1867. The association pressed Wilson to stand as Liberal candidate for Middlesbrough at the first election of 1868, but when Henry Bolckow decided to stand with Wilson's support, the position was willingly accepted.

There was considerable intermarriage within this group of ironmasters, and sons and nephews were drawn in to join their fathers and uncles while they were still very young. The ramifications of the Pease connection have already been mentioned. Other families were interconnected, too. Henry Bolckow and John Vaughan, for example, were married to sisters, and Bolckow's sister was the first wife of William Hopkins. Family ties continued to sustain the expanding economy which was based on partnership, not on dependence upon an outside and impersonal capital market.

Obligations to Middlesbrough's growing working class were stated almost in family terms during the 1850s and 1860s, although the language did not always necessarily conform to the facts. More important than the language in determining the pattern of relationships was the prevalence of high wages, the unprecedented boom conditions of the late 1860s (there were years of slump also at the troughs of the cycle) and the shared sense of growth. As a local poet sang proudly, before the town became too big:

> Then streets se cliver scan increased;
> Smash man! they numbered fifty;
> Thor's thirty butchers, man, at least,
> An' twenty tailors thrifty,
> Thor's sixty shops for rum an' beer;
> Thor's four prime shavers too, man;
> Thor's sailors, smiths and cobblers here,
> An' Cleveland poets two, man.

The two Cleveland poets were pillars of local 'culture'; its patrons were the ironmasters. Yet there were many cultural developments during the middle years of the century which duplicated developments in the new cities of America or Australia. Chapel-building was the biggest single corporate enterprise: the 'propensity to give' expressed itself most notably in this form. Churches were less popular, at first, and although one of the early non-resident incumbents had been Cobden's tutor, until the Revd Richard Bradley arrived in 1854 'it was considered hardly respectable [according to the Additional Curates' Aid Society] to be a member of the Church.' Sunday Schools were the most powerful educational influence from the start, and the Sunday School Union one of the most carefully organized local voluntary bodies. Yet the Mechanics' Institute, which acquired a new building in 1860, flourished rather longer than the Mechanics' Institutes of older towns, and its work was supplemented in 1863 by the Middlesbrough Athenaeum, 'a society for the cultivation of Literature, Science and the Arts'; in 1875 the Athenaeum took the old and respected name of 'Literary and Philosophical Society'. It had held its meetings before that date in two dingy back rooms; now it had its own premises, which were opened by Sir Stafford Northcote, the Conservative Chancellor of the Exchequer.

Two years before this, an Orpheus Music Club had been formed in Middlesbrough, and during the late 1860s both a choral society and a philharmonic society were in existence. Music was usually the first of the manifestations of popular culture; it was believed by the middle classes also – in Middlesbrough as elsewhere – that it was a perfect instrument for 'soothing the weary brow'. It is interesting to note that G.M. Tweddell in his excellent account of Middlesbrough in Bulmer's *North Yorkshire* (1883) noted with pride that the new School Board, which supplemented the schools presented by Bolckow, had just bought a piano. This, he added, was 'to be principally used for teaching the pupils vocal music, which cannot but have a civilizing influence'.

In 1870 a reading room and free library were opened under the Public Libraries Act, after inquiries had been made by the town council about the management and financing of libraries in Manchester and Birmingham. The Library Committee dreamed of an art gallery too, but it was not able to start a museum until 1890, after several years of intermittent discussion.

'Social activities' were far easier to organize. The Cleveland Club was opened in 1868 in the east end of the Exchange Building, and another middle-class club, the Erimus, was founded in 1873 with a limited membership of 300. The clientele of these clubs consisted largely of 'gentlemen in the iron industry'. Also in 1873, however, a working-men's club was opened by Bolckow; it had a quarterly subscription of 2s, and its philosophy was stated in very stilted language: 'those who contributed so largely towards the means of civilization shall partake more truly of the culture and refinement which it entailed by having opportunities afforded them for rational and civilizing pleasures'.

Fortunately, the usual language of the Middlesbrough press was hardly as stilted as this. The oldest newspaper, the *Middlesbrough Chronicle*, a monthly, was started in 1853 by Joseph Richardson, who had first arrived in the town in 1841 and had worked as a cabinet maker; an earlier venture of his was a magazine, *The Literary Pilot*. In 1855 Richardson transformed the *Chronicle* into a weekly, the *Middlesbrough Weekly News and Cleveland Advertiser*. It was a Liberal paper, but had a brief period under Conservative editorship. A further Conservative paper, the *Weekly Exchange*, challenged the most lasting of Middlesbrough's papers, the Liberal *Weekly Gazette*, which became the *Daily Gazette* in 1869.

Newspaper comments were often acrimonious; there were also local satirists. W.W.C. Seymour in 1864 wrote his *Who's Who: How is Middlesbrough Ruled and Governed?* It attacked 'the disloyal church-detesting town councillors of Middlesbrough', the 'tramp skinflint journeymen painters, penny wise and pound foolish', and 'the ranters and teetotal lecturers' who dominated Middlesbrough's life. There is evidence too that the rule of 'Middlesbrough's two kings – King Coal and King Iron' – was sometimes resented. A Parliamentary Debating Society, which flourished in the late 1870s, as in several other Victorian towns, allowed considerable scope for criticism and speculation. The resentment could not go too far, however, for there was no other basis at all for the existence of Middlesbrough.

3

It was impossible for Middlesbrough to preserve its mid-Victorian character. The sheer growth of the town made it more and more difficult for either one man or a group of families to control it. Quite apart from technical difficulties – the difficulties which led Birmingham men both to preach a civic gospel and to recruit an efficient civil service – there were many signs that the will to control of the ironmasters was being blunted as they followed the pattern of other English businessmen and chose to live in the country rather than in the town. Henry Bolckow, who in his early days in Middlesbrough had lived in Cleveland Street within five minutes' walk of the old Market, himself moved to Marton Hall, where he collected rare books and pictures. While he lived in Middlesbrough he had attended the Centenary Wesleyan chapel; in Marton he worshipped at the local parish church. John Vaughan, who died in 1868, long before the exodus was far advanced, lived in Gunnergate Hall; Isaac Wilson, who had formerly lived in 'the old town' in Sussex Street, now lived in Nunthorpe Hall, and W.K. Hopkins at the newly built mansion of Grey Towers. Their children continued to be linked in marriage, but neither the children nor the managers who succeeded them in their works, when their enterprises grew in size and were transformed into local limited liability companies, necessarily shared the feelings of the older generation about the links which bound them to the town.

The new generation certainly ceased to be as interested in the town council as the pioneers had been. As their influence declined – it did not by any means disappear – 'intermediate social classes' came into greater prominence, particularly the local shopkeepers, who gradually acquired the kind of social and political authority that they already possessed in most other Victorian cities. They had been numerically important on the council before the 1870s, but they did not provide the leadership. After 1875 the position changed. Hugh Bell did not retire from the council until 1907, but by then it had become a very different kind of council from that of 1870. Of the eighteen mayors from 1893 to 1912 only two belonged to the class of large manufacturers. In 1872 there were ten ironmasters and seven shopkeepers on the council; in 1912 there were fifteen shopkeepers and one ironmaster. In short, there had been a quiet local revolution.

The revolution did not pass completely unnoticed. The *Daily Gazette* complained as early as 1874 of 'the men with the largest stake . . . withdrawing from the Council'. Two years later it was commenting on the same kind of civil ineptitude which had been complained of in Birmingham during the rule of the 'Old Woodman Council'. 'What we deplore are the constant bickerings and personal abuse which of late years have been introduced. Scarcely can any question be settled without a scene; and too often the worst possible accusations are freely made and the business obstructed for no conceivable good.' An article of 1877 was headed: 'Decay of Municipal Life'. It asked the question, 'Where are our great manufacturers and old inhabitants now? They are fast disappearing.' In 1880 it complained of 'sectional representation'. 'Now the butchers are to the fore with some unsavoury grievance; then the publicans bumptiously demand to be heard; next the teetotallers put forward exclusive pretensions to dominate. All this is worse than absurd. It is an utter perversion of the first principle of municipal representation. Unless some great political principle is involved, the one consideration should be to elect men who by their intelligence, respectability and knowledge of the town's requirements, are fitted for a seat in the local Parliament.' Six years later the composition of the council was again condemned as 'a byeword and a reproach'.

Whatever the justice of such complaints, little attempt was made in Middlesbrough to forge a constructive plan of civic development. Improvement had depended for so long on the paternalism either of the 'Owners' or of the ironmasters that once their influence was removed the zest for improvement was reduced. Liberalism in Middlesbrough always lacked a municipal programme. A few Liberals believed during the 1880s that the day was not far distant when municipal elections, 'as in Birmingham, Leeds and other large towns', would be contested solely on political issues, but neither the old ironmasters nor the new shopocracy cared to convert Liberalism into an instrument of positive social action. The only time that they were induced to press their politics locally was when the licensed victuallers seemed to be pulling the strings of the Conservative Party too tightly. Teetotalism remained a far livelier issue than civic reform.

Even in national politics the Birmingham model was not copied until 1881. When in 1876 an attempt was made to construct a 'strong, broad and comprehensive Liberal Association', there were eight ironmasters on the provisional committee of fifteen, and no provision was made either for ward organization or for a 'general committee'. Membership of this association never exceeded 200, and it disappeared after the general election of 1880. A new association, formed in 1881, and affiliated to Chamberlain's National Liberal Federation, was representative of lower-middle-class groups and looked to Birmingham, Leeds and Darlington. It had 500 members, but it failed to win substantial support from the ironmasters.

When home rule split the Liberal Party in 1886 some of the ironmasters turned against Gladstone. Wilson remained loyal, but Bell, who had been thought of as his successor, became Unionist (he returned to the Liberal fold later on the issue of protection). Carl Bolckow moved in the same direction. The Pease family was divided against itself, the greater and more influential element remaining Gladstonian. The increase in the Conservative and Unionist vote in Middlesbrough during the 1880s and 1890s – a Unionist actually won by fifty-five votes in the 'khaki election' of 1900 – was a sign that the new community had lost its 'instinctive liberalism'. A few young Liberals at the end of the century tried in vain to break the spell by preaching a more active policy, concerned in particular with improvements in housing, health, and education.

By then the challenge to Middlesbrough Liberalism came from the left as well as from the right. In mid-Victorian Middlesbrough 'labour' had been thought of solely as an economic force: in late-Victorian Middlesbrough it began to acquire an active political personality of its own. At the general election of 1892 a 'Lib-Lab' candidate, Joseph Havelock Wilson, the general secretary of the Sailors' and Firemen's Union, won a memorable victory over W.S. Robson, the official Liberal, who was a barrister. Long before this, in 1874, John Kane, a member of the Iron Workers'

Association, a nominee of the Labour Representation League of 1869, and a supporter of the trade union 'Junta' in London, polled 1,541 votes against Henry Bolckow's 3,719, with Hopkins, the Conservative ironmaster, polling only 996 votes.

Neither Kane nor Havelock Wilson was completely independent of the Liberal Party – neither was in any sense a socialist – but their achievements, particularly Havelock Wilson's, brought to the surface new elements in Middlesbrough's political life. Havelock Wilson was reconciled with the local Liberal Association later in the 1890s – he was the sole Liberal candidate in 1895 and 1906 – but independent Labour began to emerge as a separate force on his left. Tom Mann supported the idea of an independent Labour candidate in 1891 and attacked Isaac Wilson for his opposition to a statutory eight-hour working day, the public building of artisans' dwellings and the provision of work for the unemployed. In 1906 George Lansbury was to poll 1,484 votes as a Socialist candidate. The Trades Council, founded in 1879, was for long a Lib-Lab stronghold, but a local branch of the Independent Labour Party was active in the late 1890s and there were moves after 1900 to associate the Labour movement in Middlesbrough with the Labour Representation Committee.

'Lib-Labism' was a very different phenomenon from mid-Victorian paternalism, even when it was patronized by businessmen. Its influence in local politics, however, was small, and the attempt to keep rates down or to defend Nonconformity and temperance remained the main elements at municipal elections. There was little working-class representation, and it was not until 1904 when a very short-lived Municipal Reform Association came into existence – with a Unitarian minister, W.H. Lambelle, on its executive committee – that Middlesbrough heard much local talk of 'civic reform'. Some attempts were made, however, particularly during the late 1880s, to raise the prestige of the council as a whole. In October 1881, Middlesbrough had celebrated its jubilee, but there was so much local 'distress' – the newspapers called the decline of the iron rails industry 'the death of a staple industry' – that the celebrations were somewhat muted. The Corporation refused to associate itself with the preparations for the event, which included the unveiling of Bolckow's statue, a great banquet for notabilities, and a firework display.

In 1887, however, the Corporation was directly responsible for the official proceedings which took place to commemorate the opening of the new town hall, the foundation stone of which had been laid – after long delays – in 1883. The land for the building had been acquired in 1872, when the ubiquitous Alfred Waterhouse, bobbing up once more, was appointed architect, but there had been great changes in Middlesbrough by the time that the building was started with a local architect in charge. The Prince and Princess of Wales accepted a civic invitation to open the impressive Gothic building which was described as being 'in the style of the thirteenth century suffused with the feeling and spirit of the present time'. Waterhouse was the assessor on this occasion and the chief title to fame of the architect, George Gordon Hoskins, was that he 'had designed numerous villa residences in the counties of Durham and Yorkshire'. The hall had a clock tower, 170 feet high, a large assembly room and a council chamber embellished with full-length portraits of Joseph Pease, William Fallows, Bolckow, Vaughan, and Bell. Bolckow and Vaughan figured also in the décor of the triumphal arches which were built specially for the opening.

The most active supporters of the idea of a new town hall – many of them were Conservatives – had used language not unlike that of the 1850s in Leeds. 'We hope the Council in framing their new scheme', the *Weekly Gazette* stated in 1881, 'will have under consideration the wants of the borough for fully one hundred years to come. It is also wise and prudent to enforce upon them that the building itself must be of an imposing character, befitting a go-ahead community which proposes to have as much reverence for culture as for power. . . . We have every reason to believe that there are men on the Council who will say that a ship is not spoiled for want of the proverbial half-pennyworth of tar. We congratulate the town upon the fact that it has at last been placed in a position to crown its civic edifice by providing a suitable home for its civic institutions.' The building, it was argued, would have to be of the kind that would inspire future citizens to enjoy 'the refining influence of art' and to say gratefully:

Everywhere I see around me rise the wondrous world of Art,
Buildings bright with richest sculpture standing in the common mart.

To disarm obvious criticism, it was pointed out that the building did not need to be financed from the rates; it could be paid for by a 'civic loan'. This procedure was followed, although final sanction for borrowing the money was not obtained until three years after the town hall was opened.

At the opening ceremony the Conservative mayor, Major Dixon, Middlesbrough's largest shipbuilder, who lived in Vaughan's old home, Gunnergate Hall, and whose family was related by marriage to the Bells, the Bolckows and later the Dormans, was eloquent in his praise of municipal government. 'Though our municipality is young in years, we have to the best of our ability carried on the noble traditions of freedom and self government which have ever distinguished the Towns of England.' He went on to talk of municipal institutions. 'In a Corporation which has existed for a very few years, we have institutions of all kinds to create and develop, and it has been, therefore, the pride and ambition of Middlesbrough to furnish such institutions.' Lastly, he reverted to what may be called the main Leeds theme of the 1850s:

Looking to a great future: the arrival of the Prince of Wales to open the new town hall, 1889 (MCL)

Up to this time all the Public Buildings that have been erected in Middlesbrough have soon proved themselves utterly inadequate to the wants of the place, and have not been able to keep up with rapid development. In erecting these Buildings we are doing something permanent. We have not much of a past to speak of, but we look to having a great future.

In his reply the Prince of Wales had little alternative but to extol Middlesbrough's 'Municipal Patriotism'. He could not resist saying also, however, that he had expected to see a smoky town. This remark provoked a characteristically candid comment from the mayor, which catches the spirit of late-Victorian Middlesbrough far more than the heavy rhetoric:

His Royal Highness owned he had expected to see a smoky town. It is one, and if there is one thing more than another that Middlesbrough can be said to be proud of, it is the smoke (cheers and laughter). The smoke is an indication of plenty of work (applause) – an indication of prosperous times (cheers) – an indication that all classes of workpeople are being employed, that there is little necessity for charity (cheers) and that even those in the humblest station are in a position free from want (cheers). Therefore we are proud of our smoke (cheers).

We are proud of our smoke. The Ironmasters' District from the river, 1881 (The Graphic, *1881, p. 377*)

Such pride would probably not have been expressed in this crude form and with such gusto had not Middlesbrough, like other industrial communities, passed through anxious days after the high summer of Victorian prosperity. In late-Victorian England, as G.M. Young has written, there was a chill in the air. The changes in the approach to local government in Middlesbrough can be understood only in the light of changes in the economic sub-structure of the town. The transition from iron to steel meant greater vulnerability to foreign competition; it meant also that business fluctuations, the cycles of good and bad years, were international in character. The smoke registered full employment for the worker; for the manufacturer it indicated that he was holding his own against competition. He was holding his own, however, as he well knew, in a far more interdependent world. The surviving iron industry in Middlesbrough came to depend more and more on the importation into Middlesbrough of foreign quality ores. In 1870 pig-iron production in Cleveland was self-contained; by the end of Queen Victoria's reign it was dependent on the world overseas.

The steel industry, with its large-scale plant, depended not only on foreign imports of material but on extensive outside capitalization. The partnerships of mid-Victorian Middlesbrough gave way, in consequence, to limited liability companies. Bolckow & Vaughan became a limited liability company as early as 1864 with a capital of £5½ million. The two great partners had a large financial interest in the new company, but Manchester businessmen, quite unconnected with Middlesbrough, were drawn into the flotation and were represented on the new board of directors. 'Capitalized by Manchester, but dominated by Welsh technicians' was one verdict on the incorporation. The trend towards limited liability continued throughout the 1880s and 1890s, and was associated also in its later phases with tendencies towards integration of businesses and amalgamation. Small partnerships disappeared; large integrated concerns on a national rather than a local scale became the effective business units.

This story has many different facets. In 1850, when John Vaughan discovered rich supplies of ironstone at Eston, steel was slow and expensive to manufacture. It was not used for large-scale construction, railways or ships, for example, but for tools, springs and weapons. The iron age was still at its height, and the building of the Crystal Palace in 1851 marked the triumph not only of a new material, glass, but of an old one, iron. Five years later Henry Bessemer, challenged by the military demand of the Crimean War, developed the converter process which made it possible to produce high-tensile steel in large quantities. The ore used, however, had to be free of phosphorus. Sheffield was the first British centre of the new industry, and Middlesbrough, with plentiful local supplies of phosphoric ore, lagged behind in the middle years of the century. As late as 1872 it was stated that 'no steel of any kind' was manufactured on the north-east coast. The great mid-Victorian boom of the late 1860s and the early 1870s came and went in Middlesbrough with the iron industry still supreme.

Middlesbrough had to develop its late-Victorian steel industry with imported raw materials at a time when economic conditions were unfavourable. Dividends slumped and many greatly respected firms actually went into liquidation. The local press wrote ominously of 'careless and incompetent management, reckless speculation and extravagant living'. The Bolckow-Vaughan concern, which had been founded on luck, was the first to adapt itself to the new conditions. In 1876 the first Bessemer steel plant was built by the company at Eston – it had previously owned a small steel works at Gorton, near Manchester – and 10,000 tons of steel were produced during the first year of operation. By 1879, a year of heavy depression, when there were many bankruptcies in the iron industry, steel output had risen to over 85,000 tons and the works were 'engaged to their fullest capacity'.

In the same year an important new process of steel-making was demonstrated on Teesside at the Bolckow-Vaughan works. The Gilchrist-Thomas open-hearth process permitted steel to be made from phosphoric iron ores. Enormous plant was required, and the Bolckow-Vaughan concern with Carl Bolckow, nephew of Henry Bolckow, as chairman, was ready to transform itself to meet the new opportunities. The process ultimately benefited foreign producers, however, far more than it benefited Britain.

'Middlesbrough', wrote Lowthian Bell, 'was soon besieged by the combined forces of Belgium, France, Prussia, Austria and America.' The local failures continued, Carl Bolckow himself suffering so severely in the collapse of one of his subsidiary concerns in 1891 and 1892 that he sold his uncle's collection of paintings and *objets d'art* at Christie's and disposed of his life interest in the Marton estates.

One of the new Middlesbrough firms which had the greatest stake in the future had been founded in 1870 by Arthur Dorman, born at Ashford in Kent, and Albert de Lande Long. They originally set out to manufacture iron bars and angles for shipbuilding, the most prosperous branch of the iron industry, but they acquired the Britannia Works from Samuelson in 1879, became a limited liability company ten years later, and by the end of Victoria's reign were employing 3,000 men in the iron and steel industry. In 1899 when Bell Brothers, which had remained an iron-producing concern, became a limited liability company, half the ordinary shares were held by Dorman-Long. Three years later Sir Lowthian Bell became chairman of Dorman-Long, and in the very distant future, after a sequence of amalgamations, Dorman-Long amalgamated with Bolckow-Vaughan in the strange and unforeseeable economic circumstances of 1929.

Financial and technical elements contributed to this prolonged process of integration and amalgamation. From the point of view of the citizens of Middlesbrough the changes had three important social effects. First, the increasing size of plant meant a new pattern of relationships at work. The employer receded from the workshop, and his place was taken by managers, ranging in grade from the general manager or works manager down to the foreman on the shop floor. The terms of work were set increasingly by bargaining between trade unions and employers, the employers being associated collectively in the Cleveland Ironmasters' Association and the workers in national trade unions. Second, the contribution of employers to the life of the community outside the factory was inevitably curtailed. It was not only, as we have seen, that they were usually living outside Middlesbrough. More important still, they were not as familiar with daily life there as their parents or uncles had been. A number of their managers were active in municipal politics – men like E.T. John or F.W. Mildred of Bolckow-Vaughan or T.F. Ward of Samuelson's – but as a group they were less homogeneous in outlook than their employers had been, and far less able to provide effective financial patronage for local causes. Third, the fortunes of Middlesbrough depended more and more on financial initiatives taken outside. The capital market began to count in the life of the town as its local economy was drawn more and more into the national economy. In Middlesbrough, even more than in the country as a whole, the neglected 1890s were years of change in national life, particularly in relation to the balance between provincial and national. The provincial, both in the field of

Middlesbrough's greatest ironfounder, Sir Hugh Bell, and Lady Florence Bell attend the Duke of Connaught in 1911 (MCL)

economy and culture, counted for less and the national (or standardizing) for more.

Although all these changes were noted, however sketchily, by observers at the time, it is remarkable that the best account of the texture of Middlesbrough's urban life in the new conditions was provided by Lady (Florence) Bell, the wife of Sir Hugh Bell, Middlesbrough's greatest ironfounder, in her brief but vivid study, *At the Works*, which was published in 1907. What she wrote of Middlesbrough then must have been true of Middlesbrough throughout the last part of the century, for she seized, like the French sociologist Le Play, on the central social relationships connected with 'work, place and home'. The necessity of living near the works meant renting cheap houses in unattractive rows of 'little brown streets'. 'It is a side-issue for the workman whether he and his family are going to live under healthy conditions; the one absolute necessity is to be at work.' 'There springs, and too rapidly, into existence a community of a pre-ordained, inevitable kind, the members of which must live near their work. They must therefore have houses built as quickly as possible; the houses must be as cheap, must be as big as the workman wants, and no bigger; and as they are built there arise hastily located, instantly occupied, the rows and rows of little brown streets. . . . A town arising in this way cannot wait to consider anything else but time and space.' Long working hours meant scarce leisure; and what leisure there was often was not well employed. The roughness of Middlesbrough persisted into the twentieth century. The public house was the main social institution, and drunkenness was its most common offence. More than a quarter of the workmen read books as well as newspapers, nearly a half read the newspapers only, and a quarter did not read at all. The more educated people of the country did not usually set them an example. 'Those who should be able to bring a leaven of art, of literature, of thought, to the toilers around them, are toiling also themselves; they are part of the immense machine, and it is impossible for them to judge of it with a free mind.'

The pattern of urban life in Middlesbrough seemed to her to be of a 'pre-ordained, inevitable kind', yet she discerned variety in the pattern. Some working men were tolerably secure; others, as Booth and Rowntree showed in London and York, were in poverty and want; 'the great majority were on the borderline between the two.' Social insecurity was at the heart of the industrial and consequently of the urban system. The fortunes of families depended not only on the income of the wage-earner but on the size of his family and the administrative capacity of his wife. Lady Bell was the first of the writers on Middlesbrough to turn the spotlight on the housewife. The community might appear on the surface to be aggressively masculine, but everything depended on the women. There was more variety inside the individual houses than the general vista of the street promised. 'The husband's steadiness and capacity to earn are not more important than the wife's administration of the earnings.'

Housing conditions in Middlesbrough were bad at the end of Queen Victoria's reign and the death rate was high. There had been a 'dirty party' during the middle years of the century, which argued that since Middlesbrough was 'new' it did not need extensive health legislation. 'Property owners,' wrote *Veritas* to the *Middlesbrough Weekly News* in 1859, 'away with this insidious foe – that will not allow you to build a pantry without submitting plans and specifications for the approval of an authorized architect.' The inhabitants of Middlesbrough would suffer more from eating American bacon than keeping pigs in the Mechanics' Institute garden. Baths and wash-houses, which were advocated at this time by the 'clean party', were not built until 1884. 'The great unwashed go unwashed still,' the editor of the newspaper remarked, 'and the Tees [will] receive its usual quota of bather victims, and the new cemetery its consumptive and steam-destroyed sacrifices.' It was axiomatic to the 'clean party' that 'we not only want to see factories acquired by our manufacturers and a comfortable independence for our tradesmen but to surround all classes with aids to health and longevity.' The 'permanent prosperity' of the town depended 'almost as much upon its acquiring the character of being a healthy and salubrious locality as upon its skill and industry'. What Lady Bell wrote in 1907 was anticipated nearly fifty years before by a writer who emphasized that 'healthy habitations' were necessary if people were to secure 'the attraction of their leisure hours and solace of their eye'.

Little was done, and Middlesbrough, new though it was, was distinctly unhealthy. For the years 1871–3 the death rate averaged 23.96 per thousand of the population for the borough as a whole, and it was far worse than this in the most crowded working-class districts. The infantile mortality rate was, as always, an index of lack of social control. Forty per cent of the total recorded deaths in Middlesbrough in the years 1871–3 were of children under the age of one year; deaths of children between the ages of one and five accounted for another 20 per cent.

The building of a more effective drainage system during the 1870s was a sign of 'improvement', but there were prolonged battles about rates which held back progress. In 1874, for example, after the Finance Committee of the Town Council had recommended a rate of 2s in the pound, the council as a whole amended it to 1s 6d. The Finance Committee protested, but the mayor had to give his casting vote in full council in order that the decision to set the impossibly low rate of 1s 6d could be rescinded. A compromise was struck, and by fourteen votes to eleven the council agreed on a vote of 2s. Four years later, ratepayers who claimed that they represented '£76,500 of the rateable value of Middlesbrough' petitioned the council to cut its capital expenditure on such items as water and drainage. 'These changes must inevitably cause an increase in the rates, and the subscribers . . . respectfully submit that such an increase at a time of unprecedented commercial depression, is neither expedient nor warrantable.'

From the late 1890s onwards, the annual reports of the Medical Officer of Health provided full statistics of differential mortality rates by age and by district. There was far less public interest in Middlesbrough, however, than had been shown in Birmingham twenty years before. It was not until 1900 that the Trades Council organized a large-scale conference on the housing question, which recommended that local use should be made of the Housing of the Working Classes Act of 1890. A Sanitary and Housing Reform Association, which was founded as a result of this conference, was unable to make much headway. Middlesbrough remained an unhealthy town with inferior working-class housing conditions. Geography, which favoured the town economically, did not help it socially: 'few worse sites on which to found a large and increasing town could have been found', wrote the first Medical Officer of Health. The land development of the new community had rested on speculation not on service. The Grange Farm at Linthorpe containing just over 140 acres was sold to a Manchester company for £70,000 in 1866; two years earlier 3 acres in the same township were sold at a price of £600 per acre for building sites. 'The price of

Not calculated to create a particularly favourable impression. A panoramic view of Middlesbrough from the north bank of the Tees, c. 1910 (CA)

building land', a local writer remarked in 1881, 'has more than tripled within the last twenty years, while corner sites and small lots are difficult to obtain at exorbitant prices.' The Middlesbrough Estate had proved 'a princely land speculation'. Similar comments were being made at the end of Queen Victoria's reign, when most of the development of the town centre was complete.

The face of the town reflected its history and the urges which brought it into being. A Middlesbrough guide to the town stated in 1899:

> At first sight Middlesbrough is not calculated to create a particularly favourable impression upon the visitor. Its utilitarian aspect is somewhat too pronounced. With its numerous ironworks lying between the town and the river, the town itself being built upon a low level stretch of country on the south side of the river, and its streets composed for the most part of plain brick houses, it presents essentially a business town, and little that is picturesque to attract and please the eye.

The Victorian contrast between 'utility' and 'pretensions', which is implicit in this self-assessment, represents far too simple a view of the proper relationship between art or architecture and business. It led the writer also to praise some of the more pretentious and costly late-nineteenth-century buildings in Middlesbrough and to overlook both the more simple appeal of the early buildings and the savage power of the industrial scene itself. It obscured the nature of the historical process which had made Middlesbrough look as it did. Lady Bell was more percipient. She saw that at twilight and in the night, when the sky was lit up by the furnaces, Middlesbrough could be a most impressive place to see. There was nothing in Middlesbrough to 'appeal to a sense of art or beauty' except, in its strange way, Middlesbrough itself.

The growth of the town made the first planned settlement of the 'Middlesbrough Owners' seem like a tiny frontier encampment strategically placed alongside the river. The railway line separated this Middlesbrough from the new town centre which developed around the new town hall and principal buildings, which were opened in 1887. When the plan for a new town hall was being mooted it was already known, as a newspaper put it, that 'the town is extending southwards, the iron and other works having taken possession of the ground at the east and west'. 'Should the growth go on,' the newspaper concluded, 'as there is very little doubt it will do, the new Town Hall and Municipal Buildings will in a few years be in a central position.' They were. The chief business thoroughfares of the 1840s and 1850s were Commercial Street and the streets running off Market Place to the north of the railway. After 1850, however, the area between the railway and Grange Road was developed, and after 1860 the Newport district, a factory area with long rows of working-class houses and a railway system of its own. By 1870 the main shopping centre was on both sides of the Middlesbrough railway station, and a grid-iron pattern of streets was taking shape which still gives Middlesbrough a curiously symmetrical appearance. The conditions of ownership and development dictated the form of layout, which, as W.G. Hoskins has pointed out, links Middlesbrough with very different English towns of other centuries, like Salisbury and Winchelsea. 'The planned town is an aberration, not the norm.' The absolute ownership of the first site was associated with the optimism about the future which remained strong in mid-Victorian Middlesbrough. 'The planning of a new town – laying out the lines of streets, lanes, markets, churches and house plots over a considerable area – required the investment of a large amount of capital and a greater degree of optimism than most landlords could contemplate.' *Erimus* was a very appropriate and necessary motto.

Yet the planning of Middlesbrough lacked the single purpose and persistence which had characterized the planning of Saltaire in the 1850s, and once the town split out of the original rectangle there was no inducement to retain homogeneity of style or architecture. There was no inducement either to relate working-class housing to any other criterion than nearness to work. Three main arterial roads, wider than most nineteenth-century English urban roads, cut through the rows of working-class streets south of the railway line – Linthorpe Road, the chief business street in the town, linking the railway station with the old village of Linthorpe, which was soon swallowed up in Middlesbrough itself; Newport Road cutting across Middlesbrough from the extreme west; and Marton Road on the opposite boundary, leading to Grove Hill where 'most of the gentry' who continued to live in or near

Middlesbrough had their residences. The cricket ground was at Grove Hill; the football ground, one of the best in the country, was in Linthorpe Road just beyond the point where the old large middle-class houses of early Middlesbrough were being pulled down and replaced by shops. Electric trams were not introduced until 1898, but there were horse trams along the main routes from 1876.

The large new railway station, completed in 1877, was within easy reach of the centre of the 'old town' and the new. The street names on each side of the track revealed two layers of history – Stockton Street, Wellington Street, Brougham Street and Sussex Street lying to the north between the old rectangle and the railway; Wilson Street, Bolckow Street, Vaughan Street, and Gilkes Street to the south. The name of Albert, however, was ubiquitous. A northern street, graced by the Theatre Royal (1866), was named after him, a southern road, bisecting Corporation Street, and both the new town hall and the old Exchange as great urban landmarks, and the park which Bolckow presented to the town was called Albert Park.

Many of the most Victorian of the local institutions were located on the moving southern boundary – the old cemetery, opened by the Corporation in 1854 (the first burials there were victims of the cholera), the fever hospital (there must have been almost as many writers of Victorian novels about fever hospitals as readers of novels inside them) and the 'palatial' workhouse, *the* Institution both to the Victorians and the men and women of the early twentieth century. The Prince Consort was more favoured in Middlesbrough than the Queen. Victoria Square, lying between the municipal buildings and a group of new Board Schools, was considered so uninviting – as late as 1899 – that it was nicknamed 'the Dark Continent'.

In the twentieth century Middlesbrough continued to move farther south, with housing estates flanking the most prosperous middle-class areas. 'The extremes of poverty', as Ruth Glass wrote in 1948, 'are on the northern and southern edge respectively.' The result was a social segmentation which was implicit in nineteenth-century history. The specific urban amenities of Middlesbrough, the 'urban equipment' of late-Victorian England, remained in the north – the railway station, the major shopping area, the clubs, cinemas, restaurants and public houses, the General Post Office, and the town hall – but a 'new town' without social institutions had grown up on the southern side of Albert Park. Two ways of life, as different as the contrasting ways of life within Victorian cities, were co-existing. 'People in the north live under conditions which almost compel them to be "matey"; people in the south have chosen conditions which make it possible for them to be secluded.' The complex of institutions, originally designed in some sense for all, was not at the centre of Middlesbrough but at the periphery.

Much of Middlesbrough's public building in the north was constructed during the same period that Chamberlain and his successors were remodelling the centre of Birmingham. The railway station cost £100,000 and was often compared with St Pancras; in the same year that it was opened, 1877, the Temperance Hall in Gilkes Street was also opened. Its large hall which seated 2,000 people was the biggest in Middlesbrough until the new town hall was built. The town hall cost £130,000 to build; it is interesting to compare this figure with the £2,000 which had been spent by the Middlesbrough Owners on the first town hall, 'a neat edifice of stone, designed by Mr Moffatt of Doncaster' and opened in 1846.

The shift of taste and more profound transformations of economic and social structure within the short span of Middlesbrough's Victorian history are fascinating themes for the historian. The real interest of Middlesbrough's nineteenth-century history lies, indeed, not so much in the newness of the community which was created there as in the speed with which an intricate and complex economic, social, and political sequence was unfolded. Historians of Continental cities, like Genoa, Venice, Bruges, or Amsterdam, have devoted huge monographs to sequences of change far less dramatic in character and stretched out not over sixty years but over several centuries.

Contemporary interpretations of the sequence are almost as interesting as the sequence itself. Some of them have been quoted as an introduction to this essay. There was one other interpretation which deserves special attention because of its author, Joseph Cowen, the Newcastle newspaper editor, who, as we have seen, was one of the most eloquent panegyrists of the claim of city against countryside. Cowen's *Newcastle Chronicle* was read everywhere 'from Tees to Tweed'; his powerful platform speeches and spirited lectures delivered for such bodies as the Northern Union of Mechanics' Institutions and the Co-operative Congress, were as influential in the North of England as his articles. He was a remarkable orator, at his best in great halls before large audiences, where it was said he obeyed the injunction of Demosthenes and relied upon 'continuous action' – 'action while stating his case, action in the discussion of it, and action when making his appeal'.

At the Middlesbrough Jubilee celebrations of 1881, Cowen proposed the toast of 'the Mayor, Aldermen and Burgesses of Middlesbrough and Prosperity to their Town and Trades on this Jubilee'. Surprisingly, not everybody could hear him on this occasion, but people crowded around the platform to catch his very congenial message. Wherever the British flag was flying, he began, and to whatever corner of the world English enterprise had penetrated, the fame of Middlesbrough was known.

The story, the marvellous story, of its rise is admiringly recited, and the fame of its factories is dwelt upon. The idea symbolized by its history is force – the physical, mental and moral force which enables communities to wrestle with and overcome the obstacles which circumstances cast in their way as they struggle upwards and onwards to a better state of living.

Not only Middlesbrough but nineteenth-century urban life in general was the subject of this comment. Cowen was born in 1831, about the same date that Middlesbrough was founded; his father had been largely involved at that time in the formation of the Northern Political Union, which, like Attwood's Birmingham Political Union, quickened the pace of radical agitation during the critical months leading up to the passing of the Great Reform Bill. Joseph Cowen senior started his life at the forge, and the metaphors of the forge appealed to him throughout his political career. So they did also to the son. Mental and moral force had made reform inevitable. The threat of physical force had usually been there, too. Urban life generated force, and that was its strength. 'In the great battle between movement and stagnation the cry was ever onward; and before that cry many cherished convictions and many tender prejudices had to go down. The towns of which Middlesbrough was a type were the leaders of this advance; they recorded the rise of the nation.'

Six solid 'broad brimmed, broad fronted, broad-bottomed' Quakers had cleared a swamp and made a city. They had not been inhibited by history. They trusted not in precedent but in the future. 'The steam engine had no precedent, the locomotive was without ancestry, and the telegraph centred on no heritage.' Middlesbrough was genuinely 'new', like them. 'He had a sneaking sympathy with the plaintive wail that Mr Ruskin and others so oft, so touchingly, and so eloquently raised o'er a vanished and irrecoverable past. But the facts were against them. The minister of civilization preached from the railway car and the telegraph.' There was no need to bemoan the biggest of all facts, that 'Arcadian association and romantic solitude' had retreated before the era of hammers and anvils, of looms and furnaces.

Few of Cowen's many public speeches sound more Victorian than this. But then all the accounts of the Jubilee are impressively evocative. Before the mayor could reply to Cowen, there were loud cries from a section of the audience for John Vaughan's son, 'the son of the puddler' who had made the development of the town possible. Fallows, who, with the mayor, acknowledged Cowen's toast, had been in Middlesbrough since its beginnings and he felt 'too touched to say a single word'. The proposer of the next toast to the 'Iron and Steel Trades of the District' referred to iron not only as the material upon which Middlesbrough's prosperity depended but, in defiance of Manchester and its cotton, as 'the great civilizer of the world'. The Lord Mayor of York, who was present as a guest, must have pondered deep on all these sentiments. The firework display in Albert Park which rounded off the festivities included Bengal Fire, Aladdin's Oriental Tree and the Falls of Niagara, but the *grande finale* consisted of 'a magnificent flight of two hundred coloured rockets and a monster piece of pyrotechnic art in the form of "Scenes of Middlesbrough"'.

CHAPTER 2

'JACKY' AND THE JUBILEE:
MIDDLESBROUGH'S CREATION
MYTH

Tony Nicholson

In 1880, Middlesbrough – the 'infant Hercules' and 'youngest child of England's enterprise' – woke to find itself fifty years old and thoroughly depressed. The thrusting new town which had risen out of the barren salt marshes along the southern edge of the River Tees had always been encouraged to frame its sense of identity in terms of future ambition; indeed, its corporate motto, *'Erimus'* ('We shall be'), encapsulated this dominant, tenacious faith in progress, and as long as the extraordinary growth which had so impressed Gladstone and other outside observers could be sustained, then this faith in an ever-expanding future was bound to overshadow any curiosity in its past. Now, however, things were changing. In place of the thumping optimism and sense of progress which had characterized its earlier years, there was a mood of uncertainty and anxiety. Prominent members of the community talked openly about their doubts regarding the town's economic prospects, and some outside observers began to evoke images of Middlesbrough's 'mushroom growth', hinting at the ephemeral nature of its previous expansion.

In one sense, of course, Middlesbrough's depression – both economic and psychic – was hardly unique. It was part of a wider mood of national crisis which can be traced back to the mid-1870s. The economic and social buoyancy of the mid-Victorian boom years had begun to deflate during this key decade, partly in the face of a perceived economic threat from larger industrializing nations such as Germany and the United States, and partly in a weary recognition that core domestic problems such as urban poverty and class tension had not disappeared under a liberal economic system. But if we need to set Middlesbrough in this wider national context, it also has to be acknowledged that the town occupied a special place in the nation's experience of such crisis. In essence, here was a crisis about modernization, and nowhere was there a more potent symbol of the 'modern' than Middlesbrough. Viewed from this perspective, the town's problems were not unique, but neither were they ordinary; Middlesbrough was a touchstone for the rest of the country. If 'Ironopolis' was falling by the economic wayside, what hope for other areas and industries?

The early phases of spectacular growth which had seemed to typify the halcyon years of Middlesbrough's youth, especially after the discovery of Cleveland ironstone in 1850, culminated in the 'riotous trade' of the early 1870s, a boom time when iron prices, company profits and population levels all rose to unprecedented heights; a rarefied and dizzy atmosphere which encouraged many of the more recent recruits to the iron-making capital of the world to view Middlesbrough's market dominance as natural and impregnable. By the mid-1870s, however, this extraordinary boom period had collapsed, giving way to a deep trough of economic and social depression which blighted the remainder of the 1870s, and which was still hanging ominously over the town as it approached its fiftieth birthday.

Although this depression was triggered by a severe downturn in the international trade-cycle, this was not the main source of concern; the town had experienced similar troughs during the earlier stages of its development, particularly during the 1840s and the mid-1860s, and it knew how to weather such times. No, the overwhelming mood of anxiety was rooted in a more serious structural problem which threatened the very foundations of Middlesbrough's economic future. The town's staple industry – iron manufacture – seemed to be crumbling. As late as the mid-1870s, railway contractors, shipbuilders and engineers had relied on the cheap, mass-produced iron on which Middlesbrough had built its greatness, but now these markets were turning towards steel, partly because it offered increased durability as a constructional material and partly because new production methods were reducing its selling price. Middlesbrough and the wider Cleveland iron-trade struggled to maintain a foothold in this changing world. The existing technologies of steel-making relied on the use of iron ores which were low in phosphorus, and this precluded the use of Cleveland's 'native ores' which had a high phosphoric content. Efforts to find a new method of steel production which would overcome this technical problem had resulted in the 'successful' trials of the Thomas-Gilchrist method as early as 1879, but problems still remained in applying this new technology to full production, as well as in marketing the quality of Cleveland steel to sceptical national and international consumers. In these circumstances, the Middlesbrough ironmasters were far from confident that they could dominate national and international markets by relying on their local supply of cheap ironstone – the most important natural asset which underpinned Middlesbrough's commercial greatness.

Into this unpromising situation came a bold and unlikely suggestion: that a series of Jubilee celebrations should be staged which would not only commemorate the town's fiftieth birthday, but trumpet its continued greatness. The project, initiated by a small clique of prominent social leaders within the ailing community, was designed primarily as a public relations exercise to brighten the fading image of Middlesbrough, but the planning and delivery of such a celebration also triggered a heightened level of interest in the town's sense of identity and history. Since the whole exercise was pitched at a public level and most of the events and characters being celebrated were within the personal recall of many local people, this construction of the town's history was also a very open one, with almost all sections of the community taking a part in pasting together the collective record. It was a point at which (for lack of a better way of putting it) 'elite' and 'popular' culture intertwined, and in doing so, it also became a contested process, with official and unofficial versions of the town's history sometimes coming into conflict.

At the official level, there were carefully orchestrated plans to stage public rituals and pageants which would form the central feature of a Jubilee day itself: processions of Sunday school scholars, friendly societies and social dignitaries would represent and confirm the social, intellectual and moral advancement of the community; the commissioning and unveiling of statues and portraits would honour the role of Middlesbrough's 'founding fathers'; street decorations put up in the most conspicuous places would draw attention to the finest architectural features of the developing townscape; a Jubilee banquet held in the town's most impressive building, the Royal Exchange, at which social dignitaries from Middlesbrough and the North would work their way through a wonderfully proper and predictable toast list – to Royalty, Church, Parliament, Town, Iron and Steel Trade, Municipalities of Great Britain and 'The Ladies' – would help to assure the wider world that Middlesbrough society was as loyal and respectable as any in the kingdom; a novel display of electric lights after dark would symbolize the modern and progressive character of this dynamic urban community.

Here was an ambitious programme which required considerable planning. Several committees were established to orchestrate its main strands, but overall control remained in the hands of the original clique. At the centre of this group was the commanding presence of Hugh Gilzean Reid, proprietor of Middlesbrough's principal newspaper, *The North-Eastern Daily Gazette*. Reid was a newspaper man with journalistic connections throughout the country and a truly 'modern' figure who appreciated the enormous public relations potential which could be gained by staging such a spectacle and then selling it to his colleagues in the Victorian press. It was largely through his efforts that the concept of a birthday celebration developed from a very modest and localized affair – a 'ten-and-sixpence dinner' as it was mockingly dubbed – into the major spectacle of the Jubilee Day itself. And it was largely through his professional experience and contacts that the event gained such extensive press coverage. Several editorials in *The Times* and *Pall Mall Gazette*, for example, demonstrated a remarkable familiarity with the chronological details and statistics relating to Middlesbrough's growth, and one can only assume that such information had been fed to them through carefully prepared press releases. The two most prestigious illustrated periodicals of the day, *The Graphic* and the *Illustrated London News* were both attracted to Middlesbrough and accorded every facility in covering the event. If an artist from one of these periodicals wanted to draw the spectacular panorama of industrial Middlesbrough which had caught Gladstone's imagination in the 1860s, then he was given every opportunity to gain a novel perspective: 'Our sketch of Middlesbrough was taken from the top of one of Messrs. "Bell Brothers" furnaces', crowed the *Illustrated London News* excitedly, 'and several times, when coke and ironstone were being put in, our Artist had to run into a hut for shelter from the blinding smoke and the intense heat.'[1]

The result was perfect, providing just the kind of bustling image which Middlesbrough wanted to present — a busy industrial landscape brimming with blastfurnaces, chimneys, shipping and shipbuilding, railways, telegraph wires and above all else, a smoke-filled

A commanding presence: Hugh Gilzean Reid (MCL)

sky which pronounced to the world that Middlesbrough was very much alive again. Better still were the wonderfully atmospheric images which *The Graphic* produced of the iron and steel-making process observed at closer quarters. In 'Blast Furnaces', the human scale of the puddlers, symbols of an older handicraft tradition from the iron era, was dwarfed by the surrounding canyons of massive new furnaces (Middlesbrough was already famous for building its furnaces higher than elsewhere), belching their fire and steam

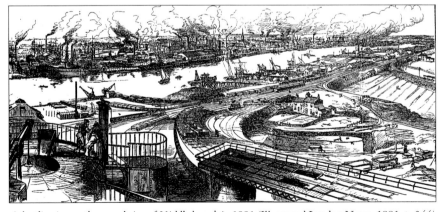

A bustling image: the general view of Middlesbrough in 1881 (Illustrated London News, 1881, p. 344)

Canyons of massive furnaces: blasting iron (The Graphic, *1881, p. 373*)

into a lowering sky. Once again, here was a landscape devoid of any traditional beauty, but one which boiled and hissed with an undeniable modern power. In 'Steel Making by the Thomas-Gilchrist Process' *The Graphic* presented Middlesbrough with the best image of all; visual proof that the new process of steel-making had developed beyond the stages of theory and drawing boards, and had taken colossal shape.

Lest the readers of these papers should come away with the impression that Middlesbrough was all furnaces and no refinement, the two papers duly obliged Reid and his friends with a series of more conventional drawings which featured the town's main civic and commercial buildings, including the private residence at Marton Hall of the Bolckow family. Reid's skilful feeding and management of the press was never openly acknowledged, but is implicit throughout. Indeed, there is visual evidence of this managing process at work during the unveiling of a statue to Henry Bolckow, one of the town's

Up-to-date steel-making: the Thomas-Gilchrist Process (The Graphic, *1881, p. 388)*

founding fathers, which took place in the afternoon of the Jubilee day itself. A surviving photograph of the event shows a special enclosure which had been provided close to the main platform for the numerous reporters and artists covering the proceedings. Drawings of the same ceremony in the *Illustrated London News* and *The Graphic* provide considerable detail of the crowds and surrounding buildings, but both edit out any visual evidence of this professional arrangement.

However, for all their impressive skills in orchestrating this kind of event, Hugh Gilzean Reid and his friends were not able to control and shape the history of Middlesbrough in any complete sense. Other unofficial interpretations were also at large, and we can sometimes glimpse them in the letter columns of the local newspapers, in descriptions and drawings of the street decorations and in repeated efforts by official chroniclers to refute what they perceived as 'popular' and misguided stories and anecdotes. Nowhere was this tension between official and unofficial versions more evident than in the central story of how Cleveland ironstone was discovered, and the place of John Vaughan in that discovery, an issue which was to lead ultimately to one

News management: published illustration of the unveiling ceremony

News management: the special enclosure for reporters and artists at the unveiling of the Bolckow statue (MCL)

of the most dramatic, unofficial 'scenes' of the Jubilee Day itself.

The idea for the Jubilee can be traced back to 1878. In June of that year, Henry Bolckow, one of the founding fathers of the Cleveland iron trade and the town's first mayor and MP, died after a long period of failing health. In many respects, Bolckow's death marked the end of a pioneering era in Middlesbrough's history. He and his partner, John Vaughan, had been associated with the years of greatest glory and prosperity, and together with Joseph Pease, the other major figure in the development of Middlesbrough, they were now all departed from the scene. If Pease had been the creator of Middlesbrough in the earliest years, it had been Vaughan's discovery of the Cleveland ironstone field in 1850 which heralded its entry into true greatness. In the years that followed this discovery, it was the firm of Bolckow & Vaughan which led the way in the expansion of the Cleveland iron trade. In doing so, they not only laid the foundations for their own personal fortunes, but assumed the status of civic patriarchs, the main providers of the town's new prosperity.

The particular nature of their business partnership had always been the stuff of industrial romance. Bolckow, coming from an educated and mercantile background, had provided the capital for the new firm while Vaughan, a skilled and talented ironworker who had risen through the ranks, provided its practical expertise. They had first met when courting and marrying two sisters, and then lived next door to each other during the early pioneering years in Middlesbrough. It hardly needs pointing out that their partnership seemed to symbolize an ideal union of capital and labour, and one moreover which was not simply idealistic but highly profitable. By the mid-1860s, the two men had made immense fortunes for themselves and for the wider Middlesbrough community and were able to retire from the active management of their concerns. Vaughan died in 1868, leaving a staggering fortune of nearly £1 million to Thomas Vaughan, his son and heir, while Bolckow survived his partner by ten years, a time during which the townspeople showered him with all the social and political honours at their disposal.

Shortly after Bolckow's burial, it was suggested that a monument should be raised to his memory and several prominent leaders of the district promised to make contributions towards the commissioning of a public statue which would be sited in the public park which Bolckow had presented to the town. However, this initiative came at a particularly bad time; the mid-to-late 1870s depression was reaching its deepest and darkest point. Ironically, it was in that very year that the unthinkable had happened – Thomas Vaughan, the son and heir to John Vaughan's immense fortune, was declared bankrupt. Although he was not alone in succumbing to this trade depression, the psychological blow which Vaughan's particular fall dealt to the Middlesbrough community was incalculable. His bankruptcy seemed to threaten the very foundations of the town, not just in the sense that his debts imposed financial strains on many local creditors, nor that there were large numbers of his workmen thrown out of employment, but also because the Vaughan name stood at the heart of a creation myth which had become central to Middlesbrough's sense of confidence and identity.

Bolckow's death was regretted deeply, but the town knew how to mourn such loss. Local newspapers appeared with their column margins lined in solid black ink; the shops and commercial premises in the town closed during his funeral day; crowds lined the route of the funeral cortège; every Middlesbrough dignitary who was able to attend the ceremony at Marton churchyard, did so; people talked about a public statue which would provide a lasting monument to a founding father's memory. Of course, it is something of a truism to observe that each age and society has its own special taboos, and it has often been recognized that the Victorians, unlike ourselves, were rather good at dealing with death. Bolckow's death was no exception; his demise provided the town with an opportunity to unite in a public display of respect, and the whole thing was carried off with considerable *éclat*. The real taboo subject which afflicted middle-class Victorian society was not death (nor, despite popular notions to the contrary, was it sex) but the awful spectre of business failure. Thomas Vaughan's bankruptcy was literally unspeakable.

Nowhere was the taboo surrounding failure more rigidly enforced than in Middlesbrough's Jubilee celebrations. Any aspects of the town's history which even hinted at failure was wiped from the official record. Such an approach was evident from the very start of planning. During one of the early meetings of the organizers in November 1880, for example, it was suggested that the Jubilee date should be set for the following month, to coincide with the fiftieth anniversary of the first shipment of coal from Middlesbrough. From an historical perspective, this was a perfectly reasonable date to adopt, but it posed awkward problems. Middlesbrough had been promoted originally as a coal-exporting port to rival Newcastle and Sunderland, but these kinds of ambitions soon proved to be hopelessly unrealistic. Indeed, by the end of the 1840s, it was increasingly evident that Middlesbrough, far from posing a threat to the established giants of the north-east, was struggling to maintain its economic position as a coal exporting outlet in the face of competition posed by a much closer rival at West Hartlepool.

What Reid and other social leaders of the town knew only too well, and what they chose to ignore in their official version of events, was that Middlesbrough and all the powerful interest groups associated with it in the 1840s – most notably the Stockton and Darlington Railway Company, the Pease family and the firm of Bolckow & Vaughan – had been brought dangerously close to ruin. The trade depression of the late 1840s almost destroyed everything and everyone: the coal-exporting trade slipped inexorably away from Middlesbrough towards West Hartlepool; the Stockton and Darlington Railway Company struggled to meet its financial obligations; Joseph Pease was brought close to personal bankruptcy and nervous collapse. By 1847, the structural weaknesses in Middlesbrough's perilous position were exacerbated by a banking panic which caught Bolckow & Vaughan at a particularly bad time. Bailiffs were sent in to take possession of their Middlesbrough works. At the eleventh hour, a messenger was despatched to Joseph Pease calling on him to bail them out. Although he was close to bankruptcy himself, Pease's public reputation was still capable of inspiring widespread confidence in the commercial world of the north-east, and he was able to bluster out the crisis, standing security for the firm and maintaining their continued presence in Middlesbrough.

Suffice it to say, the official Jubilee version of Middlesbrough's history filtered out this episode, not for its lack of dramatic potential (it had plenty of that) but because such things hinted at the mortality and vulnerability of the town and its founding fathers. Were they going to celebrate failure? Reid asked his fellow organizers, if only rhetorically. They 'should not seek to celebrate the failure of the coal trade . . . but the rise and progress of Middlesbrough.'[2] Instead of conceding the failure of the original coal-exporting trade, they chose to portray the town's transition from the 'first epoch' of coal-shipping to the 'second epoch' of iron-making as a strange mixture of untroubled evolutionary growth and magical destiny. It was acknowledged that the coal trade fell away as the iron trade prospered, but this was only to be expected in such extraordinary circumstances. Middlesbrough, after all, had now moved on to bigger and better things.

But here they encountered the real historical problem. The key factor which accounted for this dramatic transformation in Middlesbrough's fortunes was the discovery of Cleveland ironstone, the one episode in the town's history which everyone knew something about and which had been worked into a local 'creation myth', familiar to every schoolchild in Cleveland. By the time of the Jubilee, it had become a cherished part of local cultural stock, and journalists assumed that all their readers knew of it, referring to it as 'the familiar story' or 'the tale which had oft been told and needs no repeating'. In essence, the making of this myth involved an intermixing of oral and written sources, drawing ingredients from both elite and popular cultural traditions. For the most part, it operated in the realm of oral culture, a culture which, it needs to be stressed, was not exclusively confined to working people, and underwent changes and embellishments in the telling. Consequently, we have very little written evidence – apart from one notable example which we will come to later – of how the story circulated.

However, the popularity of such myths lies mainly in their use of predictable genres and formulae: they run along narrative grooves which are familiar to both tellers and listeners, and if we have only one or two fragments of the whole, it is enough to set things in motion. In effect, we can see that the familiar narrative grooves or structures which underpinned Middlesbrough's creation myth came from two principal sources. On the one hand, we can trace its original form to the classic story lines of folk-tales and fairy-tales recorded in several published collections such as the Grimms' *Kinder- und Hausmarchen (Children's and Household Tales)* which appeared throughout the course of the nineteenth century. Overlaying this foundation, however, we can also see that many of the narrative structures developed by these folk-tales were taken and reworked in another classic tradition of nineteenth-century mythologizing, the published collections of short biographies celebrating the talents and achievements of successful individuals; Samuel Smiles' *Self Help* was a pioneering work in this new genre, and one which spawned many imitators. Just as Smiles structured many of his stories of heroic individual adventure and enterprise along the lines of familiar folk-tales, so too his model of story-telling was adopted and developed by other practitioners. In Cleveland, for example, there was John Jeans' *Pioneers of the Cleveland Iron Trade* and William Hall Burnett's *Cleveland Worthies*, to mention two of the most notable. A comparison between the classic structure of fairy-tales and the main narrative structure of John Vaughan's life-story which emerged from these local Smilesean accounts might help to illustrate how close the two traditions actually were, and how easy it was for ideas and influences to flow back and forth between them:

Classic Fairy-tale Structure	*Smilesean Structure of Vaughan's Life*
• the intelligent and resourceful son of a poor family	• Vaughan is born into a labouring family
• sets out to make his fortune	• begins his life as a labourer, but rises through the ranks to become a foreman, then a manager, and finally an owner of ironworks
• experiences a series of hardships and trials	• his firm struggles to establish itself during the pioneering years of the new Middlesbrough colony
• resolves his problems when he is blessed by a stroke of good fortune	• discovers Cleveland ironstone after years of patient exploration, *or* • stumbles over a boulder of ironstone while shooting rabbits on Eston moor and immediately grasps the full significance of his lucky break
• uses his native wit and energy to make full use of his fortune	• secures very favourable royalty agreements with local landowners; superintends the construction of new blastfurnaces and becomes a millionaire
• lives happily ever after among a grateful populace.	• finally, retires to a palatial hall where he is revered as the 'founder of the Cleveland iron trade' – the provider of Middlesbrough's prosperity.

These two popular narrative traditions, similar in so many ways, diverged in one fundamental respect. While the classic structure of the fairy-tale was happy to emphasize the place of luck in transforming the hero's fortunes, Smilesean mythology claimed that success was only to be gained through perseverance, hard work and enterprise. Herein lay the fundamental difference between what was called the 'popular' version of the discovery, with its tale of John Vaughan stumbling over a boulder of ironstone while out shooting rabbits on Eston Hills, and the Smilesean version which sought to emphasize the

'Jacky': Middlesbrough's 'Smilesean' hero
(The Graphic, 8 October 1881)

years of patient endeavour and determination which Vaughan had brought to his quest. Indeed, what appears to have happened is that just as Smiles and his followers took the classic folk-tale and reworked it to suit their own purposes, so people in Cleveland took the Smilesean form of John Vaughan's life – available to them in lectures, newspaper articles and other publications – and reintegrated the classic folk-tale's emphasis on luck.

Try as they might, the combined literary spadework of ironmasters, engineers and journalists could not weed out the appeal of the popular version once it had taken root in the local imagination. Several exhaustive historical accounts were compiled which sought to tell the complex and extended story of how Cleveland ironstone had really been 'discovered'. These detailed and well-researched publications established that a complicated and lengthy process of discovery, stretching over the course of the late eighteenth and early nineteenth centuries and involving many different companies and individuals, had contributed gradually to a growing awareness of the commercial value of Cleveland ironstone. Within these historical accounts, Vaughan's discovery of the main seam at Eston was still accorded a place of considerable importance, but ceased to be seen as the single defining moment of creation. It followed from this that no single individual – Vaughan or anyone else – could be elevated to the patriarchal status of 'Founder of the Cleveland Iron Trade'. Here, in other words, were the values of historical discourse seeking to supplant the power of popular myth.

It is hardly surprising that these detailed historical accounts failed to fire the popular imagination, but even the more educated sections of local society struggled to make sense of them. Why, they puzzled, did it take so long for the value of Cleveland ironstone to be appreciated? Why had so many experienced people in the northern iron trade – furnace managers, ironmasters and mining engineers – failed to discern its worth? Their bewilderment, of course, was based on a core assumption that the ironstone which Vaughan (and others) had discovered, whether by chance or by application, was intrinsically valuable. The very concept of 'discovery' suggested that something worthwhile had been found. In reality, however, the intrinsic value of Cleveland ironstone was surprisingly low; its iron content, for example, was only a modest 33 per cent compared to the 66 per cent of the haematite ores mined in Cumbria or in the northern region of Spain, and its commercial value had more to do with a chance combination of economic and geographical factors which happened to coalesce around the town of Middlesbrough in the middle decades of the nineteenth century than with any intrinsic richness in the ore itself.

However, Vaughan's discovery of the main seam at Eston had always been represented in the most dramatic and glowing terms, largely one suspects because it came at a time when the fortunes of Middlesbrough were at such a low ebb, and any promise of redemption was welcomed with open arms. At the 'sumptuous dinner' hosted by Bolckow & Vaughan as part of the formal opening of the new Eston mines in December 1850, one local landowner caught the mood of general euphoria when he expressed the hope that the first strike of a pick in the new mines would reveal the 'philosopher's stone', turning everything into gold. It was an image which was to be repeated in countless newspaper articles and after-dinner speeches. Discoveries of gold in California the year before were still fresh in the memory, and the image of gold permeated much of the rhetoric of those early years, settling like a rich exotic silt at the base of local expectations. The first row of miners' houses built at Eston, for example, thrown up on the back-to-back principle, packed with miners, their families and lodgers, and lacking many of the most basic amenities including stairs and privies, was none the less called 'California', a name which seems to have been used without the slightest hint of irony, and which says much about the over-heated excitement of this early era. Newspaper editors delighted in dubbing Middlesbrough and Cleveland 'The New Eldorado', and Gladstone's famous image of Middlesbrough as 'an infant Hercules' added its own classical imagery to the core message: that Vaughan's discovery of Cleveland ironstone had imbued Middlesbrough (alias California, Eldorado, Hercules) with extraordinary – almost magical – richness and power. The economic expansion and prosperity which characterized the quarter century between 1850 and 1875 only served to reinforce this popular assumption. As one local commentator summed it up:

> It is like a chapter in *The Arabian Nights* to read the transformations which were subsequently effected . . . Mr Vaughan was more and more esteemed by his fellow citizens, for was it not he alone that had laid deep the foundations of their future prosperity?[23]

It has always been assumed that, once the initial euphoria had subsided, Vaughan and other ironmasters made every effort to discount this kind of popular mythology. Briggs makes the point specifically:

He [Vaughan] did not . . . stumble over a block of ironstone while out shooting on the Cleveland Hills. This legend, which he always denied, concealed the care that was taken to find good sites for ironworks.[4]

Almost all of this is true. Local ironmasters like Isaac Lowthian Bell and engineers like John Marley were at pains to point out that the firm of Bolckow & Vaughan had acquired small mining operations at Skinningrove in the late 1840s and were therefore well aware of the main seam of Cleveland ironstone long before 1850. Indeed, Marley testified on several occasions that he had visited these mines on behalf of the firm only the day before their so-called 'discovery' of the same seam at Eston, less than ten miles away. Subsequent research has confirmed these accounts, and reinforced Briggs' analysis that great care was taken in searching for the ironstone, and in siting ironworks thereafter.

However, there is no evidence to suggest that John Vaughan himself ever denied the 'familiar story' surrounding his accidental discovery of ironstone. Nor is there any evidence of him seeking to scotch the associated claims made on his behalf that he was therefore the 'Founder of the Cleveland Iron Trade'. In truth, there is surprisingly little evidence relating to John Vaughan of any kind whatsoever. His working-class background may have provided a wonderful starting point for the Smilesean accounts of his upward progress but it also meant that Vaughan, despite all his business success and monetary wealth, remained ill at ease in most social situations. He was characterized by one contemporary as:

. . . not in any sense of the word a public man; his speeches were rare, and he had not the associative feeling which brings men into society. He was emphatically an ironmaster of the olden type, thoroughly knowing his work and his workmen. . . . Kindly natured, he did not greatly cultivate social life . . . He was one of the best puddlers that Dowlais (an ironworks in South Wales) turned out, and if education had not polished the jewel, it was there . . . in the rough.[5]

In short, he was not a gentleman. Other biographies talk of his 'plodding disposition' and 'average resources', his 'practical knowledge', his 'homeliness' and his affinity with working men.[6] All of these were presented as good, sound, sterling qualities, but they were also social drags on a man seeking acceptance in a society which placed great emphasis on gentlemanly status and class; even Middlesbrough had its social pretensions. Throughout his life,

Vaughan was affectionately called 'Jacky' in the works and town, and this nickname sums up his plebeian identity.[7] Certain public offices came his way – he was made mayor in 1855 and became a JP – but even here he was often portrayed as a fish out of water. One Newcastle journalist visited Middlesbrough in the early 1860s and watched Vaughan, the magistrate, at work. A minor domestic case involving 'two women with an evident talent for disagreeing' became hopelessly confused and the journalist characterized Vaughan as looking 'as though it would be easier for him to discover another Eston mine, than to determine the question in dispute'.[8]

Even his attempts to retire like a gentleman were represented as failure:

> He rented Skutterskelfe Hall, near Stokesley, and tried to settle there, resolving to devote what was left of his life to gardening and other rural pursuits. But it would not do. His industrious tendencies were not thus to be 'cabin'd, cribb'd, confin'd'. He vented his imprisoned energies upon his flower beds by daily alterations . . . He paced the limits of his park . . . ever choosing the roads that led eastwards towards the scene of his Herculean labours; and at night he would look steadfastly to where the flaming summits of the Eston furnaces . . . were flickering against the clouds . . . and listen almost lovingly for the familiar clanging of harsh sounds – the faint murmur of a great industry which seemed to steal across the fields and meadows when the air was calm. His self-imposed banishment was an utter failure. He exhausted himself by sheer longing to be back at work.[9]

Now, whether this really happened, or whether we are reading a piece of affectionate stereotyping, hardly matters. Ultimately this is how Vaughan was represented to the wider world, and indeed to posterity. While other local ironmasters, including his partner, came from educated and gentlemanly backgrounds or acquired the necessary social graces and codes en route to their fortunes, Vaughan's plebeian background and image conspired to deny him a similar status. The emphasis which most biographies placed on his practical skills and his rapport with the workforce were hardly qualities which would guarantee him a lasting memorial in the town's formal history; a history, it has to be remembered, which was dominated during that period by middle-class values and aspirations.

In this situation, it is hardly surprising that Vaughan clung onto his myth rather than denying it. In part, he did this by remaining silent, by not aligning himself with the revisionist accounts which, while not mounting a direct attack on the myth, sought none the less to provide a more accurate account of the discovery of Cleveland ironstone. But he also did it by speaking out. The best-known and most intemperate of his public speeches on this issue came in December 1855 when he was made mayor of the town.

His appointment was a genuinely popular one among the working people of Middlesbrough, especially among his own workmen, and they marked his elevation by presenting him with a portrait. As one later commentator observed, the speech which Vaughan made in response to this gift provided a telling insight into 'the main characteristics of the man'. He thanked his audience and stressed how he valued the esteem and regard of

> men who, having witnessed the vastness of the undertakings in which I and my partner are engaged – and having had opportunities of knowing . . . the mental energy and physical exertion required to conduct these works with success – have come forward thus publicly to testify to myself their appreciation of my perseverance. I have persevered. *I believe I may, without question, assert that I am the founder of the iron trade, not of Middlesbrough alone, but of the iron trade of the North of England.*[10] (author's italics)

The sheer audacity of this claim could still raise eyebrows many years later. The *Northern Echo*, for example, quoting this passage from Vaughan's speech as part of its coverage of the Jubilee celebration in 1881, tried to make every allowance for such excesses. 'Speaking so near the time', it reasoned to itself and its readers, 'with men around him . . . who knew all about it, the claim advanced in these words would have been ridiculous if it had not been just.'[11] But it *was* ridiculous, and all those knowledgeable men around Vaughan who kept their silence, knew it. They refrained from challenging him in any direct or public fashion for a number of reasons. Partly, it would not do for employers to engage in any public spat in front of their employees; class codes forbade it. Vaughan's undoubted popularity among the working people of Middlesbrough was real enough, and this needed to be considered before any attacks were mounted against him. However, his real popularity was not the product of personal or political factors, but was based on his central role within Middlesbrough's creation myth. To question Vaughan would be to question the myth, and to question the myth would be to question the sense of destiny and purpose which the myth gave the town. The man, the myth and Middlesbrough were inseparable.

Inseparable, that is, until 1878. In that year, Thomas Vaughan's bankruptcy seemed to unravel everything from the inside. Henceforth, it seemed that no individual or town could expect to 'live happily ever after', no matter how powerful the myths which cocooned them. All those historical doubts regarding John Vaughan's claim to be 'the founder of the Cleveland iron trade' came to the fore, and the strong social taboos surrounding business failure led to Thomas Vaughan's flight from the town. Over the following years, he lived the life of an exile in various secluded houses on the North Yorkshire Moors and in East Cleveland. As the Jubilee celebrations approached, it was increasingly evident that John Vaughan, while not being written out entirely from the official Jubilee history, was being relegated to its margins. No public statue or portrait was planned to celebrate his role in Middlesbrough's growth, an omission of such glaring proportions that everyone construed it as deliberate rather than accidental.

Indeed, it subsequently emerged that considerable debate had taken place among members of the organizing committee regarding this decision. Raylton Dixon, a major shipbuilder in the town, protested against Vaughan's exclusion, but had been overruled. Not content to allow this public insult to Vaughan to pass unanswered, Dixon placed his private carriage at the disposal of Tom Vaughan and his mother on the Jubilee day itself. Tom Vaughan's reappearance caused something of a stir in itself, and the popular affection in which he and his father were still held among the labouring classes of Middlesbrough was evident throughout the Jubilee procession. 'Wherever his carriage appeared on the route, applause was loud and long continued', noted one local newspaper.[12] Reid and other prominent organizers of the event were warned that a growing tide of resentment was gathering over the treatment of the Vaughan family. The lack of any suitable memorial to John Vaughan was one source of disquiet. The lack of any formal toast to Vaughan at the evening banquet, and the relegation of Tom Vaughan and his mother to one of the lowest tables, were others.

By the hour of the Jubilee banquet, things were coming to a head. A long programme of toasts and speeches had been prepared, and a distinguished array of speakers marshalled. Unfortunately, the accoustics of the Exchange Hall proved to be 'wretched' and large sections of the audience were unable to follow the proceedings; only the Archbishop of York seemed to have the lungs and voice to make himself heard. By the time Joseph Cowen, the Newcastle newspaper proprietor, Liberal MP and prominent orator rose to propose a toast to 'The Mayor, Aldermen and Burgesses of Middlesbrough, and Prosperity to their Town and Trades on this its Jubilee', the atmosphere was strained. Cowen launched into a brilliant but overlong speech, and it was soon evident that large sections of the audience were growing restive. Sensing that he was losing their attention, Cowen cut things short and sat down. The official programme now required the town's mayor to acknowledge the toast. As he rose, however, there were loud calls of 'Vaughan: let Tom Vaughan reply' and these continued for several minutes. Small groups of people, fearing an ugly scene, began to leave their seats and move towards the exits, 'some holding back hesitatingly and looking with wonder and amazement upon the scene of excitement before them'.[13] While this was taking place, a friend advised Tom Vaughan to approach the front and acknowledge the audience. He did so, taking care to bow to the mayor and the audience, and was evidently on the point of making an impromptu speech. In a hapless misreading of the situation, the mayor stopped him and Vaughan began to walk slowly back to his seat. It was a watershed moment. The image of John Vaughan's son being turned away from

The banquet: admission by invitation (CA)

The banquet: the menu (CA)

A restive audience? The 'official' illustration of the banquet in progress reveals nothing
(Illustrated London News, 1881, p. 369)

Middlesbrough's high table was too much for almost anyone to bear. More and more members of the audience got to their feet and demanded that he be allowed to speak. Finally, amid loud cheering, he was given the floor and as one newspaper reported, 'the result was electric'.

A short emotional speech followed which ended climactically:

> I thank you all here. I thank the public; I thank the working men who showed me today that Vaughan, although absent, is not forgotten. (Cries of 'Never forgotten, Tom' and enthusiastic cheering.) It is, I am sure, your desire to show sincere respect to the memory of John Vaughan. ('Hear, hear' and a voice, 'And to his worthy successor'.) Under the restrictions of the Mayor and committee – ('Shame') – I thank you most deeply as the son and representative of John Vaughan, the puddler – (cheers) – for showing that I am not forgotten by you here; I am not forgotten by the outside public; I am not forgotten by the British working men, although I may be forgotten by those who live in marble halls; and I thank them and you most heartily for the respect you have paid to the memory of my father, John Vaughan. (Loud cheers, followed by three cheers being given for Mrs Vaughan.)[14]

A collective spasm of guilt and affection heaved through the town and neighbourhood. Within a few hours, there was talk of forming a new 'Vaughan Memorial Committee' which would organize the collection of subscriptions towards a statue. Next day, it was reported that a railway carriage full of gentlemen fell to discussing the drama of the 'Vaughan incident' and on the question being asked, 'What will you give?' a sum of £35 was immediately forthcoming. Members of the Jubilee committee who had been most closely associated with attempts to write Vaughan out of their official history were subjected to widespread abuse. On the one hand, their social snobbery was contrasted with the 'manliness', 'generosity' and 'simplicity' of both Jacky and Tom Vaughan. On the other hand, their attempts to impose historical accuracy on Middlesbrough's beloved creation myth were exposed as inept: '. . . comparative newcomers to the town have failed to understand, and have not had adequately interpreted to them, the traditions of Early Middlesbrough.'[15]

It took three more years before all the subscriptions were collected and Vaughan's statue was completed. The unveiling ceremony took place in June 1884. Among the official speakers invited to make a contribution on that day of civic atonement was John Marley, the mining engineer who had accompanied John Vaughan on the celebrated search of the Eston Hills on 8 June 1850. Once again, Marley was called upon to recite the details of that day; the town's favourite bedtime story. He did so, as he had done before, in a very correct and historical manner, stressing that he was providing them with an 'actual', 'eye-witness' account. However, on this occasion, he also offered an historical interpretation of how the popular creation myth had first arisen. During the formal opening of the Eston Mines' railway, he recalled, John Vaughan had made a casual remark that it 'was wonderful that so often as he had been out shooting over the very ground, he had never knowingly kicked his foot against a piece of ironstone'. The newspapers of that day had reported this chance remark which then passed into general circulation. Here, Marley argued, was the origin of the rabbit-shooting story which had been 'so associated with the discovery of ironstone in the popular mind'.[16] It was a clever speech which seemed to sort things out rather nicely; the historical and the mythical had been disentangled.

However, the publicity surrounding this ceremony had reached the ears of a Leeds gentleman called Henry Whitaker, and it began to stir memories. He recalled a select dinner party which he had attended near Middlesbrough in the 1860s. After the ladies had left the table, and the men were finishing their dessert, the conversation turned to the town and its locality. Whitaker's host took the opportunity to tell his guests about the rabbit-shooting story, and Whitaker was so impressed that he recorded as many details as possible in his personal journal. Over twenty years later, he dug out his old journals, copied down the story and sent it to the press. In doing so, he provides us with the only full written account of Middlesbrough's beloved creation myth. Whitaker's host began:

You are perhaps not aware that a rabbit was the cause of Middlesbrough being built, and first commencement of our fortunes. A friend of mine had got a day's rabbit-shooting from a person who owned a farm at Eston. . . . A number of rabbits were shot. One of them crept into a crevice amongst some rocks. We could see it lying dead, but could not reach it. So I went to try and find a long bramble, which I intended to wrap or twist round it, and then be able to pull it out, but I could not find one. I then recollected that when we were driving up the lane noticing a man breaking stones. He had a sledge-hammer which I went to borrow. With this I knocked off some of the rock on each side of the crevice, until the opening was so enlarged that I could introduce my shoulder, and this enabled me to procure the rabbit. I thought at the time that there was a peculiar ring or sound when the pieces of stone were falling, so I took up some of these fragments and found they were heavy; and I and my friend carried a number of these pieces to the gig which had come to a place below to meet us. And no sooner had we got home than I sent for the foreman of the foundry . . . [who] . . . took the various fragments of stone which were brought, examined and weighed them in his hand; was certain they contained metal; so he had them pounded, and then put in a crucible, and this was put into a furnace, where it remained a certain time, and when it had undergone the fiery ordeal it was found to contain some molten metal. . . . A short time afterwards we took the gig and drove over to the place where I had got the rabbit. We found there was a horizontal band of rock from about twelve to twenty feet thick, which seemed, as far as we could investigate it, to traverse the face of the hills. . . .[17]

The host and story-teller was, of course, John Vaughan.

At the end of the day, separating myth from reality is not just an impossible task for the historian, it is often an undesirable one. Myth-making was a central process in the shaping of Middlesbrough's early history, and we need to recognize its importance. It was there in the promotional work of Hugh Gilzean Reid and his friends, as well as in the 'traditions of Early Middlesbrough' with which they came into conflict. One Stockton newspaper, commenting on the Jubilee celebrations of its rival, observed how myths (like prophecies) can be self-fulfilling: 'In these days when modest merit goes to the wall, the more a community trumpets itself, the more will the world reverence it. . . . Middlesbrough has succeeded in making the world believe that she is great, therefore she is great.'[18]

By the same token, when the people of Middlesbrough chose to believe that John Vaughan was 'The Founder of the Cleveland Iron Trade', and that the discovery of Cleveland ironstone took place by accident when 'Jacky' went out shooting rabbits, then we need to take notice. Myths carry their own kind of reality.

NOTES

1. The *Illustrated London News*, 8 October 1881, p. 359.
2. *North-Eastern Daily Gazette*, 27 November 1880.
3. J.H. Burnett, *Cleveland Worthies* (1886), p. 106.
4. A. Briggs, above, p. 9.
5. Written by a 'Mr Steele of West Hartlepool' for the series, 'Northern Worthies' in the *Newcastle Weekly Chronicle*, and quoted in Burnett, *Cleveland Worthies*, p. 110.
6. See for example, J.S. Jeans, *Pioneers of the Cleveland Iron Trade*, chapter 3 and the *Northern Echo*, 7 October 1881.
7. Burnett, p. 100.
8. L. Praed, *History of the Rise and Progress of Middlesbrough* (1863), p. 18.
9. Burnett, p. 107.
10. Quoted in several biographies of Vaughan, including Burnett, pp. 99–100, and *Northern Echo*, 7 October 1881.
11. *Northern Echo*, 7 October 1881.
12. The *Daily Exchange*, 8 October 1881.
13. The *Daily Exchange*, 8 October 1881.
14. See the *Daily Exchange*, 8 October 1881 and *North-Eastern Daily Gazette*, 8 October 1881 for full accounts.
15. The *Daily Exchange*, 8 October 1881.
16. See *Weekly Exchange*, 7 June 1884 and *North-Eastern Daily Gazette*, 7 June 1884.
17. *North-Eastern Daily Gazette*, 2 June 1884.
18. *Stockton Journal*, 8 October 1881.

CHAPTER 3

THE INFANT HERCULES AND THE AUGEAN STABLES: A CENTURY OF ECONOMIC AND SOCIAL DEVELOPMENT IN MIDDLESBROUGH, *c.* 1840–1939

David Taylor

The first century of Middlesbrough's economic history has about it a mythical quality, both heroic and also tragic. There was something almost superhuman about the town's early industrialization that was captured in Gladstone's oft-quoted reference to the 'infant Hercules'. No other town in Britain could match the spectacular demographic and economic growth that transformed a small collection of farms into one of the nation's leading industrial centres. However, the life-cycle of the town, in its first hundred years at least, was not an unqualified success story. The promise of the early, rumbustious years was only partly realized as the town moved into its mature years after 1870. The economic strength of the growing 'infant Hercules' was insufficient to cleanse the Augean stables that were the town's courts and alleys. Poverty coexisted with progress in the town that Lady Bell surveyed just before the outbreak of the First World War. Worse was to follow. The interwar years were to prove a most difficult time. The industrial forces that had given birth to the 'infant Hercules' were losing their potency. The narrow industrial base proved to be the town's 'poisoned shirt'. The heroic quality of nineteenth-century industrial growth was replaced by tragedy as the town's staple industries went into decline bringing suffering to many. Yet if the town's particular pattern of development was unprecedented, in a broader sense Middlesbrough's fluctuating fortunes mirrored wider changes in the nation's economic and social fortunes and provide a commentary on the world's first industrial nation.

THE 'INFANT HERCULES': THE EARLY YEARS C. 1840–1870S

Agriculture dominated the economy and society of Middlesbrough in the early nineteenth century. The census enumerators who tallied the 154 inhabitants in 1831 could scarcely have envisaged the transformation that was about to take place. Growing demand for coal, the development of the Stockton and Darlington Railway and the navigational limitations of the Tees came together to create a window of opportunity that was to be exploited by Joseph Pease and his Quaker colleagues who became the Owners of the Middlesbrough Estate and the founders of the modern town. The extension of the railway to Middlesbrough had been completed in December 1830 and the first coal was loaded at the new staithes a month later. Success was not guaranteed as competition from Hartlepool was considerable. After a visit by Thomas Cubitt in 1836 to plan a dock, the decision to build was taken in 1838 by the Middlesbrough Owners who, in return, gained the monopoly of all coal carried past Stockton. Four years later the work was complete. Ten coal staithes, capable of loading at 16 tons per hour, had been erected and there was space for 3,000 coal wagons and 150 ships in a dock complex that covered some 9 acres in total. Impressive though this investment was, it could not safeguard the town's economic future. Indeed, by the end of the decade it was becoming obvious that coal exports were falling and the future was less than promising. Salvation was closer to hand than anyone realized.

The expansion of the railways in the region created considerable demand and in response to this an ironworks was established in 1839 by Henry Bolckow and John Vaughan with the encouragement and support of Joseph Pease. The rolling mill in Vulcan Street first started production in 1841 with an eye to the manufacture of rails for the Stockton and Darlington Railway Company. By 1846 some 20,000 tons were being produced, mainly in the form of rails and bars but the company also had machine-tool facilities which enabled the production of small and medium-sized steam engines. The support of Pease who, among other things, ensured that the orders for rails from the Stockton and Darlington Railway came their way, was essential in the early years. Demand fluctuated markedly as the slump of 1847 clearly demonstrated. With the collapse in demand production levels were well below the capacity of the company. A further problem was the supply of iron ore. However, Bolckow & Vaughan stayed in business as did other small firms in the district who were also involved in the trade. Of these, the best known was the firm of Gilkes & Wilson which was responsible for the Tees Engine Works in Vulcan Street and later, in 1852, the Tees Ironworks, which was built on a marshy site near the eastern end of the Middlesbrough Estate. Once again, the Peases were involved in encouraging the enterprise.

Fortunes were to change dramatically with the discovery of commercially viable ironstone deposits in the Eston Hills in 1850. The local iron industry was revitalized and with it came unprecedented expansion. Bolckow & Vaughan established blastfurnaces and ironworks in Middlesbrough and Eston in 1852; in 1853 the Bell Brothers set up an ironworks at Port Clarence and the Tees-side Ironworks of Messrs Snowden & Hopkins was also started; while in 1854 Sir Bernard Samuelson established a blastfurnace at South Bank and the Cochranes did likewise at Ormesby. The outbreak of the Crimean War provided a further boost, albeit of a short-term nature. By the middle of the decade there were some fourteen blastfurnaces in Middlesbrough and a further fourteen to the east of the town. The balance of economic power in the town was shifting. What is more, the new entrepreneurs were determined to maximize their position through coordinated action. In 1855 the first meeting of the Cleveland Ironmasters' Association took place in the Talbot Inn, Middlesbrough. A new presence had established itself which was to have a profound effect on the subsequent development of the town.

The growth of the iron trade was spectacular. New firms such as Fox, Head & Co. and Gilkes, Wilson, Pease & Co. entered alongside established producers. Long-term growth was punctuated by slumps in the late 1850s and mid-1860s and booms, most notably in the early 1870s when the Franco-Prussian War disrupted European production and greatly increased the demand for British iron. By the early 1870s the Cleveland District, with some ninety blastfurnaces, was producing over two million tons annually, or one-third of national output of pig-iron. Production was heavily concentrated in the Ironmasters District of Middlesbrough and further east along the Middlesbrough to Redcar railway, and the locality had clearly emerged as the major iron-making district not simply in Britain but in the world at the time.

It was not simply the number of firms nor the number of blastfurnaces that increased. The scale of production within the local industry also grew spectacularly. The early furnaces stood just over 40 feet high with a 15 foot diameter at the bosh. The cubic capacity was increased as furnaces became higher and wider thanks to the engineering skills of men such as John Gjers, Richard Howson and John Borrie. By the early 1870s, to the amazement of observers from other parts of the country, the new furnaces were now over 90 feet high and with a diameter of 30 feet. The capacity of the furnaces was in the region of 25,000–30,000 cubic feet.

Size was but one part of a distinctive Cleveland practice that was to develop in the third quarter of the nineteenth century. Technological change played a crucial role and yet, in the early years, there had been no standard pattern of production. Entrepreneurs had been attracted from different parts of the country and had brought with them different techniques. John Vaughan had worked in the Dowlais Ironworks in South Wales, the Cochranes' experience was drawn from Staffordshire, while the Bells' knowledge of iron production was based on the practices of north-east England. However, this gradually changed as blastfurnace design was improved. Somewhat surprisingly, the early Middlesbrough furnaces were open-topped which meant considerable atmospheric pollution and the loss of

The Newport Ironworks accounted for 120 puddling furnaces in 1873 (CA)

potentially valuable waste gases. Closed-top working – the bell and hopper system – was gradually introduced from the late 1850s onwards, though the ex-Staffordshire ironmasters were reluctant to adopt the new technology despite its potential for reducing costs and improving the quality of iron. However, the most important step in the emergence of a distinctive local practice was the development of hot-blast working by Edward Alfred Cowper. Furnace temperatures were greatly increased from some 700 degrees Fahrenheit to over 1,000. Within a few years rapid diffusion ensured that this was part of standard Cleveland practice. Efficient use of fuel was the key and more than offset the difficulties that might have resulted from the low quality of local iron ore. By the early 1870s the regenerative hot-blast stove, direct-action blowing engines and specially designed machinery for hoisting the vast quantities of raw materials to the tops of the giant furnaces were the hallmarks of the Cleveland practice.

The expansion of pig-iron manufacturing was paralleled by the growth in production of malleable iron via the puddling process. No evidence survives from the earliest days but it is known that in the early to mid-1850s there were two major puddling plants – the Middlesbrough Ironworks of Bolckow & Vaughan and the Tees-side Ironworks of Snowden & Hopkins – and probably a total of thirty puddling furnaces. Expansion was rapid in the next decade. In 1863 there was a total of 191 puddling furnaces in Middlesbrough including 68 owned by Bolckow & Vaughan and 55 by Hopkins & Co. A fall in demand and a disruptive strike, following a decision to cut wages by 10 per cent, checked expansion, but rapid growth resumed in the late 1860s and early 1870s. Production peaked in 1873 when the number of puddling furnaces in the town topped 400. The newly formed Britannia Iron Co., whose driving force was Bernard Samuelson MP of the Newport Ironworks, accounted for 120 of them compared with the 100 of Hopkins, Gilkes & Co. who had succeeded Bolckow & Vaughan as the second largest producers. The expansion of the railways and the growth of iron shipbuilding created the buoyant demand conditions that underpinned this expansion. However, in contrast to the pig-iron sector, technological progress played little part. Indeed, attempts to mechanize and improve the production of malleable iron were notable for their lack of success. Worse, the development of steel production spelt the end of an era which was to be precipitated by the dramatic depression of the mid-1870s.

With the rapid expansion of iron-making came an expansion of the engineering and shipbuilding trades. The earliest shipbuilding yards in Middlesbrough produced wooden sailing ships. However, as early as 1840, William Cudworth, a Middlesbrough man, launched the first steam ship, *The Fortitude*, on the Tees. In 1858 Rake Kimber & Co. made the first iron ship at Middlesbrough, the *De Brus*, while the Backhouse and Dixon shipbuilding yards, opened in 1866. In addition, there were a number of smaller manufacturing industries including chemicals, wire, tank and boiler works.

However, it would be misleading to see the local economy simply in terms of heavy industry. From the earliest days there was a diversity of economic activity that has often been overlooked. The Middlesbrough Pottery was established in 1834, the more famous Linthorpe Pottery in 1880. Skilled tradesmen such as cabinetmakers and watchmakers were a small but important element in the local economy. Entrepreneurship was not confined to industry. Retailing and even leisure developed from the earliest days as it became apparent that there was a rapidly growing and concentrated mass market developing in and around Middlesbrough.

Middlesbrough's Saturday market dated back to 1841 and by the 1860s enjoyed a reputation for being 'well supplied with all the necessaries of life'. Itinerant tradesmen were an important part of life in the early years. However, fixed-site retailing became increasingly important in the town. The third quarter of the nineteenth century saw a dramatic increase in the number of shops in the town as Table I illustrates.

Table I: Selected Retail Outlets in Middlesbrough, 1851–1911

	1851	1876/7	1901	1911
Bakers & Confectioners	14	42	97	144
Butchers	21	147	128	137
Grocers	29	120	224	240
Fruiterers & Greengrocers	1	94	93	112
Fishmongers	0	18	26	32
Fried Fish Dealers	0	0	47	90
Boots & Shoes	22	104	98	117
Drapers	7	65	69	66
Tailors	18	83	57	65
Dressmakers & Milliners	6	72	70	68
Hosiers & Haberdashers	0	33	35	28
Outfitters & Clothiers	0	0	24	26
Clothes Dealers	0	18	15	20
Pawnbrokers	0	18	21	23
Miscellaneous Shops	12	295	n/a	231

The precise figures are open to some doubt but none the less give a clear indication of the scale of expansion that was taking place in this sector of the local economy. These figures need to be related to the growth of the town. Between 1851 and 1871 Middlesbrough's population grew from about 8,000 to 40,000. Such a dramatic increase in numbers and during a time of economic expansion created a highly favourable demand environment in which the small shopkeeper flourished. However, the increased number of retail outlets did not always match the growth in population. The growth of multiple retailing will be discussed later but it is important to note that Middlesbrough shopkeepers were among the first to move into this new area of retailing from the early 1860s onwards. Equally significant was the presence of the cooperative movement. The *Middlesbrough Directory and Guide* of 1866/7 records a Co-operative Store in Suffield Street while the Middlesbrough Locomotive Co-operative Society was trading in High Albert Road from the 1870s. And finally, besides a new shopkeeper element in Middlesbrough society, there was also a smaller professional sector emerging. By 1873 there were in the town eleven attorneys and solicitors, eight auctioneers and five architects and surveyors.

Whether social progress matched economic progress is a moot point. The town enjoyed a frontier reputation – the British Ballarat, as Asa Briggs has observed – as the result of the poor facilities and spectacular disturbances such as the dock-labour riot of 1840. The riot was certainly spectacular. The need for

Defective houses, cramped together with inadequate drainage and ventilation: Hopper's Yard and some of its inhabitants in the early twentieth century (MCL)

extra hands had led to the recruitment of Irish labourers. As they arrived in the town they faced a large and hostile crowd of some 400 people. The new men were escorted from the station to the dock site by the police of the Stockton and Darlington Railway Company as the crowd, containing labourers, mainly from Lancashire, already employed in dock excavation work, tried to attack them. The arrest of one of the 'mob' did nothing to relieve tension. Indeed, such was the anger of the crowd that the local 'kitty' was surrounded and broken into and the arrested man freed. A police escort was needed the following day to get the new men safely to work. However, the departure of the police, once work had commenced, was rapidly followed by a mob attack that forced the Irishmen to flee for their lives. It took the combined action of the railway police, the Stockton Borough police and fifty special constables to restore order. Eighteen ringleaders were arrested and sent for trial at the Northallerton Quarter Sessions. The town acquired a 'frontier town' reputation almost overnight but there was nothing to match these events in the following years. It probably had an above average incidence of drunkenness and petty assaults – the town dignitaries and moral guardians certainly thought so – but the serious crime rate was below that of industrial regions in the north-west and Midlands.

The physical environment left much to be desired. The Ranger Report of 1854 painted a grim picture of defective houses cramped together, with inadequate drainage and ventilation. In some of the worst cases such as the inhabited cellars in Hopper's Yard there was 'liquid refuse oozing through the walls from the ground above'. Not surprisingly the health of the town caused concern. Outbreaks of cholera were reported in 1849, 1852 and 1853 and smallpox in 1852. However, the major and persistent killers were typhus, diarrhoea and measles. With an estimated mortality rate of 30 per thousand in 1852 and 35 per thousand in 1853, Middlesbrough was one of the most unhealthy towns in the country.

The problems of the earliest years were compounded by the very rapid increase in population between 1851 and 1871. The town had originally been planned as a community of 5,000 people living in carefully laid out streets and in well-spaced houses with substantial gardens. Such planning idealism was swept away by the influx of immigrants who flocked to the town from many parts of the country, putting pressure on housing, sanitation and other amenities. New houses were built in the back gardens of existing dwellings. An intricate system of courts and alleys developed. It is a measure of conditions in the town that the crude death rate for Middlesbrough, which was below the national average in 1851, rose to well above it by 1871.

Initially the old town had been the most overcrowded and unhealthy area but by the 1870s the western district of the town had become the site of the greatest health problems. Despite being considered by the Medical Officer of Health as unsuitable for housing because of its low-lying nature and vulnerability to flooding, this was the area which absorbed most of the incoming population, including many Irish who were housed in some of the worst accommodation in the town. Not only were conditions bad for those living at the time, they also left a legacy for succeeding generations.

THE AUGEAN STABLES: MATURITY, PROSPERITY AND POVERTY,
c. 1870–1914

The last quarter of the nineteenth century was to be a period of mixed economic fortunes. New technologies, increasing foreign competition and the vicissitudes of world trade created problems for the staple industries. Uncertainty was an ever-present reality for many employers and employees. However, this is only part of the story. Other industries grew in a less spectacular fashion while the local economy diversified as the town grew. The census figures (Table II) provide us with revealing snapshots of the town's changing economic structure. The dominance of manufacturing is beyond dispute. The concentration in industries characterized by sustained growth and a continuing high level of demand for labour boded well for the local populace, although the heavy dependence on a relatively narrow range of

Limited employment opportunities for women: washing bottles at Hodgson & Downes, Wine Merchants of Newport Road in the 1890s (CA)

industries increased the vulnerability of the town to fluctuations in the fortunes of these trades. However, the expansion of dealing and public and professional services is indicative of a gradual diversification of economic activity.

The occupational structure of Middlesbrough (and increasingly much of the Teesside region) was biased towards male employment. Unlike the north-west of England, there were limited employment opportunities for women, especially after marriage. Of all the towns with a population of 50,000 or more in England and Wales, Middlesbrough had the lowest proportion of women employed.

Table II: Occupational Structure of Middlesbrough, 1871–1911

(major occupations as percentage of occupied persons)

	1871	1881	1891	1901	1911
Manufacture	49.1	46.1	43.3	46.1	45.4
Transport	8.8	10.0	11.0	12.1	14.1
Dealing	7.4	8.0	7.8	10.4	12.3
Industrial Service	16.6	13.9	15.4	9.3	5.9
Public Service & Professional	2.8	3.9	4.9	5.5	6.3
Domestic Service	4.8	10.6	9.9	8.0	8.8

As Table III shows, within the manufacturing sector the iron and steel industries dominated, though their influence waned perceptibly between 1871 and 1911. In nearby Stockton and Darlington iron and steel manufacturing accounted for only 10 per cent and 5 per cent of the local workforce, compared with almost 20 per cent in Middlesbrough. Relatively speaking, shipbuilding, engineering and machine-making were less important in the town's economy.

Table III: Occupational Distribution within Manufacturing

(as percentage of all occupied persons)

	1871	1881	1891	1901	1911
Iron & Steel	30.9	25.0	18.0	14.0	18.4
Engineering & Machines	5.3	4.3	4.9	10.9	9.0
Shipbuilding & Vehicles	2.6	3.3	5.9	7.4	4.6
Textiles etc.	6.8	6.8	6.9	3.8	4.1
Labourers	16.9	12.2	15.1	12.7	7.5

For the town's staple industries the last quarter of the century was to be problematic. In mid-1873 began a trade depression which was to have a severe impact on the major local industries. Worst hit was the production of malleable iron. In July, Fox, Head & Co. were forced to close down the Newport Rolling Mill because of the complete absence of orders. Other closures took place in the region in the following year. Then, in 1875, Bolckow & Vaughan announced the closure of all their puddling furnaces at Middlesbrough and only months later the massive Britannia Ironworks met the same fate. Finally, in 1879 both the Tees-side Ironworks and the Ayrton Ironworks (owned by Jones Bros. & Co.) suspended payments while the Imperial Ironworks of Jackson, Gill & Co. was liquidated. The trade never fully recovered from these hammer blows. Some firms such as Bell Bros suffered less through specializing in the production of iron plates, bars and angles for the iron shipbuilding industry whose continued growth partly offset the collapse of the rail trade in the face of competition from steel. Production picked up in the early 1880s but thereafter there was a steady decline in production in the town that reflected in starker form a more general national decline in the production of puddled iron.

Pig-iron production was also badly hit by the collapse of prices after the ending of the Franco-Prussian War. In 1873 the price of pig-iron had been 122*s* 6*d* (£6.13) per ton but by 1879 it was only 32*s* 6*d* (£1.13). None the less, output continued to grow until the early 1880s when stagnation set in. However, the production of pig-iron did not collapse to the same extent as that of malleable iron but the future lay with steel rather than iron production. The development of cheap steel dated from the development of the Bessemer process in the 1850s and the Martin-Siemens open hearth process in the 1860s. The problems for Middlesbrough iron producers were compounded by the fact that the local iron ore had a high level of phosphorus which resulted in poor quality steel. This was overcome by using imported ore from Spain. However, the technological problem remained and was not solved until 1879 when the Thomas and Gilchrist process enabled the unwanted phosphorus to be removed during the refining of iron to bulk steel.

The 1880s were critical years in the transition from iron to steel production. Bolckow & Vaughan introduced four Bessemer converters at their Cleveland Works at Eston Junction which were to continue in production until 1911. In 1883 the newly formed North-Eastern Co. joined them in basic-Bessemer production. However, widespread adoption was limited, not least because of the reputation for unreliability that the resultant steel products gained. Faced with competition from abroad, where the extensive reserves of haematite were more easily and economically exploited, the steel industry in Middlesbrough never enjoyed the prosperity to compare with the heyday of iron production. In particular, the early twentieth century saw a slackening of growth.

The transition to steel production was characterized by larger and more intensive plants. The major change in the years after 1870 was the emergence of the 'big two' of Bolckow & Vaughan and Dorman Long who came to dominate the local industry by the end of the century through a process of consolidation and rationalization. From the outset Bolckow & Vaughan had expanded both horizontally and vertically to maintain their position. A similar tactic was adopted by Dorman Long which had started in 1875 by leasing the Britannia Works from Bernard Samuelson. Shifting into steel production in the 1880s, the firm took over the Ayrton sheet mills and the Cleveland wire mills. To ensure control of raw materials the company acquired Bell Bros in 1899 while in 1903 the takeovers of the Acklam works and the North Eastern Steel Co. were effected. The overall consequence of this process of consolidation was the creation of two industrial giants. In the early twentieth century Bolckow & Vaughan's capital was estimated at £3.9 million and Dorman Long's at £3.3 million.

The long-term growth of the iron and steel industry was reflected in the substantially increased export of manufactured iron and steel products from Middlesbrough. In 1870 the figure was approximately 167,000 tons, rising to 682,000 tons by 1910. This long-term trend, however, was overlain by marked fluctuations determined by the trade cycle but also by sharp year to year variations. Equally volatile was the local shipbuilding industry. There were clear signs of growth. Raylton Dixon opened a new yard in 1873 while Smith's Dock was opened at South Bank in 1908. Between the late 1870s and 1890 there was a 50 per cent increase in the tonnage of new ships launched

Diversity of activity: the employees of Brown's Brassworks pose for the camera in 1896 (CA)

on the Tees and by the early twentieth century there were some six shipbuilding firms on the river. Engineering, in contrast, was less subject to violent fluctuations. Although it was closely linked with other local heavy industries, there was a diversity of activity that gave greater flexibility, which in turn minimized the traumas of the trade cycle. Nevertheless, the closely inter-related heavy industries, with their characteristic cyclical pattern of boom and slump, accounted for some 40 per cent of the local workforce and exerted a profound (and wider) influence on the economic and social life of the town.

Given the rapid growth of the town, it is not surprising to find that the building trades were an important source of employment. Residential house building was the most important factor shaping the fortunes of the local construction industry. The rapid upsurge in numbers between 1851 and 1871 provided a massive boost and the relative importance of construction was at its peak. Thereafter, as demand slackened so did the relative size of the industry.

The preoccupation with manufacturing in general and heavy industry in particular is understandable but misleading. Nationally and locally the economy was maturing. The services sector, retailing and leisure as much as banking and finance, was taking on a new importance. The continued growth of the town, combined with a small but steady increase in working-class living standards, provided the conditions in which retailing could flourish. Indeed, it was in the late nineteenth century that a new form of retailing emerged. The sale of uniform-quality, low-priced mass-produced goods resulted in a revolution in the grocery trade, led by the new multiple stores, throughout the country. In Middlesbrough, too, a new economic and social force emerged from which was to evolve, as Asa Briggs has noted, the next generation of local political leaders. However, the economic background of these men is less well known.

As early as the 1860s, a growing number of local tradesmen were developing small-scale chains of shops. It was in the grocery trade that the first developments took place. In 1861 T. Appleton & Co. had shops in South Street, Richard Street, Corporation Road, Gurney Street and Durham Street while in 1867 George Watson had shops in East Street, Wilson Street and Wellington Street. However, the most successful local entrepreneur was 'The Alderman', Amos Hinton. Born in Tring, Hertfordshire, he moved north to Batley and then Middlesbrough as a teenager. For three years he was an assistant, living in with an established town shopkeeper, John Birk. In 1865 he returned south and spent three years extending his knowledge of the trade by serving as a butterman in a Shoreditch cheesemongery and later as a bacon-hand. Returning to Middlesbrough in 1868 he set up as a partner with his former employer in South Street, before buying out Birk's share of the business in 1871. At this time, Hinton's was one of over a hundred small shops involved in the provision trade. Unlike most of his competitors, however, Amos Hinton was not content with the ownership of a small family concern. Expansion took place at South Street where Hinton created what the *North-Eastern Daily Gazette* described in February 1906 as 'one of the largest and most convenient depots known to the provision trade in the North of England'. New branches were opened in the 1870s in Linthorpe Road and Newport Road and in the 1880s in Nelson Street, South Bank and Corporation Road, Middlesbrough. The volume of trade grew steadily, though profits were rather more variable. A second phase of expansion took place in the early twentieth century and by the outbreak of the First World War the firm of Amos Hinton & Sons (the two sons William and Humphrey having been taken into partnership in 1892 and 1898 respectively) comprised six shops and in addition an Oriental Café, opened in 1887 (incidentally, the year in which Amos Hinton became mayor of Middlesbrough) and extended in 1905 to include a billiards room. Some 230 staff, predominantly women, were employed in total. South Street dominated with its seventy-six staff and seven horsemen but almost fifty people were employed at the branch in Corporation Road.

The firm's reputation was made, in no small measure, through quality. Amos Hinton had a considerable reputation as a tea-blender. Similarly, high quality coffee, aided by Hinton's own developments in coffee roasting, added

Not content with the ownership of a small family concern: Amos Hinton in 1908 when he was president of the National Confederation of Grocers and hosted the annual conference (MCL)

Amos Hinton & Sons
Tea & Coffee Specialists

GROCERS & DRIED FRUIT MERCHANTS
IMPORTERS OF BACON, EGGS & CHEESE

———— HEAD OFFICE: ————
South Street, Middlesbrough

BRANCHES: Corporation Road, opposite Town Hall, Middlesbrough (as shown in above photograph); Nelson St., South Bank; Whitworth Road, Grangetown; High Street, Redcar; Clarence Street, Haverton Hill.

Proprietors of Hinton's Oriental Cafe and Billiard Room
Near Town Hall, Middlesbrough

Hinton's 'branch' in Corporation Road in 1908 (MCL)

to the reputation of the firm. Hinton's also provided a very wide range of groceries. However, the firm was always at the forefront of change. Amos Hinton was quick to sell imported Danish butter in the 1860s and New Zealand butter in the 1890s. American bacons, hams and shoulders were another speciality. So too was fruit. In the 1890s a new department was opened to cater for this trade and one of the great novelties was the Jamaican banana – not to be confused with its inferior Costa Rican counterpart! Modernity, good judgement of the trade and business acumen based on a philosophy of hard work and close supervision were key ingredients in the Hinton success story. The reputation for quality was essential in attracting the 'carriage' trade but for the firm to prosper as it did, it was essential as well to attract the 'shawl' trade. And this Hinton's did. Emphasizing the importance of being 'servants of the public' the firm provided cheap but consistent quality produce. Good service and the building up of customer loyalty was another factor stressed by Amos Hinton. Good service required good staff. Shopwork generally entailed long hours and Hinton's was no exception, especially at the weekend when the shops stayed open until 9 p.m. on Fridays and midnight on Saturdays. However, the Hintons took a paternalistic view of their responsibility to the staff. There was a close working relationship with their employees and the firm was known to pay well and to offer a greater degree of job security than was common in this highly competitive trade. Recruitment and training policy was concerned with creating a steady flow of people who moved between departments, learning the various facets of the trade, and who moved up through the company as their experience increased. Promotion was not guaranteed but it was unusual for Hinton's to recruit outsiders into senior positions in the shops. Concern for the shop staff was reflected in the early introduction of a half-day holiday in 1881. Significantly, the firm had a high percentage of long-serving employees.

The Hinton story has to be put in the wider context of the late-nineteenth-century retailing revolution which was itself part of a process of economic diversification and maturity. Middlesbrough, not least because of its rapid growth and relative prosperity, witnessed some important changes in the years between 1870 and 1914. Given the volatile nature of the local economy, the dependence of shopkeepers on the purchasing power of an overwhelmingly working-class population, heavily concentrated in these volatile trades, and the highly competitive nature of the retail trade, it is not surprising to find that there were marked annual fluctuations in this sector of the local economy. As a consequence figures for an individual year can be misleading. However, by averaging out figures over the trade cycle we can obtain a clearer picture of long-term trends.

Table IV: The Growth of Food Retailing, 1865/74–1907/13

A: Average Number of Retail Outlets (over trade cycle)

	1865–74	1874–83	1883–90	1890–1901	1901–07	1907–13
Bakers & Confectioners	24	33	54	73	71	127
Butchers	79	93	127	114	133	132
Grocers	95	116	164	178	211	205
Fruiterers & Greengrocers	39	39	82	83	101	96
Fishmongers	5	11	25	53	89	118

B: Retail Outlets per 10,000 Population

Bakers &						
Confectioners	6.1	6.1	7.1	8.7	7.8	12.1
Butchers	19.7	17.0	16.7	13.6	14.6	12.6
Grocers	23.6	21.1	21.6	21.3	23.1	19.5
Fruiterers & Greengrocers	9.8	7.2	10.8	10.0	11.1	9.1
Fishmongers	1.2	2.0	3.3	6.4	9.9	11.2

The figures in Table IV throw some interesting light on the economic and social development of the town. The long-term increase in absolute numbers points to a strengthening of this aspect of the town's economic life. What is more, it is clear that the number of multiple retailers was increasing. In the 1880s William Woffenden & Son had three shops in Middlesbrough and two more in South Bank and Grangetown. In the same decade Charles Ephgrave, another future mayor of the town, had three shops in Linthorpe Road, Newport Road and Cannon Street. The former had disappeared by the end of the century and the number of Ephgrave shops had dropped to two at the same time. Others were more successful, most notably Pybus Brothers who were ex-employees of Hinton's and supported by their former employer. Starting up in the late 1890s they had two shops in Linthorpe Road and Prince's Road. By 1913 they had six outlets, there being two new shops in Parliament Road and two in Newport Road.

It was not simply in the grocery trade that such developments took place. Butchers such as Eastman's and Nelson's had a dozen or more shops each by the early twentieth century. What is more, the introduction of cheap imported meat into the country was reflected by the presence of such firms as the American Fresh Meat Company, the New Zealand Mutton Company, the River Plate Fresh Meat Company and, above all, the British and Colonial Meat Company, which boasted fourteen shops by the outbreak of the First World War. Examples could be multiplied from other branches of the food trades. In bakery and confectionery Forbes had three outlets in the 1890s and six a decade later, while Spark's had three in the immediate pre-war years. Sutton Brothers, greengrocers and fruiterers, expanded to four shops in the early twentieth century. Finally, in dairying the delightfully named Rustic Dairy Company operated a number of outlets around the turn of the century.

However, when related to the increase in population the picture is less optimistic. The number of retail outlets per head of population does not show signs of a significant long-term improvement. The one exception to this is the number of fishmongers and, even more so, fried fish dealers. Overall, however, the retailing revolution in Middlesbrough is less muted than might be expected. There is, nevertheless, one important qualification to make. The simple comparison of numbers is misleading in that there was a qualitative difference to retailing by the late nineteenth and early twentieth centuries. The advent of local multiples such as Hinton's, of regional and national multiples such as Maypole Dairies, which had two stores by 1913, and Home and Colonial, which had three outlets in the town, and the presence of several Co-operative stores, meant that there was a wider range of foodstuffs available, of better and more consistent quality and at a lower price. Price competition undoubtedly influenced small shopkeepers, though improvements in quality, including hygiene, were probably less marked.

In comparison with other towns and cities in the region, Middlesbrough was well provided for in terms of food retailing. Even in the 1870s, with the exception of Newcastle, Middlesbrough had more food retailers per head of population than Stockton, Darlington, Durham or Sunderland. This was particularly so with regard to butchers, grocers and provisions dealers, fruiterers and greengrocers and, to a lesser extent, fishmongers. However, figures for the early twentieth century suggest that this lead had not been maintained in all areas.

The picture regarding non-food retailing (Table V) is far less striking. Generally speaking, expansion came later and was less

The revolution in retailing: one of Middlesbrough's first multiple stores was Dickson & Benson (MCL)

spectacular. Indeed, in certain trades there was an absolute decline in the number of outlets in the early twentieth century, reflecting the general downturn in the economic well-being of the town at that time. None the less, there were success stories to be found. The first multiples in the men's clothing trade had emerged in the 1880s but the major development of the early twentieth century was the emergence of the wholesale bespoke multiple shop retailers. The dominant figures here were Montague Burton and Stewart's, the 'King Tailors' of Middlesbrough. Although overshadowed in the historical record by the better-known name of Burton's, Stewart's were the leading firm by size and scale before the First World War with some eighty branches. Stewart's filled the gap in the market between the very cheap clothes, with all the risks of wrong size and inappropriate style, and the expensive product of the bespoke tailor. Measuring and fitting were part of the service but, unlike the bespoke tailor who gave his price on completion of the order, Stewart's offered a fixed price. The 20*s* suit was their speciality and it is significant that their new shops were concentrated in working-class areas. A new market was emerging and being met by the 'King Tailors'.

Table V: The Growth of Non-Food Retailing, 1865–1913

A: Average Number of Retail Outlets

	1865–90	1890–1901	1901–7	1907–13
Boots & Shoes	43	95	104	120
Drapers	40	65	82	74
Dressmakers & Milliners	39	61	47	45
Hosiers & Haberdashers	16	21	22	18
Tailors etc.	51	92	109	111
Chemists	14	16	20	20
Newsagents	16	41	48	54
Tobacconists	18	42	52	59

B: Retail Outlets per 10,000 Population

	1865–90	1890–1901	1901–7	1907–13
Boots & Shoes	10.5	11.3	11.4	11.4
Drapers	9.6	7.8	9.0	7.1
Dressmakers & Milliners	9.5	7.3	5.1	4.3
Hosiers & Haberdashers	3.8	2.5	2.4	1.7
Tailors etc.	12.5	11.0	12.0	10.5
Chemists	3.5	1.9	2.2	1.9
Newsagents	3.9	4.9	5.3	5.1
Tobacconists	4.3	5.0	5.7	5.6

The retail revolution, exemplified by the regional and national multiple stores, was to be seen, albeit to a lesser degree, in this sector too, as the pages of the local trade directories bear witness. As with food retailing, regional and national multiples began to appear. Alongside the Public Benefit Boot Company were to be found more familiar names such as Freeman, Hardy and Willis and the London Boot Company. In the clothing trade names like Hepworth's and Dunn's made their appearance.

Putting these figures into a regional context throws up some interesting contrasts. In the mid-1870s Middlesbrough compared favourably with the other towns and cities of the north-east of England in quantitative terms. It was better provided with boot and shoe shops than any other major centre and its provision for men (as reflected in the number of tailors, clothes dealers, newsagents and tobacconists) was better than anywhere, other than Newcastle. However, as in other branches of retailing, by the early twentieth century others had caught up.

Finally, it is also important to note the growth of a variety of occupations and professions which further underline the maturation and diversification of the local economy. Leisure was an increasingly profitable area for entrepreneurial activity. The increase in free time and the rise in living standards meant that a growing number of working-class people (more men than women, it has to be said) had the ability to partake in commercialized leisure activities. The theatres, music-halls and early cinemas in the town are more commonly discussed in terms of the social and cultural development of the town. However, these were also important business ventures and their continued existence is evidence of their profitability. This is not the place to write about the entertainment that was provided in such establishments but suffice it to say that, from the early travelling showmen who visited the town in the 1840s to successive generations of entrepreneurs who invested in bricks and mortar, the leisure industry has had a small but important part to play in the economic, let alone social, life of the town.

But what of the working men and women of Middlesbrough in these years? To what extent did they benefit from the economic growth of the town? There seems little doubt that, in broad terms at least, working-class living standards rose both quantitatively and qualitatively in the period 1870 to 1914. Estimates of real wages for the town's major industries suggest a steady long-term improvement. The iron and steel trades suffered considerable annual fluctuations, as wages were tied to prices through the operation of a sliding scale whereby the economic fortunes of employer and employee were bound together. There were also sharp short-term variations in earnings that meant that uncertainty was an ever-present feature of life. Some branches of the industry, notably puddling, never recovered the prosperity of the early 1870s boom years. But even in this shrinking sector real wages increased in the long term from 1880 onwards. In other industries, notably engineering and building, the Victorian years were a period of steady improvement, rarely punctuated by the sharp rises and falls experienced in the iron and steel trades. However, the early twentieth century saw a check to this long-term improvement and it was only after 1908 that real wages resumed their upward trend. On the other hand, it is not possible to speak confidently about the overall experience of the unskilled and often casually employed labourer.

These general trends need to be qualified in another way. Within any industry there was a range of occupations, each with its own rate of pay. While it might be the case that each occupation experienced the same general trend this did not mean that all workers (and their dependants) were equally well off. For example, there were at least twenty-six different types of worker to be found in the Cleveland blastfurnaces, each paid a different rate depending upon his position in the hierarchy. Keepers, who accounted for less than 10 per cent of the total workforce, were the best paid. In 1905 their wage rate was 60s (£3) a week. Metal carriers were paid 50s (£2.50) while mine fillers received 42s (£2.10). Lower down the scale, slaggers received 37s (£1.85), keeper's helpers and enginemen 35s (£1.75) and coke fillers 31s 6d

(£1.58). Less fortunate were weighmen who received 24*s* 6*d* (£1.23) a week while ordinary labourers received only 19*s* (95p). In percentage terms each of these occupational categories had experienced a similar increase since 1870. However, this meant that in absolute terms the gap between the best and worst paid had increased and with it had increased relative deprivation.

Rising real incomes, which tie in with the growth of retailing and leisure catering for the working classes, suggest an optimistic interpretation of developments. However, there are a number of other indicators that point to a more pessimistic conclusion. There may have been more money to spend on consumer goods but the conditions in which many people lived and worked did not improve significantly, if at all.

The predominantly working-class district of the northern (and oldest) part of the town had a prolonged history of speculative and largely unrestricted building which gave rise to the complex network of narrow, ill-lit and ill-ventilated courts and alleyways. By the end of the nineteenth century the sheer age of much of this property meant that it was in very poor structural condition. In contrast, housing in the western part of the town, which bore the brunt of population growth in the years after 1870, was influenced by building regulations. The adoption in 1855 of the 1848 Public Health Act was followed by the introduction of wider-ranging building regulations which prevented any further development of culs-de-sac and alleyways. The critical change came with the introduction of byelaws in 1875. This prevented the worst excesses of poor construction and congestion occurring. Moreover, there were not the physical constraints on expansion that existed in the north. Finally, in the east of the town a different social mix – upper working class and middle class – resulted in a more generous spacing of houses than elsewhere.

The town's rapid growth put immense pressure on existing housing stock and made a nonsense of well-intentioned plans for controlled urban growth. Nevertheless, from 1871 to 1911 the number of inhabited houses more than kept pace with the growth in population. As a consequence, average household size fell from 5.78 to 4.29 in these forty years. In percentage terms Middlesbrough's experience of improvement was in line with other towns locally and nationally. However, the above-average family sizes and the large number of lodgers that characterized the town made probable a problem of overcrowding.

More detailed information in and after 1891 provides a more sensitive indicator of the adequacy of the housing stock by giving details of overcrowding. The definition of overcrowding used was a simple one: more than two persons per room in a house constituted overcrowded conditions. By this standard, in 1891 some 13,412 people, or almost 20 per cent of the town's population, lived in overcrowded conditions. By 1901 this total had been cut to some 10,000 people, equivalent to 12 per cent of the population.

But in the next decade the situation deteriorated. The figures for 1911 show 13,513 people, or almost 13 per cent of the population, suffering from overcrowded conditions. In the Marsh and Cannon wards the problem was at its most acute. Financial hardship, rather than a shortage of housing *per se*, was the major cause. The single casual labourer and those with very large families were most vulnerable. Compared with the national average overcrowding was a greater problem in the north-east. However, conditions in Middlesbrough were not significantly worse than in nearby Stockton and Darlington and clearly better than in Newcastle, Gateshead and Sunderland.

There was another aspect to the housing problem in Middlesbrough. Too many, rather than too few, houses in a relatively small area created problems. The older, northern part of the town revealed clearly the consequences of such congestion. The insanitary conditions of Olive Street and Princess Street, for example, were a result of the densely packed nature of the housing development and the proximity of sanitary facilities to the doors and windows of the houses. The sanitary and medical officers were clear that housing density was the major cause of the town's ill-health and in 1901 they adopted a policy of 'loopholing' whereby congestion was relieved by the demolition of property at regular intervals throughout the most badly affected areas.

The sanitary condition of the town also left much to be desired. Once again, the story was one of original good intentions being swamped by the sheer growth in numbers. Sewerage was an obvious matter for concern. The main drainage system of the borough was planned in 1869 and implemented in 1873 for an estimated population of 40,000. By the turn of the century the population was in excess of 100,000 but the drainage system was largely unchanged. Sewage flooding, exacerbated by the low-lying location of the town, was a recurrent problem. In the older parts of the town catchpits were the major form of sewage disposal. These were cesspools, as much as 6 feet in diameter, about 10 inches below the road surface. High tides and heavy rainfalls led to constant flooding of streets and basements in parts of the Marsh, Newport, Cannon and Vulcan wards. The situation was compounded by the fact that catchpits in the back streets were not regularly emptied. Only when they became an obvious nuisance were they emptied. The persistence of the problem is illustrated by the fact that between November 1878 and August 1895 there were twenty-two cases in which houses in the Marsh Road area were flooded by sewage. The scale of the problem is illustrated by the fact that a heavy sewage flood, such as that of 12 November 1901, could involve as many as 400 houses and over 2,000 people.

Domestic sanitary arrangements were also problematic. Water-closets were relatively few and largely confined to middle-class areas. Conservancy methods of excrement disposal (the privy midden and pan closet) predominated. Theoretically emptied once a fortnight, in practice less often,

Liquid residue from the privy midden?
A passage adjoining Bridge Street, c.
1900 (MCL)

the custom was to throw the contents of the privy midden (often located close to back doors and pantry windows) onto the street to allow the liquid residue to soak away before scavengers removed the solid remains. The attendant fouling of the air compounded the air pollution from local industry. As late as 1869 over 90 per cent of all houses in Middlesbrough had privy middens and it was only during the First World War that the last one was abolished. The pan closet which gradually replaced the privy midden was only marginally better. Emptying them was easier and less hazardous but the problem of pollution remained considerable. In 1912 there were still some 15,000 pan closets in use in the 23,000 houses in the town. The immediate pre-war years saw a belated drive to replace them with water closets. Not surprisingly, areas of poor sanitary conditions and poor health were coterminous. Diarrhoea, dysentery and enteric fever were more prevalent in districts such as Newport and Marsh. It is also no coincidence that these were the areas with the highest infant mortality rates.

Air pollution has already been alluded to in our earlier discussion of sanitation. The scale of the problem, especially in the northern part of the town, is beyond dispute but its relationship to the town's health is more difficult to assess. Water supply was another worry. In quantitative terms, Middlesbrough was inadequately supplied. In many courts and yards there was but one tap for a dozen houses. Not surprisingly the water was used for a variety of washing and cleaning purposes. In qualitative terms, there were problems. The Tees had been directly linked to the typhoid epidemic of 1890/1 and there was a general and persistent concern that the supply was always impure.

To some extent these dilemmas were tackled by local government action but there was never the same sense of urgency about sanitary questions in Middlesbrough as, for example, in Sheffield or even Leeds. The appointment of a full-time medical officer of health in 1893 was important in creating a greater awareness of the scale and nature of the problem but even this in itself was insufficient to guarantee action. Finance was the crucial stumbling block and the situation was made worse by the fact that from 1866 to 1918 the so-called Ironmasters' District, which had the greatest concentration of property and of sanitary problems, enjoyed a differential rate, paying only three-quarters of the full rate. There was a sharp contrast between the advice of the medical officer of health and the actions of the council. An investigation in 1900 into conditions in St Hilda's identified 671 houses as injurious to health and recommended the destruction of at least 150 and as many as 299. The recommendation was never acted upon. Nowhere was this failure to act coherently and systematically more starkly seen than in the Nile Street area.

From 1871 onwards the general mortality rate for the town fell, notably in the early twentieth century. However, when allowance is made for sex and age structure, it is more accurate to talk in terms of stabilization. Furthermore, a number of very important qualifications have to be made. First, the reduction was not as great as in other towns. Locally, the contrast between Stockton and Middlesbrough, which had clearly existed in 1871, was even greater in 1911. Relatively speaking, Middlesbrough was an unhealthy place in which to live. In particular, respiratory diseases were far more prevalent in the town than elsewhere. Indeed, such was the scale of the problem that a special inquiry was made in the early twentieth century and a special report delivered to the Local Government Board in 1908. It transpired that the greater part of the difference in mortality rates between Middlesbrough and the other 'Great Towns' could be explained in terms of Middlesbrough Pneumonia, a particularly virulent and widespread local affliction. Second, for certain age groups (that is children under five and adults over forty-five years of age) mortality rates actually increased before 1900. In other words, in absolute terms, the situation was worsening for these vulnerable groups in society. Only Burnley and Wigan were more unhealthy places to live for children under five. Third, in certain districts, notably in the north of the town, mortality rates increased in the late nineteenth century. Conditions in the western part of the town had stabilized after the 1870s, in the east of the town they improved but in the north matters deteriorated. The combination of a heavily concentrated population, many of whom were poorly and irregularly paid labourers, living literally next to (if not actually within) industrial sites led to a long-term increase in mortality. Infant mortality rates were particularly high. So much so that the Local Government Board ordered a special inquiry into the question in 1915. The starkness of the contrast between different wards in the town can be appreciated from the following figures. In the immediate pre-war years (1911–14) the average death rate per 1,000 births in the town was 251. In the Newport ward the figure stood at 303, in Cannon ward 329 and in St Hilda's 369. In contrast, in the wards of Ayresome and Grove Hill the figures were 146 and 147 respectively.

Overall, in many respects housing and sanitary conditions had scarcely improved between 1870 and 1914. Indeed, in some areas conditions may have deteriorated. Structurally unsound and congested housing, antiquated and unhealthy sanitary arrangements and poor health were a feature of at least four wards and affected the lives of between one-third and a half of the town's population. And yet it is one of the peculiarities of late Victorian and Edwardian Middlesbrough that its housing and sanitary problems did not result in a worse state of health. One can but conclude that the rise in real wages noted above and its resultant impact on the diet of the town helped to offset the environmental problems that threatened the health of the people of Middlesbrough. It is no coincidence that the most vulnerable members of society, such as those dependent on casual employment, lived in the most overcrowded and insanitary districts of the town and suffered the worst standards of health. Furthermore, there was a polarization in working-class living standards. For those unable to move out of the vicious cycle of irregular and/or inadequate pay, poor housing and poor health the relative deterioration experienced by a large minority of the town increased.

THE AILING HERO: THE INTERWAR YEARS – DEPRESSION AND RECOVERY?

The outbreak of war in 1914 had a dramatic effect on local industry. Increased demand revitalized the heavy industries which still dominated the local economy. Shell steel for the army, plates for naval vessels and rails for military operations in France were in demand. Plant was increased to meet the needs of war but the upturn in fortunes was a mixed blessing. Without denying the short-term fillip to employment, the wartime and post-war boom distorted patterns of production and obscured the structural changes that were taking place in the economy as a whole. In addition, the war years provided an opportunity for foreign competitors – notably but not exclusively America – to greatly strengthen their position. Although it was not immediately apparent, Middlesbrough in 1919 entered the post-war era with excess industrial capacity at a time of slackening demand and increased foreign competition. The long-term trends which had propelled Middlesbrough to fame in the nineteenth century had run their course. New economic forces were in play and the traditional structure of the local economy was becoming increasingly inappropriate to the world of the 1920s and 1930s. The transition from old to new was to be difficult.

Unfavourable long-term trends were compounded by short-term fluctuations. Two very severe downturns in economic activity, in 1921–3 and 1929–32, resulted in sharp increases in cyclical unemployment which was superimposed on the structural unemployment that beset the town throughout the interwar years. Economic conditions were unfavourable and smaller firms went under. In 1930 the Clarence and Newport Iron and Steel Company ceased operation. Larger firms responded by rationalizing and amalgamating but with mixed success. Bolckow & Vaughan never recovered their former position. For much of the 1920s the firm operated at little more than 50 per cent capacity and losses mounted. The onset of further depression in 1929 led to amalgamation with the more successful firm of Dorman Long. Having diversified their production, and having won the prestigious contract for the Sydney Harbour Bridge in 1924, Dorman Long built up a reputation in structural engineering that enabled them to win a series of important contracts which kept the firm afloat. Even so, at the depth of the depression of the 1930s the firm was operating at 30 per cent capacity. Government protection against cheap imports was introduced in 1932 and this, combined with a ruthless reorganization of production, led to better times from the mid-1930s. The industry was also relocated, with coastal sites becoming dominant as greater fuel efficiency and the use of imported ores lessened the dependence on coal supplies.

Shipbuilding on the Tees shrank dramatically in the 1920s. Demand, so buoyant during the war years, collapsed. Raylton Dixon & Co. closed in 1922, though the yard was taken over by a new firm, Cleveland Shipbuilding Co. There was no revival in demand as world trade stagnated in the 1920s and early 1930s. Government intervention to reduce surplus capacity led to the closing of most shipbuilding yards on the Tees. Engineering did not suffer so badly. However, there were problems, especially for those heavily involved in marine engineering. In 1930 the leading firm in the town, Richardson Westgarth, shut down. All was not gloom, however. The growth of the local chemical industry had been stimulated by the demands of the First World War. Amalgamations led to the creation of Imperial Chemical Industries in nearby Billingham.

As in the pre-war years, there was a significant retailing sector that has not been commented on by historians. The trends that had emerged in the late nineteenth century continued. Multiple retailing became an increasingly common feature of many branches of the trade, though it was in the grocery trade that it was most highly developed. The growth of firms such as Amos Hinton & Sons and Pybus Brothers bears witness to the continuance of favourable demand conditions.

Hinton's opened eight new branches and a bakery in and around Middlesbrough in these years while existing branches increased their range of activities through a bakery and the sale of cooked meats. Staff numbers rose from around 230 during the First World War to 679 on the eve of the Second World War. During the difficult years of the 1920s the amount of capital employed increased by some 150 per cent from £52,000 to £126,800. Net profits as a percentage of capital employed averaged just under 14 per cent, though there were some marked year-by-year fluctuations. Net profits continued to grow during the early 1930s, even though turnover had fallen by some 10 per cent, but thereafter profits fell until the last year of peacetime trading.

Despite these occasional bright spots the interwar economy in the town was dominated by unemployment. During the 1920s and 1930s, with the exception of the boom year of 1921, unemployment in Middlesbrough was always in excess of 6,600. The worst year in the 1920s was 1926, the year of the General Strike, when the total was in excess of 18,000. During the 1930s the unemployment total for the town only once fell below 10,000, in 1937. At the trough of the depression in 1932 over 21,600 people were registered as unemployed. Although Middlesbrough was not as badly affected as Stockton, levels of unemployment in the town were consistently double the national average.

The consequences of these economic changes on the population of the town were varied. Some were fortunate. A single man, or a married man with no children, in employment, particularly if he were in one of the more successful trades, was in a stronger position than a married man with a large family in one of the declining staple industries beset by sharp fluctuations in economic activity and the threat and reality of unemployment. For the former, these could be good years as the cost of living (and especially food prices) fell and the range of cheap consumer goods increased. For the latter, these could be years of hardship for which there was little precedent in the town's history.

The contrast between employed and unemployed was at its greatest in the 1920s. The scales of benefit under the various Unemployment Insurance Acts and the Board of Guardian relief scales for the able-bodied were as much as 50 per cent lower than the prevailing wage rates for local workers such as blastfurnacemen. The gap narrowed markedly in the 1930s until there was little to choose between the two experiences. Fortunately, the cost of living fell sharply, particularly in the early 1930s. For employed and unemployed alike the standard of living (in quantitative terms, at least) was worse in the 1920s. Indeed, for the unemployed and their families the 1920s were years of considerable suffering involving inadequate diets, insufficient footwear and clothing and sub-standard housing. Women in particular were likely to have an inadequate diet but teenage boys and men in physically demanding jobs would also suffer some degree of nutritional deficiency, even in the 1930s.

The effect on the town's health is difficult to gauge but it is likely that unemployment and low incomes held back improvements that were taking place in the country at large. The crude death rate fell from around 15 per 1,000 in the early 1920s to under 13 by the late 1930s. At the same time the town's infant mortality rate fell from about 110 per thousand to about 80. Killer diseases associated with environmental conditions, such as diarrhoea, diphtheria, scarlet fever and enteritis, were in decline. Thus, in an absolute sense, Middlesbrough became a healthier place in which to live than before the war. However, marked variations were still to be found within the town. The death rate per 1,000 population in St Hilda's was almost three times as high as that in Grove Hill in 1921. Local differentials diminished over time but even in 1939 the death rate in the worst ward (still St Hilda's) was more than twice that in the best (Linthorpe). Moreover, the town had higher than average mortality rates. This was a particularly significant fact because, given the age structure of the town, one would have expected to find a death rate *below* the national average. The death rate in the early 1920s was some 25 per cent higher than the national average and the infant mortality rate almost 50 per cent above. By the late 1930s these differentials had fallen to approximately 10 per cent and 25 per cent respectively. Again, this represents improvement but of a highly qualified nature.

The fall in mortality rates was the product of a number of factors. Unlike before the war, the town authorities took a more positive role during the 1920s. A concerted effort was made to clear drains and remove 'nuisances'. The housing problem was also tackled with greater vigour. A programme of house building on the outskirts of town was adopted by the council in the 1920s which resulted in the completion of 2,756 houses by 1930. A more direct attack was made on slum housing thereafter and particularly after the 1935 Housing Act came into operation. By 1937 the number of people classified as living in overcrowded conditions had been reduced from 2,100 to 900 since 1934.

There was also great concern with the problem of unhygienic foods. The milk supply came under greater scrutiny as it was accepted that infected milk was a common carrier of tuberculosis. Similarly, more attention was given to the question of the sale of infected meat. However, the small number of legal actions taken suggests that the direct impact of council policy was limited.

Specific attention was also aimed at the problem of infant and maternal welfare. Six centres were set up offering advice and care before and after birth. Only a small number of women took advantage of these facilities but it was estimated that by 1937 one-third of mothers had had some contact with one of these centres. Another initiative was the phasing out of 'handy women' or unqualified midwives at births and their replacement by qualified midwives. Within four years (1924–7) the number of births attended by a 'handy woman' had been cut by 60 per cent. Even more encouraging, at least to the medical officer of health, was the fact that a health visitor called on 96 per cent of babies born in 1931. Finally, in 1937 a municipal midwife service was established and in that year 2,513 births out of 2,898 were notified by midwives. Important as these initiatives were, their immediate impact should not be overstated.

The interwar years saw the end of an era. As in the country at large, the economic structure that had served the town so well in the nineteenth century was no longer suited to a rapidly changing world. Middlesbrough had too many links with the old industries and not enough with the new. The town suffered from high levels of unemployment, which persisted through the two decades. Unemployment brought with it a low level of income but, whereas in the 1920s the unemployed were distinctly worse off than those in employment, after 1930 the difference was largely eroded. The town also suffered from its pre-war inheritance of inadequate housing and sanitation. However, despite these problems the interwar years were not wholly gloomy. The environment of the town was improved and so was its health. There was still much to be desired. Conditions in certain wards remained shockingly bad. The town as a whole was unhealthier than average. And yet the fact remains that there was progress — less than was hoped for, less than might have been expected but progress none the less. In the space of a hundred years the town had been transformed. The boom of the mid-nineteenth century and the steady growth of the late-Victorian and Edwardian years were not offset by the depression years of the 1920s and 1930s. Despite that, in economic terms, the industries that had once made Middlesbrough great were past their peak. The seeds of a new future had been sown but there were few signs of new growth before the Second World War. Social change was equally dramatic. The unprecedented urban growth of the nineteenth century had created a town characterized by high wage levels but poor housing and sanitary conditions. The improvement in real wages was bought at considerable cost to the health of the workforce. After the First World War there was no return to the high wages and profitability of Victorian times but, somewhat paradoxically, there was an improvement in workers' environmental conditions and their health. The no-longer infant Hercules was losing some of his strength; and the Augean stables were no longer as filthy!

CHAPTER 4

THE FRONTIER REVISITED: THRIFT AND FELLOWSHIP IN THE NEW INDUSTRIAL TOWN, *c.* 1830–1914

Jim Turner

From its beginnings as a planned new town in the 1830s Middlesbrough has often been portrayed as a harsh and unforgiving environment peopled by gritty individuals, the great majority of whom have struggled to make the best of it in the face of periodic economic uncertainty. A visitor to the town in 1843 wrote that, 'The population in one year has decreased by upwards of 1,000. Large numbers are to be met who have not had a day's work for these twelve months.' Even early attempts to boost the new settlement's reputation – a ' . . . vigorous, muscular, blazing, booming, sweltering town' observed Praed in the early 1860s – cannot disguise even in times of prosperity the oppressiveness and rawness of the place. In the year 1867 the Poor Law Relieving Officer for the Middlesbrough district reported ' . . . hundreds of children (of ironworkers) are running about bare legged without any education; they are mostly Irish and Welsh.' Twenty years later distress in the town had become so deep and prolonged that the chief constable put himself in 'telegraphic communication with the police centres of various towns so that he may be able to summon at very short notice a sufficient force of police to quell any rising that may occur'.[1] In 1911 the Liberal MP C.F.G. Masterman posed the question, 'Why indeed, the cynical might ask, should any children be born in Middlesbrough at all, considering the more than dismal picture which investigation discloses of existence in that feverish industrial centre?' On becoming the town's first Labour MP in 1924 Ellen Wilkinson wrote: 'Here capitalism reveals all its hard ugliness and the struggle for bread is bitter. Middlesbrough is a book of illustrations to Karl Marx.' Visiting in 1933 the writer J.B. Priestley described its development as 'more like a vast dingy conjuring trick than a reasonable town'. Neighbouring Stockton was 'better-looking' than Middlesbrough which was 'dismal, even with beer and football' and lacked 'civilized gaiety'. For Gordon Comstock, the anti-capitalist hero of George Orwell's novel *Keep The Aspidistra Flying* published in 1936, the 'real poor' were ' . . . the unemployed in Middlesbrough, seven in a room on twenty-five bob a week'.[2]

As one might expect, prosperous local industrialists and civic dignitaries in the expanding new town took pride in what they saw as their own creation – a place devoted entirely to trade and commerce, a challenging 'frontier' which offered everyone willing to exercise persistence and mainly exertion, a chance to get on. Lady Bell in her Edwardian description of the town wrote, 'The main object of his [the workman's] life is to be at work: that is the one absolute necessity', and that the whole environment '. . . is designed for the working hours of the people who live in it, and not for their leisure'.[3] Middlesbrough's utilitarian appearance resulted from its economic achievements as the country's leading iron and steel producing centre – the noise, the dirt, the poverty, the ill-health, and the sacrifices to be made were, it was argued, the price to be paid for progress. 'It is in the nature of things,' stated Sir Hugh Bell, a local ironmaster and the husband of Florence Bell, that human welfare will suffer at times because ' . . . we must be alternately slowly climbing up the incline . . . tumbling over the precipice at the top, rolling down the foothills, crawling along the valley, and then beginning the thing over again.'[4] Belief in this kind of natural law helped the better off explain away any form of negative description or critical judgement of the town's development likely to be encountered – workers should accept the inevitable. Some local employers went further by openly urging cooperation between workers and bosses through the introduction of profit-sharing schemes. In return for not taking industrial action, the workforce would enjoy a share of any company profits on top of wages, these extra amounts acting as 'savings' when trade was bad and earnings had to 'naturally' fall. One such local example was set up at Newport Rolling Mills in the late 1860s. The owner Jeremiah Head was warmly applauded by Samuel Smiles, the influential Victorian propagandist of self-help with whom he corresponded. 'Save all you can . . . provide for old age, read good books,' said Head to his employees but the partnership failed, Smiles was informed, because the men were 'greedy' and 'insufficiently educated to appreciate the advantages' of the scheme. Undoubtedly the employees did not share Head's acceptance of natural law or believe that in practice there was much to gain in the long run from an 'experiment' which Smiles was assured was in no way 'sentimental . . . [and] without in the least relaxing discipline, or sacrificing any true principle of business'.[5]

Those who have commented on Middlesbrough's phenomenal growth from Joseph Pease's vision of a planned ('grid-iron') industrial settlement to what Florence Bell saw as a centre of 'Titanic industry' (best seen at 'twi-light and night') have often been struck by how relentlessly the demands of industry appear to have created an urban drabness and uniformity in the town. Residential areas, we learn, were merely industrial adjuncts or annexes while one architectural historian spoke of '. . . interminable rows of two-storeyed cottages . . . [while] outside the centre hardly anything calls for perambulating'. As late as 1945 Max Lock's Survey and Plan of the town argued that rapid industrial growth had been ' . . . at the expense of adequate social services which its status as the capital of the Tees-side and Cleveland area demands'. Three years later Ruth Glass reported that severe urban problems had continued to be experienced during the first three decades of the twentieth century as a legacy of rapid expansion when ' . . . crowds of immigrants were hastily and miserably housed near their places of work'.[6]

Earlier contemporary judgements of what had taken place tended to link physical conditions directly with social relations: the hostile environment acted as a disintegrating force on the community and bred 'intemperance' and 'immorality'. Females, we learn, were particularly brutalized by their experiences and sought refuge in 'evil' habits: house drinking among women, one report claimed, had 'very considerably increased' in the town during the 1870s with ' . . . many wives putting down drink money as "groceries" and "sundries" in shop-books to keep their husbands in the dark'. In 1894 a writer in the *North-Eastern Daily Gazette* spoke of the 'appalling increase' of gambling among working-class women in Middlesbrough – 'Sweeter to them is the hum of the betting ring, and the clink of glasses in the dram-shop, than the cooing of innocent babies.' Florence Bell's portrayal of the women is more knowledgeable, less exaggerated and more sympathetic but the themes are the same: betting, drink, 'wasteful' expenditure and 'sheer ignorance' hinder a majority of women, whose domestic management is seen as the key to family welfare, from being able to cope in a 'relentless' world. The remedies for self-improvement were simple, it was claimed, and, by the turn of the century, were increasingly available in the town thanks to the wise guidance and generosity of a 'charitable elite' made up of wealthy men and women like Sir Hugh and Lady Bell; schools, churches, a Free Library and Reading Rooms, theatres, tea rooms and coffee houses, and teetotal workmen's clubs opened by local industrialists for persons in their employment. Florence Bell's own personal contribution was a 'Winter Garden' in Dundas Street which opened in October 1907. Reading and writing tables, garden seats and tile-top tables, a bandstand and refreshment stall were introduced and the 'garden' motif developed with tubs of plants, a rockery and hanging baskets. In the local press Lady Bell was reported as saying that her scheme was a sensible way of giving to the workmen a 'modest luxury' and a 'healthy' experience which they could not normally get, but that it would be ' . . . wrong to give them a necessity, which they were bound more or less to obtain for themselves'. This is a revealing comment: in a harsh and hostile environment the stability of the ironworker's life and that of his family would best be achieved through individual effort and self-help. Working hours were disciplined; the problem was, leisure time was not, and it was in this area alone that the more fortunate could set a good example.[7]

Valuable as it remains as a social document of Edwardian Middlesbrough, Lady Bell's study nevertheless forms part of a long tradition of writing about

WINTER GARDEN
DUNDAS STREET, MIDDLESBROUGH.

ADMISSION
ONE
PENNY
❖
OPEN
from
9 a.m.
till
10 p.m.

THIS Institution provides, at small cost, Comfort, Refreshment and Recreation for the worker and his wife and friends.

Warmth
Refreshment
Games
Pictures
Music
Library
Concerts
Recitals
and
Entertainments

FUNDS are earnestly appealed for. Please send CONTRIBUTIONS, however small, to the Secretary, MISS F. BEALES, WINTER GARDEN, MIDDLESBROUGH.

A sensible way of giving to workmen a modest luxury and a healthy experience. The Winter Garden, opened in 1907, still going strong in 1926 (CRL)

the history of the town and its population which emphasizes the passivity of local response to hardship and a disposition to grin and bear it when the trade cycle required one to do so. This enduring perception of the Middlesbrovian seems to have originated from the 'frontier' legend with which the town has always been associated, or at least since Ravenstein made the comparison with towns of the American West in 1885. For successive waves of migrants – predominately male, young and from all parts of Britain and beyond – aggressive industrialization on Teesside provided the opportunity and freedom for self-advancement. Meanwhile, adjusting successfully to a coarse and demanding environment was a calculated risk which each newcomer took. A doctor who inspected Middlesbrough in 1853 reported that ' . . . the town is built without any regard whatsoever to the conditions necessary for health' but although we are told that this and similar comments deeply offended the city fathers, we might speculate that for the bulk of the workforce at the time it was an unremarkable state of affairs.[8] However, while the frontier analogy in respect of Middlesbrough has proved useful (and we will employ this concept again later) it has at the same time encouraged us to view the new industrial town as a 'mere colony' or assemblage of strangers which existed for economic purposes alone. This description of the internal structure of the town in the nineteenth and early twentieth centuries is misleading, of course, for it ignores the overwhelming evidence of close cooperation, mutual aid and fraternity practised by the population from the earliest days of the new settlement. The development of these activities forms the subject matter of the remaining part of this chapter.

Briggs' passing comment that 'Friendly societies had been active in the town from the start'[9] is historically correct, but it does raise problems for those interpretations of the town's history which portray a bleak landscape largely devoid of any indigenous working-class institutional and cultural activities beyond the beerhouse and the gambling ring. However, there does exist extensive documentary evidence that these societies quickly became a commonplace feature in neighbourhoods and in the workplace. The term 'friendly society' remains an ambiguous one for the urban historian where, even in studying their presence in just one town, we are faced with a wide variety of forms, each laying claim to 'friendly' status for different and sometimes conflicting reasons. The legal status of these organizations remained uncertain for much of the nineteenth century but, although an increasing number of clubs sought legal protection of their funds against defrauding members and officials, a large proportion of small local societies preferred complete independence and remained unregistered. One contemporary authority defined friendly societies as 'insurance clubs based on mutual principles' and attempted the difficult task of classifying them.[10] Utilizing this classificatory approach allows us both to appreciate the diversity of this form of associational life in one town and explore how different types of society worked to meet varying needs within the local population.

We begin our survey of societies in the town by focusing on the 'Affiliated' Orders, branches of which were organizationally linked at three levels. The basic unit was the lodge to which individual members belonged. Above the lodge was the district, a number of lodges in a given area governed by representatives from the separate lodges. In turn, districts were organized into an Order, sometimes called a Unity. The original lodges and subsequently the Order headquarters were located in Lancashire, South Yorkshire, and the Midlands but in practice the Orders remained loose federations with both districts and individual lodges retaining a great deal of independence. One of the earliest lodges of an Affiliated Order in the town was the Joseph Warburton Lodge of the Oddfellows (Manchester Unity) which opened on 21 November 1835 at the King William IV Inn in West Street. Of the nine founding members there was a joiner, a tailor, six potters and the innkeeper. The lodge was named after a Staffordshire potter who came to Middlesbrough around 1834 when earthenware manufacture first began in the town. It is probable that he was manager of the pottery but acted as an honorary member of the lodge, not becoming a full subscriber until 1847. Early records reflect the lodge's growing sense of identity and purchases were made to consolidate this: it was resolved that 'the chairs of the lodge be decorated', 'that a common flag be purchased for lodge purposes' and 'a small colour be got for the lodge and caps (cost 28s) for the officers and supporters'.[11]

In 1842 a second Oddfellows lodge was established, the Rose of England, at which time it was decided to form a separate Middlesbrough district. The first district meeting was held at the Baltic Tavern, Commercial Street, on 27 June. The district membership totalled 109 and within four years it stood at over 200. Lodge minutes show that at this time a considerable number of new members joining the Rose of England lodge were mariners. In the early 1840s there were three failed attempts to form new Oddfellows branches in the town but the original lodges continued to flourish, expanding their membership at more or less the same percentage rate between 1842 and 1855

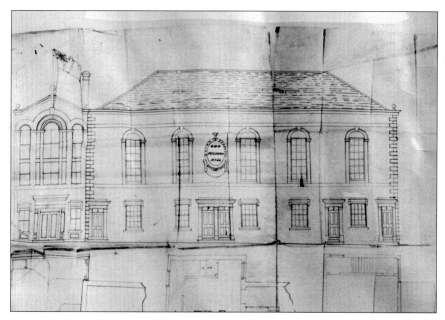

By 1861, when they had four lodges in the town, the Oddfellows had built a hall in Bridge Street West
(CA)

as the population increase for the new town as a whole. In 1856 two new lodges opened and another the following year. Ten years later the district membership was 700 and by the turn of the century stood at over 2,500 organized into nine lodges. Membership peaked at 2,844 in 1908. In 1888 a successful Juvenile Society, connected with the district, was formed for males aged three to sixteen. Girls were admitted ten years later and by 1910 total membership was nearly 380. A lodge for adult females, The Lady Bell, opened in 1912.

This dramatic growth in one Affiliated Order was mirrored also in the successful establishment of others. A Trade Directory for 1884 identified fifty-eight lodges in Middlesbrough belonging to eleven different Orders, six of which had the word 'Oddfellow' in their title (the same source had listed thirty lodges in the town affiliated to nine Orders, five using the term Oddfellow, in 1871). This survey, however, did not include temperance Orders which were very popular from the 1870s or a number of minor affiliated organizations. In 1907 Florence Bell estimated that in the town there were '. . . nearly 200 branches of various friendly societies' but it remains unclear whether she is referring to non-affiliated local clubs also. Space permits us only to focus briefly on the other major Affiliated Orders besides the Manchester Unity which attracted large memberships. A lodge

Above: Elaborate symbolism: the 'logo' of the Order of Druids (JJT)

Left: The open display of brotherliness: a parade of the Free Foresters was an added attraction at a fireworks display (CA)

of the Ancient Order of Foresters, 'Court' Tees, opened in 1834 and membership had reached 220 by 1874. When a separate district was formed in 1903 there were over 600 individual members. By the mid-1880s we find lodges of the Grand United Order of Oddfellows with a total of 899 members. A district of this Order was set up in 1871 but individual lodges made an early appearance in the town: the North York lodge started in 1841 and three more were established in the next eight years including a lodge serving Tees-side Ironworks. By 1838 the Sheffield Order of Oddfellows had two lodges operating in the town. There were several Orders set up locally describing themselves as 'Druids', the earliest forming districts around 1860, while later in 1904 members of the Jewish community in the town opened a lodge of the Hebrew Order of Druids. Temperance Orders locally emerged at about the same time as the first Druids. Of the two major organizations of this type in the area we find a Middlesbrough 'Grand Division' of the Sons of Temperance opening in 1868 (by 1907 eight lodges had a total of 1,503 members) and a Cleveland district of the Independent Order of Rechabites, a number of whose 'tents' met in the town centre, forming in 1870.

Why were the Affiliated Orders so successful in establishing themselves in the new town and, in most cases, sustaining their growth? No doubt their

Regalia: a sash of the Order of Druids (JJT)

elaborate ceremonial practices and use of regalia together with their emphasis on conviviality and open display of 'brotherliness' appealed to many local men who worked long hours and lived in drab 'mean streets'. However, an important additional reason for their progress lay in the special benefits which as regional or national organizations they were able to offer. The provision of 'travelling relief' to members helped individuals in search of work through meeting the cost of bed and board for each day on the tramp. In 1842, for example, the Middlesbrough district of Oddfellows set a figure of 3*d* per day. Each lodge appointed a Relieving Officer who on production of the correct password would pay the travelling member of their Order or in some cases assist those in difficulty. In July 1843 the Rose of England lodge of Oddfellows in Middlesbrough gave 2*s* to a 'distressed brother on travel'. Similar assistance was available through 'clearance' cards whereby a member of a distant lodge could, after prior agreement between the branches involved, join a new lodge if he wished to settle in a town where work was available and he required assistance in getting established. Sometimes communication broke down although 'brotherly' generosity might prevail: the minute book of the Joseph Warburton Oddfellows lodge in Middlesbrough recorded on 7 October 1844 that a brother ' . . . have a gift of 5*s*, he being out of work and having travelled upwards of 200 miles to get his card (he not being aware that he was not entitled to it), the lodge sympathised with him and awarded the above.' Such benefits would be of great practical value to migrant workers attracted to the boom town of the 1840s and membership not only facilitated mobility into the area but would allow movement out when trade declined. In the meantime their presence in the town increased the need to open new lodges or to alter the frequency or timing of meetings. Clearly those from the Midlands, like the Staffordshire potters who set up the first Oddfellows' lodge in the town, brought with them a tradition of friendly society membership.

Before the arrival of branches of Affiliated Orders in Middlesbrough during the 1830s when the new coal port and town were established, we find in the area that was to become known as 'Teesside' (incorporating parts of South Durham and historic 'Cleveland') a friendly society tradition with a long history. Using records of society rules deposited with local Justices of the Peace (an Act of 1793 having encouraged societies to enrol and provided them with some legal recognition) and Poor Law returns for 1803 and 1815 we see that nearly every village in the area had at least one benefit club, while in places like Darlington and Stockton, societies were a common feature of town life. Middlesbrough's first town planner and patriarch Joseph Pease helped form a Woolcombers' Sick Club for his employees in Darlington in 1813 to which he and his brothers were subscribing members. In Stockton it was recorded that ten societies had a total membership of 620 in 1803. The oldest of these which met at the Black Lion Inn started in 1742 and remained in existence until 1883.[12] Purely local societies were of two types: permanent and dividing. The former provided a permanent fund into which members paid contributions and drew benefits while the latter would disband at the end of each year and be re-formed after the remaining money had been shared out equally.

In Middlesbrough the earliest local permanent club appears to have been the North Yorkshire and South Durham Local Mariners Association formed in 1834. By 1841 the membership was over eighty, drawn mainly from Hartlepool, Stockton, Whitby and Middlesbrough itself. Permanent societies for men following the same skilled trade became relatively common and included, for example, separate clubs for blacksmiths, locomotive enginemen and firemen, and policemen in the town. Many of the men who flocked to Middlesbrough looking for work in the 1850s and 1860s were in fact drawn from the town's rural hinterland and further afield in the North Riding. In the Cleveland district a farm agent reported in 1867 that agricultural labourers had ' . . . all gone to the ironworks'. Plenty of documentary evidence has survived to show that most agricultural workers were already members of friendly societies and it is likely that a number retained their membership and the benefits arising from this after they settled in Middlesbrough. For those for whom continued membership had become impractical because of the distances involved, there would be a keenness to join one of the new clubs in the town in order to maintain thrifty habits.

Of local societies in Middlesbrough, the most popular type was the yearly club. By the end of the nineteenth century most public houses in the town had one or more annual clubs which met on the premises. Compared with lodges of Affiliated Orders, yearly societies were short on ritual and ceremony, less exclusive and more concerned with conviviality. They proved attractive because, as a savings bank, they did not lock up a member's savings for an indefinite period as permanent clubs did. The promise of an annual dividend, usually distributed at Christmas or New Year, enabled a member, for example, to ' . . . meet rent due, to buy clothes, articles of furniture'. The unskilled, older people and those not in perfect health were more likely to obtain entry than in other types of club. The typical share out for clubs in the town around 1900 was about 17s per individual with each club having an average of seventy members. One of the earliest societies of this type, which met at the Slaters' Arms in Northern Street, was the Wherryman's Yearly Club made up of those who earned a living rowing passengers across and along the River Tees. In December 1890 the 'Ally Sloper' Social Benefit Society held its first meeting at the Excelsior Hotel in West Street. The name was taken from a character in a popular comic magazine called Judy (a rival to Punch) which first appeared in 1867. The cartoon Ally was poor and always in debt: a figure the club members could laugh at and identify with at the same time.[13]

The dramatic growth in the number of yearly societies in the town, particularly in the late nineteenth century, attracted criticism from a number of quarters. Other types of club, most notably the Affiliated Orders several of which were experiencing a fall in membership by this time, complained of 'unfair competition' from annual societies whose low rates of contribution and flexible entrance rules undercut them. It was often argued that these clubs were financially unsound and that savings were squandered through the payment of 'wet-rent', a compulsory amount of money allotted for drink each meeting-night. Lady Bell criticized this practice as did a number of religious organizations, which set about combating this 'evil' by setting up their own yearly clubs which met on church or other teetotal premises. The local Church of England was particularly active in this area: All Saints' opened a yearly benefit club for its church members and congregation in 1886 and St Columba followed in 1890. Three years later an unsuccessful attempt was made to amalgamate the clubs at all the Protestant churches in the town into one society. However, in 1896 a branch of the Church of England Benefit Society was established in All Saints' parish. This was an Affiliated Order which operated a 'clearance' system for church members but was a permanent rather than yearly club. Branches of the Catholic Benefit Society ran similar schemes, the first opening at St Paul's in South Bank in 1872.

By the 1890s friendly societies and the 'drink question' had become a major issue in local politics and received wide coverage in the local press. The representatives of teetotal societies were always keen to press their case: a town councillor and long-standing member of the Poor Law Guardians ' . . . wondered if ever a Rechabite had come before them for Relief. He had no recollection of such a case.' In their defence the yearly societies and other clubs meeting on licensed premises argued that there was a shortage of alternative and affordable accommodation in the town. Furthermore, publicans were often club members themselves and many acted as society treasurer. By stipulating the amount of 'wet-rent' to be spent and imposing fines for drunkenness the societies, it was claimed, were regulating drinking habits in a sensible and realistic way. A local journalist and member of a friendly society in the town wrote: 'For twelve years I have regularly attended at my lodge (in a public house) and I never yet saw a man get the worse for drink. I have seen . . . twenty men sit and discuss questions from 7 to 10 without a single drop of drink coming into the room.'[14]

As an alternative to the public house many societies originated at and met at places of work. Employers in the iron trade on Teesside were generally enthusiastic about encouraging their men to set up clubs or provident funds. Management usually contributed annually to society funds which were further increased by the paying in of money from fines regularly imposed for breach of company rules during working hours. By agreement weekly club contributions could be taken out of wages. A scheme of this type operated at Tees Iron Works from 1859 where for 4*d* per week a worker could obtain 8*s* a week sick pay, medical attention and £4 in case of death. Fox, Head and Co. at their Newport works encouraged their men to join a Labourers' Fund or the Puddlers' Society instead of relying upon 'gatherings' among the workers when an individual was injured or killed at work, such methods being unreliable and amounts collected variable. In a number of instances we find the total membership of a lodge of an Affiliated Order worked for one company. Thus, the Ironopolis lodge of the Sheffield Independent Druids in Middlesbrough, which was formed in 1896, had nearly 700 members all of whom worked at the North Eastern Steelworks in the town.

In contrast with County Durham where all-female friendly societies were very common, particularly catering for coal miners' wives, there were relatively few women's clubs in the Teesside towns although Stockton boasted three as early as 1803. Affiliated Orders were slow to introduce female lodges and among the major societies only three in Middlesbrough had taken this step before 1914. Temperance Orders allowed women in earlier but the numbers remained small. Most women's involvement with friendly societies was through their husband's membership. Male members chose to pay into Orphans' and Widows' Funds while widows themselves might continue to receive benefits other than an initial lump sum through payment of a small weekly contribution. Any club member marrying was to register his wife, whose acceptance into the fund was determined by the lodge doctor. In the largest societies in the town we find a majority of male members subscribing to funds for widows and orphans – in 1894, for example, 1,009 (67 per cent) out of 1,506 men of the Royal Order of Shepherds did so.

Two classes of friendly society which women themselves often did belong to were Burial and Collecting societies which aimed to provide 'respectable interment'. A number of burial clubs were established at Sunday schools. The Brougham Street Chapel in Middlesbrough formed a death club in 1856. Mothers paid a penny a week to provide £1 on the death of a child. Within three years half of the 120 scholars were in the scheme. In the second half of

The Pearl Assurance Company, its Middlesbrough offices here having seen better days, began as a Collecting Society (LP)

the nineteenth century there was official concern at the work of burial societies and their influence on infant mortality and neglect. While Lady Bell in her survey spoke with sympathy about women with very large families, she did believe that ironworkers' children died in some cases '. . . due to the fact that the child's life has been insured'. In 1895 a local children's society discovered that in the previous year in nearly a quarter of cases of neglect the child was insured for an average of £6 10s 0d. By this date, however, the work of local burial clubs had been largely taken over by collecting societies.[15]

An Act of 1896 defined a Collecting Society as one that received contributions by means of collectors at a distance of more than ten miles from their registered office. The growth in this form of life insurance in Middlesbrough was very marked in the last quarter of the nineteenth century. In 1871 only one agent of a major collecting society was recorded as working in the town but by 1890 this had risen to eighteen, twelve of whom were Prudential agents. During the 1880s, for example, one society increased its business in the town five-fold as life insurance for the whole family became more popular. Analysis of membership of 200 working-class families in Middlesbrough with the General Friendly Collecting Society shows that each had taken out at this time an average of four policies.

One local figure, George Carey, successfully set up his own life insurance company. Working in the town for many years as a collector for several of the large national collecting societies like The Pearl led him to believe that these societies were 'very tight – cruelly so' with the collectors who worked for them. Too often clients themselves were treated badly as societies sought to minimize or ignore their obligations to policy holders. Carey's new company, The Trade Union Friendly Collecting Society, opened for business in April 1905. He described it as 'a working class club run by working men' with every agent having to belong to a trade union. This new venture with its offices in Kensington Road, Middlesbrough, soon proved popular on Teesside, collections doubling in the first five years. A committed Socialist and Labour councillor for Middlesbrough, Carey was born in Barnstaple and was dismissed from his first job in the local Eston mines for his trade union activities. His life insurance company, he claimed, ' . . . had no shareholders, was a mutual club serving the people'.[16] Meanwhile, other forms of local life insurance had begun to develop, in particular newspaper insurance. In 1896, for instance, the Middlesbrough-based *Northern Weekly Gazette* started an insurance scheme which required no contributions other than placing a regular order for the paper with a newsagent. Death and disablement benefits were payable. The first claim awarded was to a widow and her six children after the husband had died from a fall at the North Eastern Steelworks. Between 1903 and 1906 the paper paid out on 110 claims (£1,100). Other local newspapers soon followed suit with rival schemes.

A branch of the National Deposit Friendly Society opened in Middlesbrough in 1897 and a district office serving South Durham and North Yorkshire was established in the town in 1902. The 'deposit' type of friendly society which grew rapidly after 1900 in urban areas combined life insurance, sickness benefit and a personal savings scheme. By 1911 membership on Teesside stood at 2,300. Collecting and deposit societies were often accused by the representatives of other forms of society of not being 'friendly' or 'mutual' but merely there to provide individual insurance. However, this was not true of the National Deposit Friendly Society locally where we find regular and well-attended social gatherings and annual picnics with regalia worn.

Having described in some detail the range of different types of friendly society in Middlesbrough before 1914 we now need to say more about who actually joined these clubs. Our best detailed surviving information on this relates to Affiliated Orders. Normally entrants had to be eighteen and no older than forty-five although it was possible to enter over this age if in good health and willing to pay higher contributions. Age on first joining was usually about twenty-two with the average age of the whole club membership around thirty-five although, with increased life expectancy, the latter rose sharply, creating financial problems as more older men remained on permanent sickness benefit. Turning to occupation, the three largest groups joining two Oddfellows lodges in the town in the early 1840s were potters, mariners and joiners. One in ten of all new members entering seven large societies between 1860 and 1870 were mariners. The picture of the thrifty mariner is supported by local evidence for other ports in the area. Lady Bell, however, took a negative view. The sailors in the port of Middlesbrough had '. . . no responsibility for their words or deeds . . . they seem to bring to the whole world a kinship of lawlessness and disorder'. An earlier report had stated that Middlesbrough sailors generally worked on coastal or the Baltic trade and ' . . . their habits were better than those elsewhere who worked longer routes'. More frequent visits to their home port would allow them to maintain their membership. Bell's description applies more accurately to local dockers where the general opinion appeared to be that as a class they were 'improvident' with few joining friendly societies. The casual nature of local dock labour would have made regular saving difficult anyway. Nevertheless, annual societies and informal 'share-out' clubs existed most notably at the Smith's Dock Company in South Bank and these grew in popularity in the 1920s and 1930s.[17]

Over a quarter of those initiated into the Victoria Oddfellows lodge in the town between 1898 and 1910 were labourers, who formed the largest occupational group. Ten per cent of entrants into two other Oddfellows' lodges in the same period were ironworks' labourers while general labourers and clerks formed the largest groups joining a Rechabites' tent. Such evidence would begin to contradict the popular view that the unskilled were thriftless or that fellowship did not cross class lines. Moreover, labourers acted as lodge secretaries although only one, who worked in an iron foundry, achieved Grand Master status in the local Oddfellows (Manchester Unity). Surveying ironworkers as a whole group at the turn of the century, Florence Bell found that 39 per cent in Middlesbrough belonged to no benefit club at all while of the remaining 61 per cent two-thirds subscribed to one club and a third to two or more societies.[18] Combining this with other evidence would suggest that generally local ironworkers were thrifty but not to the same degree as mariners or indeed miners in the Cleveland ironstone district. In the industrial 'villages' of Eston, South Bank and Grangetown in east Middlesbrough there were at least thirty-three friendly societies with a total membership of 3,200 in the early 1890s. Allowing for overlapping membership we find therefore one-third of the eligible male population in terms of age belonging to a society in this district.

What was the wider social significance of friendly societies in Middlesbrough? What part did they play in community building? At society meetings it was often claimed that the individual thrift and mutual help practised by members made them 'better husbands and true Christians'. In addition, it was argued, working men could ' . . . become acquainted with the mode of conducting business, in filling the offices of committee men, chairman, secretaries etc. which qualify them for the right discharge of the higher duties of citizenship'. An inspection of printed society rule books would lead us to believe that friendly societies were strictly non-political and non-sectarian organizations which, outwardly at least, were keen to foster an image of respectability in the community. The public face of society activity – parading the town in regalia, processions to church or chapel, demonstrations to raise funds for local hospitals and other good causes, annual balls, soirées, outings and picnics, sports galas, open-air singing contests and so on – masked, however, the more secretive and serious side of club life. Lodges of Affiliated Orders in particular sought to enhance their social exclusiveness and individuality in a number of ways: employing passwords (which were frequently changed), appointing officers (with titles like 'Tyler'

The public face of society activity: the regalia of the Grand United Order of the Knights of the Golden Horn (JJT)

or 'Beadle') to guard the lodge door on meeting nights and bar entry to outsiders, threatening members with expulsion from the club if they divulged details of society business, awarding 'degrees' to those showing themselves knowledgeable of the signs, symbols and ritual of the Order. The often elaborate systems of rules and fines operated by many societies to prevent 'malingering, drunkenness and disorderly behaviour' were more about safeguarding club funds and encouraging members to make sacrifices for each other than satisfying middle-class opinions about self-improvement.

By the last quarter of the nineteenth century the town's local dignitaries and prominent citizens were all keen to be associated with one or more societies and often acted as honorary members. This was not simply patronage, but a recognition of the size, popularity and influence of the friendly society movement locally. In some cases self-interest operated: doctors competed with each other to act as well-paid society medical officers, clergymen joined to meet and (hopefully) offer spiritual guidance to the large numbers of working men who rarely went to church, Guardians of the Poor and town councillors saw opportunities to nurture their electorate. In December 1878, for example, Samuel Sadler the Mayor of Middlesbrough was publicly accused of 'giving away of his substance as a catch for votes' at a parliamentary election by buying drink extravagantly at a lodge meeting of the Order of Shepherds. For their part the societies themselves sought to stress their independence and dignity. As one local official put it, a club existed ' . . . to provide against the contingency of having to accept assistance from the soup kitchen, and that kind of charity given by "Lady Bountifuls" seeking a reputation for benevolence and who did not understand there were societies of working men whose objects were to assist each other in avoiding such charity'. In practice societies were generally tolerant of individual members' activities outside lodge hours as long as such behaviour did not threaten the club's reputation in the community or lead to ill-feeling or divisions within the membership itself. Members were fined or sometimes expelled for fighting, using abusive language, or being drunk in public. Individuals were censored or applauded for their behaviour: in 1843 the Rose of England lodge of Oddfellows resolved to ' . . . take an emblem back from Brother Williamson until he start to work' while five years later the same lodge severely reprimanded its senior officer (who was officially on the club sick list) in front of the assembled membership ' . . . for going out to gather mushrooms while receiving the gifts of the lodge'. In 1844 a member was given a vote of thanks ' . . . for the manly manner he has acted in not laying himself on the Lodge fund while sick'.

Regardless of their position in the wider community, society members were expected, while carrying out society business and activities, to treat each other as equals. In the small 'walking' town of the 1840s this was more easily achievable with workers and a small middle class living in close proximity. Two of the town's future leading ironmasters, Henry Bolckow and John Vaughan, joined the Rose of England lodge in 1845. In 1847 Bolckow was proposed as treasurer for the Oddfellows district but never took up this position. By the mid-1850s there was suburban development to the south of the town as villas were built to the specifications of the growing middle class while the more wealthy like Bolckow and Vaughan moved from the town centre to outlying areas like Marton. With this mobility came a change in membership from ordinary to honorary status. It was the democratic ideals of societies as well as the practical benefits of membership which attracted many working-class men in the town. In Middlesbrough friendly society membership overlapped with involvement in political radicalism as well as trade unionism. Six leading Chartist activists in the town in the 1840s were also prominent Oddfellows holding official lodge and district positions. One was John Anderson, who worked in a local iron foundry. In 1848 he was elected Grand Master of the district, the only labourer to achieve this prestigious status. The printer John Jordison was the town's leading middle-class Chartist and member of the same lodge, the Joseph Warburton, and by 1861 we find him and Anderson, both now town councillors, working together administering the district funds.

Although friendly societies in Middlesbrough had in total a far greater membership than trade unions in the town before 1900, dual membership was common because of the complementary nature of the benefits offered. Societies provided sickness or old-age benefits while unions insured workers against unemployment. In practice it was often difficult to distinguish the two organizations: unions often grew out of friendly societies and were keen for various reasons (not least legal) to stress their 'provident' rather than industrial activities. Like many unions the lodges of affiliated friendly societies provided the important benefit of travelling relief for those looking for work.

Later in the nineteenth century we can identify other radical traditions, notably secularism and republicanism, recruiting from the ranks of local Oddfellowship. A key local figure representing both these traditions was William Blakiston, a pattern maker employed at Bolckow & Vaughan ironworks. In the 1860s he was the leading secularist organizer and fund raiser in the area. In 1859 he helped establish a Political Reform Association in the town and in the following year convened a popular lecture programme held at the Oddfellows' Hall in Bridge Street West on the theme of republican 'heroes'. The same year he was elected Grand Master of the Middlesbrough district of Oddfellows (Manchester Unity). An intriguing character, Blakiston apparently worked as a spy for the United States federal government during the time of the American Civil War collecting evidence on illegal trading with 'rebels' in local ports like Stockton, Hartlepool and Middlesbrough.[19]

Having described the dramatic growth and consolidation of friendly societies in the town we can now, in the light of this evidence of widespread thrift through mutual aid, return to our opening theme and re-examine Middlesbrough's enduring reputation as a 'frontier' town. Analogies with towns of the American frontier appear to have been more common than comparisons with, for instance, northern industrial cities like Manchester, Liverpool or Leeds. Historians have also ignored comparisons with new towns which developed at about the same time and for similar reasons: for example, the iron 'colony' and shipbuilding community of Barrow-in-Furness (a link suggested by Briggs) or Coatbridge in Scotland, which began to develop as an iron-town about 1830.

In some respects this preoccupation with change in the United States rather than in Britain remains puzzling. Joseph Pease's original planned town consisted of a small square of streets set at right angles to each other on a plot of 500 acres which immediately faced the river to the north, the railway to the south and industry on the other two sides. Within a decade unplanned and hasty housing development had spilt out of this grid the size of which was distinctly un-American. Touring the United States in 1862 the novelist Anthony Trollope was struck by how each new town 'with noble avenues and imposing streets . . . is laid out with an intention that it shall be populous. The houses are not all built at once, but there are the spaces allocated for them.' Milwaukee, a new settlement with about the same population as Middlesbrough at the time, had ' . . . room apparently for double that number'. Thirty years earlier the English author Harriet Martineau visited the young town of Chicago growing on the shores of Lake Michigan. 'It looks', she wrote, 'raw and bare. The houses appeared all insignificant and run up in various directions, without any principle at all.'[20] In fact Chicago began life as a planned settlement in the same year as Middlesbrough. In 1830 a Canal Commission (established to decide on a canal route to link Lake Michigan and the Mississippi River and the location of a new port at its northern end) drew up a grid system plan on a plot of land covering one square mile, an area of similar size to Joseph Pease's original planned community on the banks of the Tees. Unlike the latter, however, the young Chicago was built on the edge of a vast unexploited prairie and it was the way this was developed as the town grew, with land divided into rectangular plots prior to building, which led to the dominant grid pattern. In this and other American frontier towns the ' . . . primary purpose was not to found communities but to sell lots'.[21] The establishment of urban centres in frontier America was based upon an abundance of free land rather than, as in Middlesbrough's case, commercial and industrial enterprise on small plots of bought land.

The early American frontier had an average population of two people per square mile (later revised by historians to six when pioneer settlement came to an end in the 1890s) but in 1831 the new town of Middlesbrough already had nearly 200 persons per square mile and by 1841 this had risen to 3,540. By the latter date the town had a greater number of persons per house (6.2) on average than most other English northern industrial towns[22] and certainly higher than early American new towns at the same stage of their development. Briggs' 'turbulent urban frontier' was a crowded place but one key characteristic it did share with new American townships, at least in the early decades, was a preponderance of males in the population. The demands of heavy industry in Middlesbrough in the iron and steel mills, engineering works, shipyards and docks required men to be both tough and reliant upon each other; and belonging to all-male friendly societies, as many adult males did, reinforced this masculine solidarity. For women there remained few employment opportunities outside the home and so they were less likely to be drawn directly into the life and activities of the many work-based friendly societies. The last three decades of the nineteenth century in America have been described as the 'Golden Age of Fraternity' when millions of adult males fled the female-dominated world of the family home and joined fraternal organizations like the Oddfellows and Foresters. In new settlements like San Francisco which, even more quickly than Middlesbrough, were created on what had been almost empty land, numerous mutual-aid clubs were soon flourishing which were exclusively male and which, we are told, assumed a woman's place was in the home.[23]

It was during the first decade of the existence of the new township of Middlesbrough that Alexis de Tocqueville visited the United States.

Drawing upon his experiences and observations he wrote his famous book *Democracy in America* in which he discussed at length the importance of voluntary associations in this unique frontier society. In a democratic world with no feudal past or aristocratic dominance individuals pursued their own self-interest, but quickly came to learn that by combining with others and assisting each other their future was more likely to be secure in the long term. 'The principle of self-interest rightly understood', wrote Tocqueville, 'produces no great acts of self-sacrifice, but it suggests daily small acts of self-denial.'[24] As free and democratic associations whose members contributed small regular contributions to a central fund and treated each other as 'brothers' in times of need, friendly societies epitomized this principle in action. On the urban frontier of early Middlesbrough the first generation of settlers came to organize themselves in the same way for the same reasons and under similar conditions. Most workers were more or less equal in the local (industrial) market-place but equally prone to misfortune and the uncertainties of the trade cycle. The new town possessed no rich and powerful aristocrats in its midst and the industrial elite which emerged later was quick to move out, coming to play a diminishing role in civic affairs. Meanwhile collective effort in the form of friendly societies (as well as cooperative societies and trade unions) provided opportunities for local people to act in socially responsible ways, to practise a rudimentary form of citizenship.

Clearly the evidence presented in this chapter of the growing size and scope of mutual activity undermines that version of Middlesbrough's 'frontier' history which describes an urban landscape which began and continued to be populated by aggressive, selfish workers, who struggled to survive and compete in a harsh industrial environment. Experience of the latter taught people the necessity of self-reliance but also recognition that they were not self-sufficient. In an influential essay published in 1893 the American historian F.J. Turner persuasively argued that 'frontier' conditions promoted the values of both self-help (competitive individualism) and mutuality (neighbourly help and trust) and that survival depended on recognition by pioneers of their interdependence. Frontier settlers he described as 'social idealists' – working hard to better themselves and build communities at the same time. Much of the ritual language, the words of club songs, the meaning given to the symbols and slogans that embellished flags and other regalia, together with the professed aims of friendly societies expressed in rule books reflected this form of idealism. By the last quarter of the nineteenth century almost every small American town or growing 'city' had an Oddfellows' Hall or similar building where friendly societies met.[25] Like Middlesbrough's own Oddfellows' Hall which opened in 1854, this form of institution came to symbolize a 'civilized' community with a wide range of 'respectable' working-class club life. Like the new savings banks, churches and chapels and town halls, it was an important physical reminder of an emerging urban identity increasingly shared by townsfolk (regardless of their birthplace), and built and sustained by cooperation. Interestingly, one early chronicler of Middlesbrough's development castigated its working men ' . . . for want of co-operative sense and social courage' because, unlike the men of Rochdale and Tyneside, whom he had visited and found 'growing powerful and rich', they did not believe at the time in Co-operative Stores. By focusing on his own particular remedy for poverty this historian of the town's progress, like many others before and since, chose to ignore the significant day-to-day contribution of mutual effort via the activities of hundreds of local friendly societies which played a key role in alleviating many of the harsh consequences of living in a 'smoke dried, iron bound' town.[26]

A.J.P. Taylor once described Manchester as 'truly a frontier-town . . . squeezed into the south-eastern corner of Lancashire'[27] and in the same way Middlesbrough has always been and continues to be indisputably a border settlement. Geographically sitting on the northern edge of Yorkshire it remains, in spite of its economic and administrative past as a 'Teesside' or 'Cleveland' town, a place with a distinctiveness and independence all its own, having successfully resisted all attempts to date to treat it as a county capital, Yorkshire 'outpost' or Durham dormitory town.

Today the friendly societies have more or less disappeared while the handful that remain in the town function mainly as local agencies of large and purely commercial insurance companies. In one or two instances activities include voluntary and charitable work. However, two remaining mutual-aid organizations do provide us with a direct link to the past. The St Pauls Mutual Aid Society in Middlesbrough was established and registered under friendly society legislation in 1888 and still operates today as a source of investment and loans for its 1,600 members, many of whose parents and grandparents were members. Known locally as the 'Mut' it remains non-profit making and pays a dividend out of any surplus funds. The year 1887 saw the formation in Middlesbrough of the Grand United Order of the Knights of the Golden Horn, a mutual-aid society with a strong emphasis on conviviality and a love of regalia. At least 140 lodges or 'encampments' of the Order were set up in the South Durham and North Yorkshire region, a small number of which remain open today. Meetings are characterized (after the transaction of business) in time-honoured fashion by singing, monologues and the telling of jokes. For bad language, disrespectful behaviour and introducing 'outside topics' members are fined and must contribute to the 'Harmony Bowl'. From a General Fund, members experiencing hardship can draw benefits. These two organizations represent the vestiges of a long tradition of fraternity and mutual support, a collective movement which played an important part in the town's development.

NOTES

1. *Stokesley News & Cleveland Reporter*, 1 July 1843; L. Praed, *History of the Rise and Progress of Middlesbrough* (Middlesbrough 1863), pp. 1–22 (Landor Praed was the pseudonym of G.J. Holyoake. Nationally a leading secularist in the 1850s and 1860s and much influenced by the ideas of the socialist Robert Owen, he was a frequent visitor to the north-east and especially Middlesbrough); British Parliamentary Papers (BPP), *Royal Commission on Children, Young Persons and Women in Agriculture*, 1867, p. 273; *The Daily Exchange*, 24 February 1886.

2. C.F.G. Masterman, *The Condition of England* (1911), p. 90; Quoted by Betty Vernon, *Ellen Wilkinson* (1982), p. 76; J.B. Priestley, *English Journey* (1934), p. 340; G. Orwell, *Keep The Aspidistra Flying*, 1936 (1962), p. 98.

3. Lady Bell, *At the Works: A Study of a Manufacturing Town*, 1907 (1985), p. 8.

4. BPP, *Royal Commission on Labour*, Testimony before Group 'A', 22 July 1891, First Report, pp. 73, 83.

5. Samuel Smiles, *Thrift* (1880 edn), pp. 219–22.

6. N. Pevsner, *The Buildings of England: Yorkshire, The North Riding* (1973), p. 253; M. Lock, *A Plan for Middlesbrough: The Proposals in Outline* (1945), p. 6; R. Glass (ed.), *The Social Background of a Plan: A Study of Middlesbrough* (1948), p. 51.

7. Evidence of J.W. Pease, June 1877, to Select Committee on Intemperance, Q. 8480; *North-Eastern Daily Gazette (NEDG)* references quoted by Major Seton Churchill, *Betting and Gambling* (1894), pp. 42–44; Bell, *At the Works*, ch. VI; *NEDG*, 11 October 1906.

8. E.G. Ravenstein, 'The Laws of Migration', *Journal of The Royal Statistical Society*, 48 (1885), 215; *The Times*, 10 October 1853.

9. Briggs, above, p. 6.

10. J.M. Baernreither, *English Associations of Working Men* (English edn, 1889), pp. 171–230.

11. For the quotations and references to local friendly societies in this and the following three paragraphs see J.J. Turner, 'Friendly Societies in South Durham and North Yorkshire, *c.* 1790–1914' (unpublished University of Teesside PhD thesis, 1992).

12. Darlington Reference Library, *Combers' Sick Association records* (1813–1830), D/XD/95/1 and D/HP/40; J.J. Turner, 'Early Friendly Societies in North Yorkshire and South Durham', *Cleveland and Teesside Local History Society (CTLHS) Bulletin*, 50 (Spring 1986), 64–70.

13. For a short history of the Ally Sloper comic strip character see *The Guardian*, 20 August 1987.

14. *Northern Review*, 9 October 1886.

15. Bell, *At the Works*, p. 194; *NEDG*, 22 July 1896.

16. *Letter & Account Books*, Trade Union Friendly Collecting Society, Middlesbrough.

17. Bell, *At the Works*, p. 18; W. Ranger, *Report to the General Board of Health: Middlesbrough* (1854), pp. 15–16; *Smith's Dock Monthly Journal*, 1919–1933.

18. Bell, *At the Works*, pp. 118–20.

19. P. Barton, 'The Southerner', *CTLHS Newsletter*, 38, August 1991 (no pagination); for a discussion of working-class radicalism in mid-century Middlesbrough see K. Flett, 'Progress and Light: Secularism and Radicalism on Teesside after 1848', *CTLHS Bulletin*, 56 (Spring 1989), 16–24.

20. A. Trollope, *North America*, 1862 (1992), p. 80; H. Martineau, *Society in America*, I (1837), pp. 259–60.

21. D.W. Meinig, *The Shaping of America: A Geographical Perspective on 500 Years of History*, II (1993), p. 249.

22. M. Walsh, *The American Frontier Revisited* (1981), pp. 19, 60; R.P. Hastings, 'Middlesbrough: A New Victorian Boom Town in 1840–41', *CTLHS Bulletin*, 30, pp. 2, 6.

23. Briggs, above, p. 25; P.J. Ethington, *The Public City: The Political Construction of Urban Life in San Francisco, 1850–1900* (1994), pp. 368–9.
24. Quoted by L. Siedentop, *Tocqueville* (1994), p. 91.
25. F.J. Turner, *The Frontier in American History* (New York, 1962), pp. 348–9; B. Lee and R. Reinders, 'The Loss of Innocence: 1880–1914', in M. Bradbury and H. Temperly (eds.), *Introduction to American Studies* (1981), pp. 179–80.
26. L. Praed (George Holyoake), *History*, p. 14.
27. A.J.P. Taylor, 'Manchester', in *Essays in English History* (1977), p. 313.

CHAPTER 5

THE EVOLUTION OF A POLITICAL CULTURE: MIDDLESBROUGH, 1850–1950

Richard Lewis

The most important factor shaping the emerging political culture of Middlesbrough in the mid-nineteenth century was the exceptional nature of the town's origins and growth. Unlike neighbouring Stockton, which had a municipal tradition which went back two or three centuries, Middlesbrough sprang from a hamlet of 150 souls to a county borough of over 90,000 within seventy years, an experience virtually unparalleled outside the 'new' world. Its political development was also shaped by the economic basis of the town's growth, from a minor coal-exporting centre in the 1830s to being the world's iron and steel smelting centre by the 1870s. Inevitably the sheer drama of this transformation affected the growth of a distinct character in the political life of the growing town. In the second half of the nineteenth century, Middlesbrough acquired a political life and personality which reflected the economic, social and demographic realities of its spectacular rise. But this political culture was not just the mirror of its industrial and commercial roots, it was also the product of other less material pressures, such as the key personalities, and the rivalries of various non-commercial interest, religious, ideological and ethnic groupings. These various elements constructed a political culture which was distinct, and which gave Middlesbrough its sense of identity.

One of the more appropriate aspects of recent developments in the study of modern British political history has been a resurgence in interest in the role of local and regional factors in the political processes. Many historians still prefer to see politics as the activity of a remote elite, operating in the hothouse atmosphere of Westminster and Whitehall, and others have tried to explain even local patterns of activity in terms of inexorable forces shaped by 'objective' factors growing out of economic and demographic change, over which local experiences, circumstances and variations have little or no role in the actual formation of events. For these historians, politics may be acted out in the theatre of local life, but the script is written by an absent, anonymous and impersonal author. Renewed interest in the significance of the local political culture has produced a new perspective on local activity, which gives a greater role to and emphasis on such factors as, among others, the individuals involved, the nature of election campaigns in particular constituencies, the state and quality of party organization in the districts concerned, and the impact of ethnic and religious factors in an area or region.

This renewal of interest is particularly valid with regard to the period of this survey, 1850 to 1950. With the formation of the municipal borough of Middlesbrough in 1853, and the parliamentary borough in 1868, there was created an electorate which was too large simply to be held in the pocket of one man or small group of men, but which was still small enough to be influenced by personal factors. After 1867 the political process was based on a mass franchise, but one limited in a way which retained an intimacy which was soon lost when all adult men and women gained the vote in the interwar years. While the fabric of local political life had features which we would recognize today, there were crucial differences. In particular, the public meetings mattered, attendances were often very high, and they could affect the outcome of a campaign in ways which would be virtually unthinkable today. The press coverage was provided, almost exclusively, by the local press; the national daily paper was still to emerge as a real force in popular culture and politics. The canvassing of voters was more significant before 1918 when the electorate was smaller, more easily identified, and when the canvasser could often be your employer, landlord, foreman or some other influential local figure – or his wife or daughter. This, combined with residual doubts as to the truly secret nature of the ballot (introduced in 1872), made the whole electoral process much more significant for those engaged in it, either as party activists or voters, than it would appear today. Also in an age before television, or even the wireless, the local political processes were the only ones which could effectively engage the average adult. Perceptions of the 'national' campaign would be hazy and remote to most electors. The 'national' campaign was really the aggregation of the local experiences, whereas today the local campaign is essentially a minor adjunct to the televisual dogfight. There was another crucial difference – the nature of party organization. Today party labels denote quite rigid, and readily understood political entities, whatever the ambiguities of policy and ideology. This was not so much the case in the period before 1918, when the nationalization of political life, triggered by the huge extension of the electorate, and the growth of mass forms of communication, led to party labels becoming more concrete and less subject to the subtleties of local control and distinction. Although 1918 was a watershed, many features of the earlier political culture remained. It can be argued that it was not until after the Second World War that Middlesbrough, along with the rest of England and Wales, became part of a genuinely national political culture, where local patterns of political behaviour were finally overwhelmed. That is why this study does not end until 1950, when television news firmly established a new political imagery for the mass of the population which had little to do with public meetings or door-to-door canvassing.

In its earliest years when the new town of Middlesbrough was still a small company-dominated settlement stuck at the end of the famous Stockton to Darlington railway line, it is inappropriate even to write of it possessing anything resembling a distinct political culture. The Owners of the Middlesbrough Estate exercised total control over every facet of life in the community. The bulk of the inhabitants were unskilled labourers drawn from the local countryside, whose main concerns were employment, and fear of competition from those, such as Irish immigrants, who might undercut the price they could obtain for their labour. Politically the town was run by the Owners, whose mixture of entrepreneurial and religious, mainly Quaker, zeal fostered attempts at social control, which were in later years to breed forms of popular resistance which were to contribute significantly to a distinct political culture for the town. Studies of Chartism on Teesside have shown that in Middlesbrough the virtual exclusion of all sections of the town's population from any element of political life bred a broad-based coalition of support for reform, but one which in reality was a middle-class dominated movement directed as much at challenging the authority of the Owners as it was directed at national constitutional change.

It was the dramatic development of the iron smelting industry from the 1840s which transformed the town, not just economically and demographically, but also politically. The demand for incorporation, achieved in 1853, became the focal point for the development of a distinct political culture. It occurred just as the expansion of the iron industry established the power of the ironmasters in the new community. The period from the early 1850s until the end of the 1880s has often been portrayed as the era of the 'Ironmasters', who dominated the town's politics in a way that was more comprehensive than that exercised by the Owners. This power was derived not just from the naked exercise of economic control, but from the fact that they enjoyed genuine support from a population who saw them as the authors of the town's spectacular growth and success. Middlesbrough's self-image, as one of the great success stories of Britain's mid-Victorian age of prosperity, was carefully cultivated by the personification of this success in the lives and careers of the owner/managers who created the iron trade. Certainly in all the various focal points of political activity the ironmasters were always a significant, not infrequently dominant, element. From the creation of the borough ironmasters were prominent in the affairs of the council, with the first mayor being the man often credited with creating Middlesbrough as the great industrial prodigy of Victorian Britain, Henry Bolckow. In the following decades he was to be succeeded in that office by several other notable figures in the early development of Teesside's iron industry such as John Vaughan, Isaac Wilson, Hugh Bell and Edward

Williams. Bolckow also became Middlesbrough's first MP being returned unopposed in 1868. He was succeeded in Parliament by Isaac Wilson, and by Edward Williams' son Penry in 1910. It was a prominence in the affairs of the town which has led many commentators to see the latter part of the nineteenth century as an era when the town was run by and for the owner/managers of the iron trade. Some writers have seen this in heroic terms, these leaders of industry bringing their undoubted entrepreneurial talents to bear on the affairs of the new and rapidly expanding town, and giving it a sense of civic pride and distinct commercial personality. Others have seen it as a period in which these men exploited the district, creating an unplanned urban sprawl indiscriminately mixed in with industrial activities which provided work, but also polluted the environment in ways which led to the town's having a reputation for bad health, poor sanitation and high mortality rates.

As is often the case, neither the heroic nor the exploitative interpretation will stand up to very close examination. The individual who personified the era of the ironmasters more than anyone else was Bolckow, the town's first mayor and Member of Parliament. When the town celebrated its Jubilee in 1881 the centrepiece of the occasion was the unveiling of a statue to the man commonly acknowledged as its real founder. Yet far from being representative Bolckow was exceptional. His commitment to the new town was real, but few of his fellow ironmasters followed his lead. A study of the political activities of the eighty or so men who can be defined as ironmasters, active in the district in the 1850–90 period, has revealed that few took part in the municipal affairs of the town. Only twenty ever sat on the council, and only nine of them were members for more than ten years. The later generations of ironmasters had even lower levels of participation; only three 'non-pioneers' played any part at all. Certainly there was always an iron trade presence on the elected bodies of the town – the borough council, board of guardians and school board after 1871. But they were almost always outnumbered by others, and small business and especially retailing tended to eclipse them numerically if not in the quality and quantity of influence that individuals could command. When the great boom period of the mid-century gave way to prolonged recessions and the challenges of new technologies and foreign competition it appears that the commercial leaders of the iron trade had neither the will nor the time to devote to civic affairs. By the Edwardian era only one prominent figure in the iron and steel industry was on the borough council, which was otherwise dominated by small business and professional men. This was a process no doubt reinforced by the growing split between ownership and management roles reinforced by the trend towards limited liability companies in the trade later in the century. Edward Williams, who presided over the 'flotation' of Bolckow & Vaughan in 1864, was rare in being both a 'manager' and a prominent figure in the local community. It also appears that when ironmasters did take an active part in municipal affairs it was because their commercial interests were at stake. A sudden surge of participation in the mid-1870s seems to have been related to the question of whether the low-rated 'ironmasters' district of the town should have this privilege withdrawn. This might seem to reinforce the critical interpretation of the ironmasters' influence, yet the picture is more subtle and complex. Some were active to protect their commercial interests, others accepted a broader social responsibility and supported a more equitable distribution of the rate burden. The ironmasters never constituted a monolithic political entity; there were personal, commercial and indeed political rivalries which often overrode any notional solidarity among them.

In defence of the ironmasters it has been suggested that their commitment was embodied in their philanthropic generosity. Yet with the exception of Bolckow's gift of Albert Park, little in the town can readily be traced back to the munificence of the leaders of the iron trade. However, if the ironmasters failed in the test of philanthropic generosity they can perhaps be acquitted of full culpability in regard to Middlesbrough's poor health and mortality record. Here the 'ratepayer mentality' of the small businessmen and householders of the town, who actually dominated the council, seems to have been a much more significant factor than the rapacity of the iron trade. The poorly planned, badly drained and insanitary condition of the 'infant Hercules' was down to the shopocracy not the ironmasters. Even here the picture is far from clear-cut. As another study of Middlesbrough in the 1850–1914 period has shown, advances in technical knowledge, such as the germ theory of infectious and contagious diseases, were often transmitted to holders of public office in an imperfect and convoluted manner, which often led to decisions being made on the basis of inadequate understanding of the scientific basis of ill-health. Infant mortality, exceptionally high in Middlesbrough well into this century, was still ascribed to the ignorance and incompetence of working-class mothers, rather than the social irresponsibility of town councillors anxious to keep down the rate burden, by even well-informed medical officers of health. It

Bolckow presides over all he surveys, especially Albert Park; a cartoon from Dominie, 1875, *Middlesbrough's own short-lived* Punch
(MCL)

John Dunning as seen by Dominie *in 1875 (MCL)*

is a complex story made even less comprehensible if driven by a desire to seek out heroes and villains – in truth Middlesbrough's political life had few of both.

Hostility to the political influence of the ironmasters came from several disparate sources. Within the politically active coteries of small businessmen and professional people in the town in the second half of the nineteenth century there was never a sense of deferential acquiescence to the power of the leaders of the iron trade. John Dunning, a former borough surveyor for Middlesbrough, became an active councillor in the 1870s and acted as a leader of opinion among those seeking to check the power of the ironmasters. He also championed the cause of 'economy' in local government expenditure, often against the more ambitious ideas of the ironmasters. In the surrounding countryside the local gentry viewed the rising power and wealth of the Middlesbrough iron trade with a mixture of excitement and apprehension; they saw opportunities for material gain, but feared the loss or dilution of their status as leaders in the community. The Pennymans of Ormesby Hall are the classic example. Living on Middlesbrough's doorstep, James Stovin Pennyman, educated as an engineer, took a lively interest in the commercial and technical development of the rising industrial settlements on the banks of the Tees and in the surrounding hills, and he certainly had no qualms about socializing with the wealthier ironmasters who became his neighbours. However, with his interests in North Ormesby he strove to curb the spread of the borough of Middlesbrough and its less compliant political culture.

There is one other point that needs to be made about the role of the major employers in the political life of late-nineteenth-century Middlesbrough. While the movement to joint-stock, limited-liability companies increasingly separated the ownership of capital from the management of Middlesbrough's industry, those leading capitalists that did continue to reside in the area belonged to a network of commercial and political influence which was much wider than the populous, but geographically very small, town of Middlesbrough. By the end of the Victorian era hardly any major businessmen actually lived in Middlesbrough. This is well illustrated by the two Unionist (Conservative) candidates elected for the parliamentary boroughs of Middlesbrough and Stockton in 1900, Sam Sadler and Robert Ropner, whose wealth was made from chemicals, and shipbuilding/owning respectively. Both men lived close to one another in some style, in Eaglescliffe and Preston-on-Tees. The commercial and political elites were living and socializing at an increasing distance from the realties of Middlesbrough, and the other industrial communities on the banks of the Tees.

The triumph of the Conservative Sam Sadler in the 1900 election was a severe blow to the town's reputation as a stronghold of Liberalism. Municipal life in the new town in its early years never operated within a rigid party political framework; interests and personalities transcended ideology and party labels. Many writers, including Asa Briggs, have noted the inability of Middlesbrough Liberals to sustain effective local organization, yet it was almost inevitable that any parliamentary representative from the town in the 1860–90 period would take the Liberal whip. It is difficult to believe that Bolckow would have been returned unopposed in 1868 if he had stood as anything but a Liberal candidate. But his candidacy reflected neither the basic power of the ironmasters, nor the robust strength of popular Liberalism in the town. On the contrary it mirrored the limited clout of the former, and the essential instability of the latter. Bolckow was seen as a figurehead rather than an ideologically committed Liberal; radicals in the town despaired of him. His heavy German accent and poor oratorial skills made him an unappealing candidate. He regarded his sojourn in Westminster as a reward for services rendered, rather than as a platform to project the aspirations of Middlesbrough radicals. Interest groups associated with popular Liberalism – Sabbatarians, temperance men and advocates of Anglican disestablishment – found his successor and fellow ironmaster Isaac Wilson equally frustrating. E.T. John (later himself to become a radical Liberal MP), one of the few leading figures in the Teesside iron and steel industry to evince a genuine interest in political ideas, helped establish in the 1880s a local debating society to facilitate an understanding of 'the principles of party struggles', for he despaired of the fact that in Middlesbrough 'Strict party organizations do not flourish on either side'. In fact by the late 1880s Middlesbrough Liberalism was in some difficulty. The industrial and commercial elites of Teesside were as afflicted by the crisis in national Liberal politics as elsewhere. Some former supporters among the ironmasters, such as Hugh Bell, defected to Unionism over the Irish Home Rule issue, though Bell himself was later to return to the Liberals in support of Free Trade. Even Henry's heir, Carl Bolckow, and Thomas Vaughan the son of John, switched to Toryism. But many more of the rising industrialists with interests outside iron and steel, such as the chemical magnate Sam Sadler, and the shipbuilder Raylton Dixon, who founded the Middlesbrough Conservative Club, saw the

Tory party as their natural home. By the 1890s a Teesside-wide network of Unionist influence and connection flourished, which enabled Thomas Wrightson with his heavy engineering interests in Thornaby, and Arthur Dorman, the steel maker, to collaborate effortlessly with gentry Tories such as the Pennymans of Ormesby Hall, or the aristocratic Londonderrys of Wynyard Hall. The local Liberal press soon noticed that these networks underpinned organizational structures which the Liberals found almost impossible to match. The Conservatives thus constituted a major undercurrent in the political culture of Middlesbrough, which was probably always a minority element but made up in social coherence, and unity of purpose and organization, what it mostly lacked in sheer numbers.

The essential instability of Teesside Liberalism in general, and in Middlesbrough in particular, grew out of the fact that its component parts were not socially or culturally harmonious. It was essentially a disparate mixture of business radicalism, militant Nonconformity and the emergent political ambitions of organized labour. Indeed the only element within Middlesbrough's political culture which lent any coherence to the rather nebulous set of attitudes and ideas which constituted poor Liberalism was the main local daily newspaper. Hugh Gilzean Reid was the founder and early editor of the first daily, and soon the main, newspaper of Teesside, the *North-Eastern Daily Gazette*. He was an entrepreneur of vision and ambition to match any of the pioneers of Middlesbrough, whom he lionized in his much quoted early history of the town, *Middlesbrough and Its Jubilee*, in 1881. Reid's genuinely humble origins lay in the farming community of north-east Scotland near Aberdeen, where he acquired a radical political outlook, a Nonconformist religious conscience, and a burning desire for self-improvement. It was a classic combination which resonated well with the better-off, and aspirational working-class elements of Teesside society in the latter decades of the Victorian era. Although Reid always sought to give full coverage to all political persuasions active on Teesside, his paper was unambiguously Liberal in its outlook. It was the voice of what he described in his 1881 history of the town as 'a decidedly Liberal constituency'. An advocate of extending the democratic franchise, he was active in the establishment of consumer and producer cooperation, sympathetic to trade unionism, a supporter of Irish Home Rule and a champion of the peaceful resolution through arbitration of international conflicts. He was a Baptist lay-preacher. Yet he was also a major capitalist, soon acquiring other local newspaper titles in the Midlands, and in addition becoming a director of a local iron foundry. He embodied all the key elements of late-nineteenth-century popular Liberalism, a cause he felt no qualms in promoting through his journals. His paper always backed the official Liberal candidates in parliamentary elections. Reid was himself briefly a Liberal MP for the Aston Manor constituency in Birmingham in 1885.

While there had been attempts to establish Conservative titles to oppose the domination of the area by Liberal/radical journals such as the *Gazette* and the Darlington-based *Northern Echo*, it was only in the aftermath of the Home Rule/Unionist split of 1885/6, that they made any headway with the creation of the Darlington-based *North Star*, and the transfer of political allegiance of the formerly Liberal weekly, the *Darlington and Stockton Times*. Although the *Gazette* retained its ideological stance it found itself continually forced to offer a lead at a time when Liberal political hegemony in the Teesside industrial communities was being threatened by a rising Conservative challenge, and deepening divisions within the already fragmented and ill-organized forces of the Liberal party within the area. It was the *Gazette* more than the short-lived and rather amorphous Liberal organizations of the area which sustained the Liberal creed in industrial Teesside.

The better organized forces of Conservatism (commonly known as Unionists at the time) on Teesside began to make significant advances from the late 1880s; they took the Stockton seat for the first time in 1892, and in the 'Khaki' election of 1900 they captured both the Teesside borough constituencies. It was a far cry from the 1870s when Teesside in general, and Middlesbrough in particular, seemed to embody the key tenets of Gladstonian virtues – economic enterprise, individual and voluntary collective improvement. The drift of commercial and industrial wealth from Liberalism to Unionism is well illustrated by the growing complaints from Liberal spokesmen in the local press about the undue influence being exercised by Tory employers and their agents over their workforces. This was often followed by demands that the practice of door-to-door canvassing should be made illegal – another sign of the relative organizational weakness of the local Liberal party. Yet the underlying causes of Liberal decline were grounded in the essentially informal coalition which made up the forces of 'progress' in the area.

Middlesbrough was a new town. It was a town of immigrants, drawn primarily from the surrounding rural hinterlands of Yorkshire and Durham, but also in significant numbers from further afield. There were substantial elements within Middlesbrough's population from Ireland, Scotland and Wales. The Irish and the Welsh in particular contributed to the political character of the town, not just numerically, but because they embodied another key element in the political culture of Middlesbrough – religious affiliation. The Welsh were predominantly Nonconformist, and therefore shared the political aspirations and perspectives of the large indigenous dissenting community. The Welsh migrants to the town were brought to the area to fill a niche role in the iron industry, whether as semi-skilled puddlers, or as foremen and managers. Two of the most important figures in the later development of the great Bolckow & Vaughan company, the general managers Edward Williams and Windsor Richards, were products of this settlement. Thus, while they were always overshadowed numerically by the

Irish component of Teesside's population, the Welsh constituted a distinctive and influential element within the political culture, often, as with E.T. John, offering leadership to the local Nonconformist congregations and articulating their political demands.

In 1910 both Teesside borough seats sent to Parliament products of this community in the persons of Penry Williams (son of Edward Williams) for Middlesbrough, and the Welsh-born Baptist, Jonathan Samuel (a former puddler) for Stockton-on-Tees. Significantly both regarded themselves as radicals, and both claimed a special relationship with organized labour. It was to be a short-lived triumph for the Welsh, since there was no sustained migration from Wales after the 1870s, and they were soon assimilated into the wider Teesside community. However, if anything, they constituted a rather divisive element in popular Liberalism. The demands of the Nonconformists tended to alienate as many voters as they won over. The influence of the temperance movement provided many opportunities for the local Conservatives to portray themselves as the defenders of the recreational rights of the working man; the demands by the Sabbatarians for Sunday closing of various popular facilities had a similar effect. It was in the field of education, however, that the aspirations of the chapelgoers proved to be most divisive. Education at that time was still bedevilled by deep religious sectarianism, and the desire of the Nonconformists to check the influence of the state church, the Anglican Church, led them to adopt a very aggressive stance towards all forms of state financial support for church schools. This, however, brought them into direct conflict with another key element within the political culture of Middlesbrough and Teesside, the Irish Catholic community.

From the 1840s there had been a growing Irish migration to Teesside, the Roman Catholic Irish being the main constituent of this population movement. By the 1870s they were outnumbering the Welsh by three to one, and in the later years of that decade the Catholic Church made Middlesbrough the centre of one of its new dioceses for the north of England. Catholicism became a factor in the political life of the town. In some other parts of the country such a large population of Irish immigrants would have triggered the growth of an anti-Catholic and anti-Irish backlash among the host, predominantly Protestant, population. There were outbreaks of anti-Irish feeling from time to time, but sustained hostility does not seem to have developed on the same scale as in Liverpool or Glasgow. That is not to say that there were not attempts by some local politicians to play on anti-Irish feelings. The shipbuilder and active Conservative, Raylton Dixon, was a sponsor of a local South Bank based Orange Lodge in the 1880s. A more sustained attempt to use anti-Irish and anti-Catholic sentiment for electoral purposes occurred in the early 1890s when the Thornaby and Stockton based heavy engineering magnate, Thomas Wrightson, founded an organization called the British League, which soon established branches throughout Teesside. Aimed at working men, it was overtly monarchist and imperialist in its aims; partly social, partly propagandist in its activities. Its sectarian nature was revealed by rules which specifically excluded Catholics and Jews from its ranks. In an early example of what today would be called investigative journalism, the local Liberal press pursued the main agents of this organization, senior employees of Wrightson's company, and in the end the more offensive aspects of the British League's rules were amended. However, there can be little doubt that playing the anti-Irish card assisted Wrightson in his capture of the Stockton constituency seat in 1892, and certainly heightened community tensions in the rest of Teesside. The local Catholic community, overwhelmingly working class, was never fully assimilated in the period of this study; denominational schooling and the institutional strength of the Catholic Church – so very different from the fragmented Nonconformist churches – ensured that. They did, however, through the rise of another component of the political culture in Middlesbrough – organized labour – gradually become fully integrated into the system.

Although the predominantly Liberal ironmasters liked to think of themselves as enlightened and progressive employers, there was always a tension in the relationship between the masters and the men – the term men is valid here, since there were few opportunities for female employment in the trades of Teesside. Dr Malcolm Chase has traced the early history of industrial relations on Teesside from disputes in the much larger-scale enterprises of the iron industry from the 1840s. The insurrectionary and the collective self-improvement features of Chartism were both present in Middlesbrough, and both played a role in the early growth of working-class political activity in the town. Retail cooperation, such a feature of mid-Victorian proletarian activity elsewhere, does not seem to have flourished in Middlesbrough, though it was more successful in Stockton from the late 1860s. It was trade unionism which provided the base for the growth of working-class engagement with the local political processes.

The 'frontier town' quality of Middlesbrough, with its narrow-based, boom/slump economy, and its overwhelmingly male population, made industrial relations an area of social dislocation in the new community. When this was combined with pressures on the owners and managers to secure a good return on, what was by the standards of the time, very high levels of capital investment some conflict between capital and labour in industrial Teesside was almost inevitable. From the 1860s there were major bouts of industrial action, culminating in 1866 in a five-month 'lock out' of the ironworkers. The workers were eventually starved back to work, with wage reductions of between 5 and 10 per cent being forced on them. It was a bitter defeat which checked the growth of effective trade unionism in the iron industry, which was further complicated by ethnic divisions between the declining 'puddling' foundry trades, dominated by English and Welsh migrants to the area who lost out particularly badly in the 1866 dispute, and the newer and more buoyant blastfurnace trades, where the Irish Catholic community was well represented, which suffered a less severe reverse. It was also a defeat which left a legacy of bitterness and resentment which prevented the growth of an effective Liberal electoral machine where middle-class radicalism and working-class aspirations could combine harmoniously. It was only the fear of an emerging popular Conservatism, fed by anti-Irish Catholic sentiment, which allowed radical elements in the town to accept Bolckow's unopposed return in 1868.

The fragility of the social basis for popular Liberalism in Middlesbrough is well illustrated by the early and repeated attempts by champions – some self-proclaimed – of organized labour to secure direct representation of the working class of the town in Parliament. The enfranchisement of the town as a parliamentary borough was accompanied by the extension of the vote to working men householders, which made the proletarian element of the electorate sufficiently large to make the return of representatives of organized labour at least feasible. Indeed, one of the first serious attempts to gain a seat in the House of Commons by a trade union backed candidate occurred in 1874, when John Kane, general secretary of the largest iron industry trades union stood for the Middlesbrough constituency. Backed by the Labour Representation League, Kane's campaign was hampered by the fragmented radical working-class political movement in the town. The power of the ironmasters in a still relatively small electorate (the total poll was only just over 6,000) was probably sufficient to discourage many ironworkers from voting for the union leader. This was the first general election where the secret ballot was used, and its absolute secrecy was still doubted by many. However, Kane's candidature broke the brittle unity of the industrial and commercial elite of the town, something which had prevented a Conservative challenge in 1868.

The election of 1874 exposed the true nature of popular politics in Middlesbrough. There was a solid block of popular support for the ironmasters, grounded in a belief in the Gladstonian tenets of free trade, and cautious institutional and religious reform. It was powerfully reinforced by deference to the economic power of the main employers. Against this there was a small but not uninfluential coterie of Conservatives, who were anxious to protect the privileges of the established Church and hostile to constitutional change and to the aspirations of Irish nationalism. The Tory ironmaster, W.R.I. Hopkins, who considered putting himself forward in 1868 but had acquiesced in Bolckow's unopposed return, became their standard bearer in 1874. Standing outside these two groups there was a body of opinion which felt unrepresented. It included some middle-class radicals, disgruntled advocates of temperance reform, who were unimpressed by

Bolckow's activities regarding the drink question, and above all it consisted of a growing number of working men who felt sufficiently independent of their employers to support a 'Labour' candidate. This was no mean action at a time when being an MP was still surrounded by a social snobbery which saw only the wealthy and/or the well-bred as suitable candidates for such a public office. The *Gazette*, which by 1874 had already established itself as the main newspaper on Teesside, threw its weight fully behind Bolckow's candidacy, giving little space and even less credence to the claims of John Kane. Despite other financial and organizational problems which surrounded Kane's challenge, the trade union leader still managed to take nearly 25 per cent of the vote. The Tories took less than a sixth of the ballot. It represented not just a milestone in the embryonic development of the political ambitions of organized labour, but also showed how far Middlesbrough's political culture had moved from its company-town origins. The hold of the Liberal establishment over the electorate was real enough, as long as the Liberals could produce some acknowledged 'pioneer' of Middlesbrough's development, such as Bolckow and his immediate successor and close political ally Isaac Wilson, as their candidate. The local Labour movement did not try to challenge the employer-dominated Liberal caucus in Middlesbrough again until 1892 when Isaac Wilson retired from politics.

Trade unionists in Middlesbrough established a trades council in 1870, and the unions of the iron, engineering and shipbuilding trades focused their energies on improving the wages and conditions of their members through their industrial rather than their political strength. It was not until the late 1890s that the first acknowledged 'Labour' candidate was returned to the borough council. The latter decades of the nineteenth century formed a period in which the iron and steel trades saw little sustained industrial conflict, and most disputes were resolved through arbitration and the operation of a sliding scale which related workers' wages to the selling price of their product. It was a period in which the unions of the iron and steel industry established their reputation as being well organized, but essentially non-militant in their tactics. Many on Teesside saw the unions as basically benefit clubs, or friendly societies, which helped their members in times of sickness and unemployment. This contrasts starkly with the mining industry where a break with sliding scales and automatic arbitration at the end of the century was to turn miners into the focus of militancy, and the cutting edge of demands for major social and economic change. In Middlesbrough the demands of organized labour tended to be limited and non-ideological, fundamentally ameliorative and piecemeal which could be accommodated within the existing order of things.

The essentially pacific strategy of the main agencies of organized labour in the Teesside area does not mean that the working-class voters of Middlesbrough were entirely reconciled to the political hegemony of the employer-dominated Liberal organizations. When the general election of 1892 was called, the local Liberal elite decided to import a wealthy barrister, W.R. Robson, as their nominee. The town was going through one of its periodic economic depressions, and many working men were being faced with penury, and the ignominious relief systems of the Poor Law. They might have been willing to accept the nomination of a venerable local employer; they were less happy about the credentials of a wealthy outsider. Instead a group of trade unionists made an approach to James Havelock Wilson, the mercurial and highly theatrical leader of the seamen's union. He had already made a name for himself in Labour circles as an effective propagandist and advocate of social reform, and by 1892 was ready to enter national politics. Playing on the still very informal party structures of the time, he managed to force himself into the selection process for the Liberal candidate by encouraging hundreds of unemployed working men to take up free membership of the local Liberal association, then organizing a mass meeting of Liberal 'supporters' where he ran a 'poll', shrewdly using press reporters as 'scrutineers', of those present which, not surprisingly, came down strongly in Wilson's favour. The local Liberal elite cried foul and still endorsed Robson as the official Liberal candidate.

Wilson stood on an independent Labour ticket and came top of the poll with 4,691 votes, pushing the official Liberal, Robson, into second place with 4,062. The shattering nature of the Liberal defeat was made more painful by the relative success of the Unionist candidate, the former Liberal ironmaster, Hugh Bell, who gained 3,333 votes which revealed how the underlying strength of popular Conservatism had grown since 1874. It was the first time that an independent 'Labour' candidate won against official Liberal opposition, the other two 'Labour' members elected in that general election, Keir Hardie and John Burns, having only Unionist opposition. However, unlike Hardie, but alongside Burns, Wilson was soon reconciled with official Liberalism, took the Liberal whip, and was the official Liberal candidate in 1895 and 1900. In this stance he seems to have reflected the desires of his working-class supporters who were more interested in the direct representation of Labour rather than in the creation of a new party. Representation of the trade union interest through the agency of the Liberal party was known at the time as Lib-Labism, and in this regard James Havelock Wilson epitomized the dominant strain within trade unionist and working-class political activity in the 1890s. The advocates of independent Labour representation, such as the socialist Keir Hardie were still very much in the minority. Wilson and Hardie were to become bitter enemies; the austere, teetotal, ideological enemy of capitalism Hardie, against Wilson, a man willing to compromise his professed principles, ready to do deals with the political representatives of big business, whose personal behaviour frequently betrayed a susceptibility to attractions of the lifestyle of the successful capitalist.

Relations between Wilson and the Liberal establishment in Middlesbrough were never easy. The *Gazette*, after denouncing his tactical sharp practice in 1892, decided to throw its weight behind him, praising the man's undoubted talents, and, above all, supporting the logic of Lib-Labism, of keeping organized labour within the broad boundaries of popular Liberalism. Tensions remained, however, and during the general election of 1900, called by the Unionist government at the height of the Boer War, when imperialist and jingoistic sentiment was at fever pitch, the local newspaper had to engage in special pleading for Wilson's cause. It stated that although there were many Liberals who felt that the town should be represented by a figure prominent in the affairs of one of the chief commercial activities of

James Havelock Wilson: Middlesbrough's Lib-Lab MP in 1895, whose susceptibility to the attractions of the lifestyle of the successful capitalist made him a bitter enemy of Keir Hardie (MCL)

the area, Wilson's personal contribution to the maintenance of good relations between Capital and Labour outweighed such considerations. Wilson's slightly unsavoury reputation by the late 1890s, in particular persistent rumours, propagated assiduously by the Unionists, about his fondness for alcohol, eroded support from the still powerful Nonconformist and temperance lobby in the town. Despite these problems it still came as a shock when it was reported that Middlesbrough, the former stronghold of Gladstonian Liberalism, had returned a Conservative, in the shape of the local chemical magnate Sam Sadler. While it is easy to see Wilson's narrow defeat (Sadler's majority was only fifty-five) as part of the 'Khaki' election landslide for the Unionists, there can be little doubt that it reflected a further undermining of the complex social foundations of popular Liberalism in the town, and a change in its political character. Sam Sadler was part of the new generation of local capitalists, unattached to the 'pioneers' and with a finger on the pulse of popular sentiment. He made frequent allusions in his campaign to his connections with Middlesbrough football club, and set himself up as the defender of the popular pastimes of the working men of the town, having the licensed victuallers very much on his side. The 1900 election was therefore a milestone in the development of the political character of the town. Employer-led popular Liberalism had given way to a loose and uneasy coalition of interests, middle-class radicalism, the temperance and Nonconformist lobbies, and the demands of organized labour. It was an aggregation of disparate and often conflicting interests, which even the best endeavours of the *North-Eastern Daily Gazette* found impossible to reconcile fully. As a result the Unionists, still just a very large minority within the broad electorate, were able to make the breakthrough. As long as organized labour was prepared to stick with the party, then recovery for the Liberals was possible, but from the late 1890s there were forces in the town striving to break the old links and create a new and independent force.

Socialist and republican radicalism had flourished briefly among some working-class activists in Middlesbrough, and in the ironstone mining districts of east Cleveland, in the early 1870s. Certainly this radical element may have assisted the drive for Kane's challenge to Bolckow in 1874, though Kane himself was no socialist. Ethnic divisions between the English and the Irish radicals of Teesside weakened this embryonic movement, and the shock of the Conservative victory of 1874 seems to have driven many working-class radicals back into the Liberal fold. The rebirth of socialist radicalism in Middlesbrough in the 1890s was led less by working-class activists than by a small coterie of middle-class ethical socialists, closer in outlook and approach to the Fabian Society than to the union activists on the Middlesbrough trades council, with whom they tried to establish a working political alliance, with very limited success. After clinging to a precarious existence from its inception in 1895, the local branch of the Independent Labour Party (ILP) was only rescued from oblivion in 1900 by the energy, drive and the money of three middle-class radicals – known disparagingly by some working-class activists as the 'Linthorpe Gang' – Charles Coates, his sister Marion Coates-Hansen, and her husband Frederick Hansen. By 1903 this group dominated the branch and shaped its activities and its outlook. Threats of resignation by them, and the consequent withdrawal of funding, always kept the rest of the membership in line. This made the establishment of an effective political alliance with the trade unionists of the town even more problematic, as Coates and the Hansens made little attempt to hide their disdain for the non-socialist trades union leaders in the town. They made even less effort to disguise their absolute loathing for J. Havelock Wilson, and when he was readopted as the official Liberal/Labour candidate for the town in 1906, they were determined to mount a challenge. The local trades council decided to support Wilson's nomination, and the national executive of the recently formed Labour Representation Committee, the forerunner of the Labour Party, felt unable formally to endorse a candidate in opposition to Wilson. The Middlesbrough ILP decided to go ahead with its own candidate. Using funds from the wealthy Coates family and other wealthy benefactors, George Lansbury a radical socialist activist from

The canvassing card used by Sam Sadler in the 'Khaki' election of 1900. Canvassing was a novel development and helped the Conservative secure his majority of just fifty-five (CA)

London, later a leader of the Labour Party, and a close friend of the Hansens, was persuaded to stand.

The contest exposed the limited extent to which the attitudes of the rank and file working-class elector had changed in the years since 1892. The loose Liberal alliance of middle-class radicalism, Nonconformity and organized labour, which had unravelled somewhat in 1900, was re-established by universal hostility to the policies of the Unionist government. There was no constituent element of the political culture of Middlesbrough which felt alienated from the representatives of the major parties. The large Irish Catholic vote in the town, which Lansbury tried to win over, remained steadfastly loyal to Wilson, and were not attracted by Lansbury's advanced socialist ideas – nor one suspects by his strong advocacy of female enfranchisement. Indeed the Irish Catholic community was already beginning to integrate itself into the political culture of the town through the increasing intrusion of the local Labour movement into the electoral scene. Lansbury secured only just over 8 per cent of the vote, and Wilson was swept back to the Commons with over 50 per cent of the poll, the defeated Sadler still securing a higher vote, though smaller percentage, than in 1900.

A more culturally attuned effort to capture the seat for Labour occurred in the election of January 1910 after Wilson retired. The ILP, now more under the influence of local trade unionists than before 1906, brought in Pat Walls, leader of the blastfurnacemen's union, and like many of his members in the Middlesbrough area a Catholic of Irish extraction. This candidacy did enjoy official endorsement from the national Labour Party, and the local trades council. The local Liberals tried desperately to find a prominent local trade unionist to carry the Lib/Lab banner in this overwhelmingly working-class seat, but to no avail. In the end they adopted the ironmaster, Penry Williams, who – despite being a president of the Ironmasters' Association – claimed to be the 'Liberal and Labour' candidate. Walls was nearly to double Labour's poll, and its share of the vote, but he still came third and Labour did not contest the seat in the December election of 1910. Williams could still play on claims to be the true 'local' candidate; the threat from a reactionary Conservative Party in the crisis elections of 1910, over the 'People's Budget' and the House of Lords Veto, blended in well with his claims to embody a radical party not unsympathetic to the 'reasonable' demands of organized labour – the incongruity of an ironmaster claiming to be a representative of 'Labour' looks more obvious today than it did at the time.

Popular Liberalism on Teesside at this time seems to show few signs of any long-term decline; its cultural underpinnings were, if anything, stronger in 1910 than they were in 1890. But beneath the surface there were signs of change, the Labour Party in Middlesbrough making slow but significant progress. Election to the small businessman-dominated borough council, and the Board of Guardians, allowed a number of Labour men and women to earn a reputation for public service which slowly raised the party's credibility and weakened the cosy 'non-partisan' traditions of Middlesbrough's municipal life. When a family prominent in the Catholic community, the Careys, joined the ILP and the Labour Party in Middlesbrough in the 1900s, a powerful new element was created which allied the political aspirations of organized labour with the integrationist ambitions of the Catholic community. By 1914 there were six Labour members on the borough council of forty-four members; it was a small but significant element which seems to have established itself by that time as an integral part of the political culture of the town.

There has been much historical debate about the impact of the First World War on the political life of Britain. Certainly changes brought about by the terms of the 1918 Reform Act were to alter the electoral scene in Middlesbrough. The splitting of the seat into two, East and West, ended the organic link between the municipal and the parliamentary politics of the town, although the parliamentary constituency had always been slightly larger than the municipal borough. The huge increase in the size of electorates after 1918 – by 1929 the two seats had over 80,000 electors between them – destroyed the older patterns of electioneering. The nationalization of political life through the rapid growth of mass-circulation daily press, followed by the advent of radio and the cinema newsreel in the 1930s, reduced the essentially local element in the electoral processes. Political parties became more formal, and centrally controlled in their organization, and locally more like electoral machines for the national party leaderships. The full impact of these changes has yet to be fully analysed and understood, but they all seem to have eroded the importance of the peculiarities of political culture in different constituencies.

Marion Coates-Hansen, wearing the robes of the Women's Freedom League, who were active in local government in the early twentieth century (Dorman Museum)

The extension of the parliamentary vote to women, although carried out in two stages to those over thirty and householders, or the wives of householders, in 1918, and to all women over twenty-one in 1928, also affected the political culture. In Middlesbrough the campaign for female suffrage had been led by the same middle-class radicals who spearheaded the demands for Labour representation. Marion Coates-Hansen and her sister-in-law Alice Schofield-Coates (who was briefly imprisoned in Holloway for her suffrage activities) were very active campaigners, mainly through the militant, but non-violent, Women's Freedom League, a breakaway from Emily Pankhurst's Suffragette movement. Both women had been involved in local government long before 1918, and in this regard they represented a movement into local government, and the local political culture, by women which was significant long before the law accepted them as full members of the wider political nation.

From the 1890s female participation in local government in Middlesbrough became a part of the political scene. It was initially confined to the Board of Guardians (fifteen women were elected to the board between 1895 and 1918), who administered the Poor Law system in the town, where it was felt their particular talents in dealing with the interests of children and the aged poor could be deployed without undermining their femininity. There was little erosion of the male domination of other agencies of local government, especially the borough council where no women were elected until 1919. The women elected as guardians tended to be drawn from the middle classes, the wives and sisters of medical practitioners, solicitors, accountants and businessmen, who, at least at first, regarded their membership of the board as less an extension of the political aspirations of women, than a logical extension of the traditional involvement of middle-class women in philanthropic activity. The essentially non-partisan approach, which was, at least nominally, a feature of Middlesbrough council politics, was particularly stressed with regard to female candidates for the Board of Guardians. It was thought that the rough and tumble of parliamentary politics was peculiarly unsuitable for the delicate female temperament, whereas local government, the 'domestic work of the nation' a distinct and separate sphere, was a legitimate area for female participation. In Stockton and in Darlington some women were elected to the Elementary School Boards before they were abolished in 1902, but in Middlesbrough they remained a male preserve, though one woman, the head of a local private school, was co-opted on to the borough education committee, which replaced school boards, in the Edwardian era.

The separate spheres arguments used against female participation in the parliamentary political processes were especially disingenuous, as both parties from the 1870s showed no scruples in using women as foot soldiers at election times. The Conservatives were the first to see the value of female canvassing of male voters in the expanded electorates of the later nineteenth century, and the Primrose League had a very substantial female membership which local Unionists used very effectively at election times. The local Liberal press was often full of complaints about the ubiquity and impact of the Primrose League 'dames' at election times. Indeed the leading local Conservative, Charles Dorman, ascribed the narrow victory of Sam Sadler over Wilson in 1900 to the 'enthusiasm of the ladies'. The Liberal women's organizations were active in Middlesbrough, but the constantly expressed desire that they should be more involved in canvassing work suggests that they were not as effective in that regard as the Unionist bodies. Both female organizations were divided on the issue of female suffrage, but the Liberals, being the party of government when this issue became more salient, were affected by deeper divisions on the matter. Not all women active in local government in Middlesbrough actually supported female enfranchisement. May Hedley, elected to the Board of Guardians in 1895, actively campaigned against the extension of the parliamentary franchise. Even more ironic was the fact that her brother, Penry Williams, MP for Middlesbrough from 1910, actively supported female suffrage. Such limited evidence as exists suggests that these women reflected popular sentiment among the Middlesbrough population, female as well as male, in opposing female enfranchisement.

The end of the war saw the arrival of women for the first time on the borough council. Yet, as in so many other facets of the popular culture of

Middlesbrough, older patterns of behaviour still survived the dramatic changes of the post-war period. Although the overtly partisan activists of the ILP, such as Alice Schofield-Coates and Marion Coates-Hansen, did secure election to the council early in the interwar years, many of the women who became councillors in this period, such as Mrs H.M. Levick, were driven mainly by the same sense of social and community service as those women who had served on the Boards of Guardians before 1918. Even Alice Schofield-Coates and Marion Coates-Hansen, who did much to establish the Labour Party as an organizational force in the town in the 1920s, often deployed the argument that women had special qualities to bring to local government, and often, by choice, tended to serve on committees dealing with maternity and child welfare issues. There is little disguising the fact that these Labour stalwarts were, in terms of background and education, from the same social strata as the other females who broke into local government in the early years of this century.

It is perhaps remarkable that given the rather unenthusiastic support for female enfranchisement displayed by the Middlesbrough population, one of the Middlesbrough constituencies should, in 1924, be one of the first in the country to return a woman as its representative, in the shape of the radical socialist and feminist, Ellen Wilkinson. Precisely how Miss Wilkinson obtained the Labour nomination for the seat remains a bit of a mystery. Her links with the town were tenuous to say the least, but she undoubtedly benefited from the fact Middlesbrough East was a genuine three-way marginal at a time when the party system was still in a very plastic condition following the deep divisions among the Liberal leadership in the latter stages of the First World War. The 1918 general election saw the splits made more profound by Lloyd George's decision to maintain his coalition with the Conservatives into the election, and to endorse Unionist candidates, even when they were standing against official Liberal nominees. The official Liberal Party, including its leader, the former prime minister H.H. Asquith, was virtually wiped out, returning fewer members than the Labour Party, which became the *de facto* opposition to the Lloyd George coalition. Yet Middlesbrough was one of the few places where Asquith's party was unchallenged by a coalition candidate. Faced by only Labour opposition the new constituencies returned two Liberal members. Unlike many other urban and industrial centres in Britain, the Liberal Party in Middlesbrough did not go into a catastrophic decline. It remained a major group on the borough council until the 1930s, and secured the election of its candidates for the Middlesbrough West seat in every election in the interwar period. In Middlesbrough East, a solidly working-class constituency, the situation was more fluid, but the Liberals still held the seat in three out of the seven contests between the wars. Precisely why Liberalism in Middlesbrough was so resilient requires further investigation, but elements within the political culture of the town offer some clues. Popular Conservatism, among both working-class and middle-class voters, was always a significant but never a dominant force. Labour had still to translate itself into the broad communally based political movement that it became in many other industrial areas, especially in the coalfields where it swiftly displaced Lib-Labism as the natural home of working-class voters. Labour members on the council in the interwar period continued to function as a sectional interest group, much as they had in the immediate pre-war era. Liberalism in Middlesbrough, which still straddled the old components of the business community, the chapels and, unofficially, some elements of organized labour, could be successful in straight fights, attracting Tory votes against Labour, and Labour votes against Tories. Often, in three-cornered contests, Liberals won as the largest minority element in a first-past-the-post electoral system. Thus, ironically, local Liberal candidates benefited from a voting system which was, nationally, to assist in the destruction of the Liberals as a party of government.

In seeking to explain the remarkable success of Ellen Wilkinson in the 1924 general election, this fluidity in the electorate needs to be set alongside other factors within the political culture of Middlesbrough which made her victory possible. The early 1920s had been a period of great difficulty for the staple industries of Teesside, the post-war boom had collapsed into prolonged depression, and the export markets for the products of Middlesbrough's steel works, foundries and shipyards had all but dried up. The first Labour government proposed restoring economic links with Russia, which had been virtually severed following the Bolshevik revolution of 1917. In the fevered 'Red Scare' atmosphere of the time, the opposition parties, including the Liberals, and the pro-Conservative press sought to use this move as evidence of Communist sympathies among the leaders of the Labour Party. In frightening many middle-class voters into supporting the Conservatives, this strategy was successful and Labour lost the general election. However, on Teesside the idea of re-establishing links with the old trading partners in the Baltic region was attractive, irrespective of their political colour, and many working-class voters supported Wilkinson in the hope that her party could bring work back to the town. Thus the older traditions of Teesside reasserted themselves, and certainly mattered more than the conversion of the Middlesbrough voters to socialism and feminism. Ellen Wilkinson did build up a personal vote. A very capable representative of her economically stricken constituency, she held the seat with an increased majority in 1929, but lost it in the anti-Labour landslide of 1931.

Middlesbrough East returned to the Liberal fold in 1931, but in the three-cornered contest of 1935 the split of political sentiment within the constituency fell narrowly in Labour's favour, with their candidate gaining a majority of sixty-seven. The Liberal vote fell to just over 12 per cent of the poll, which reflected the extent to which the town was beginning to mirror the patterns of political polarization to be found in the rest of the country. In

Middlesbrough West, since the Liberals held the seat on only 36 per cent of the vote, against Labour and 'National Labour' opposition, there must be doubts that the seat would have been held against an official Conservative candidate.

This would seem to suggest that the local political culture was beginning to succumb to the processes of nationalization discernible from the end of the war, but even in 1935 the town could still display traits which went back to the traditions of its early political development. The successful Labour candidate in 1935 was Alfred Edwards. A self-made and extremely successful businessman, he was also an active Rotarian and Christian Scientist. He made frequent visits to the United States on business, and in all respects he would have fitted the model of an ideal Conservative candidate. An effective publicist, he made good use of the various local platforms that his business and Rotary connections offered him, even making use of his reputation as an accomplished local sportsman in his youth. He was elected as a Labour councillor in 1932, after a very brief membership of the party, and his meteoric rise was crowned by his selection as the parliamentary candidate for the Middlesbrough East seat in 1933. Yet his appeal to the people of Middlesbrough was basically the same as that of the Liberal and Conservative businessmen who had previously represented the town, and who had portrayed themselves as champions of the local economy and as the bringers of work to the town. A critic, on essentially religious and ethical grounds, of the more humiliating facets of the existing mechanisms of poverty relief, his political outlook was idiosyncratic and ideologically incoherent. He was friendly with left-wingers such as Aneurin Bevan, but would speak and write warmly about politicians from other parties. In this regard Alfred Edwards was in a long line of Middlesbrough MPs who found that the formal endorsement of a political party was necessary for electoral success, while their attachment to a party in ideological terms was often slender. In

Alfred Edwards, elected Labour MP for Middlesbrough West in 1935, photographed top right on a Rotary outing in 1934 to Fort Dunlop, Birmingham; a Rotarian whose attachment to the party was ideologically slender and who was expelled in 1948 (RL)

1948 these innate tensions came to a head, and Alfred Edwards was expelled from the Labour Party for actively campaigning against the state ownership of the steel industry.

Labour had little difficulty in recapturing the seat in 1950, but by that time it was also the dominant element on the borough council, and the processes of assimilating Middlesbrough into the wider national political culture were virtually complete. Alfred Edwards was closer in spirit, temperament and outlook to Henry Bolckow than he was to the men and women who were now politically active in Middlesbrough. Indeed the Alfred Edwards affair was essentially a throwback to an earlier political age, and the 1945 election marked the point at which the political culture of Middlesbrough was integrated into the national political scene. If personal factors had been important in securing the election of Alfred Edwards in 1935, in the election of 1945 he was returned as the nominee of the national Labour Party. His loss of that status guaranteed his defeat in 1950. While personalities, and the particular social and economic structure of the town, could still give colour and emphasis to electoral contests in Middlesbrough, the local political culture was by the second half of the twentieth century subordinate to, and a mirror of, national political life.

CHAPTER 6

LEISURE AND SPORT IN MIDDLESBROUGH, 1840–1914

M.J. Huggins

During the nineteenth century there were mixed views about industrial towns like Middlesbrough. Some Victorians defended them, praising them for their economic and social achievements. Others were afraid of the problems of their teeming, uncontrolled life, and bewailed the less than respectable pleasures of some inhabitants. In the 1860s, for example, shortly after William Gladstone described Middlesbrough as an 'infant Hercules', the *Middlesbrough Weekly News* was expressing grave concern about drink, prostitution and the resulting 'moral condition of Middlesbrough'.[1]

Modern historians of Victorian urban life reflect these attitudes. Some have stressed the extent to which the leisure of the urban working classes was affected by urbanization, industrialization and bourgeois hegemony, as traditional leisure patterns weakened and were replaced by new secular commercial leisure forms.[2] Some writers have laid more stress on leisure continuities.[3] Yet others have stressed the Victorians' new cultural institutions and the development of municipal and socio-religious provision, catering for the respectable middle and working classes. Even in devoting a whole book to leisure in Bristol between 1870 and 1914, Helen Meller focused mainly on those citizens who provided more cultural facilities, while excluding 'the day to day experiences of the majority of citizens'.[4]

Writers on Middlesbrough's broader leisure pattern have also given more attention to the respectable groups. Lillie's book on Middlesbrough, for example, paints a sanitized, earnest view of nineteenth-century life and leisure, very much in the town booster tradition.[5] Asa Briggs brings a more impartial and comparative perspective, although his discussion of 'culture' focuses on respectable, 'world of the mind' areas like libraries, mechanics' institutes, or museums, and his judgements on 'the roughness of Middlesbrough' and on the leisure of its working class as 'not well employed' should not be allowed to inhibit further academic exploration of these aspects.[6] Middlesbrough was a Victorian new town, created and expanded significantly by migrant male labour, and dependent largely on labour-intensive heavy industry.

Both factors were very influential in determining its leisure patterns. Initially *apparently* dominated by 'respectable', Quakerite 'rational' recreations, Middlesbrough nevertheless also quickly developed a very strong but predominantly less respectable pattern of working-class leisure. While these less respectable patterns became more generally acceptable towards the century's end, they were only partially tamed.

Briggs does, however, stress two important influences on leisure activities in Middlesbrough. First, railway developments contributed through the growth of trips, seaside holidays, and inter-town sporting competition, and in terms of access to national news and sport. Secondly, a governing elite bound together by civic office, philanthropic work and involvement in religious life was very active in attempts to channel and control leisure, and cooperated across religious and political barriers up to and beyond the 1870s. Their success, however, was very limited.

A chronological analysis of leisure and sport indicates three main phases, closely linked to Middlesbrough's economic and social development, and revealing the various cultural and social responses by its citizens to the changing urban environment. The first stage covers the 'turbulent urban frontier' from the 1830s to the end of the 1850s. At this point commercial leisure was limited, largely because of the constraints of population size, and because both working- and middle-class leisure was restrained and shaped in part by the dominant governing elite of leading citizens – the Owners of the Middlesbrough Estate, the ironmasters and other industrialists. This elite exercised substantial paternalistic power over the pace and direction of leisure forms. Where possible, respectable, 'rational' activities such as membership of the Mechanics' Institute which might further the appropriate behaviour of the workforce were supported, and less respectable but widespread activities such as betting, gaming, or drinking were subjected to police pressure. During the mid-Victorian period, from the 1860s to *c.* 1874, population growth allowed an expansion of commercial leisure provision such as theatre, music-hall, or seaside trips for the lower-middle- and some working-class groups. It was a time of economic boom and industrial growth, and the paternalistic influence of the ruling elite was beginning to slacken. The growing numbers of company managers, shopkeepers, builders, bankers, lawyers, architects, auctioneers, medical practitioners and other businessmen and professionals also led to a strengthening of independent, respectable middle-class leisure forms, alongside a more widespread clearly secular and less respectable leisure culture. The year 1874 saw the beginnings of the anxiety of alternative slump and boom which characterized the next forty years in Middlesbrough. The role of commercial leisure expanded, as did that of sport, both now linked to national patterns. Some sports worked hard to maintain a respectable, amateur, middle-class ethos, others embraced professionalism, while the sporting press contributed to an ever-growing interest in spectatorship and betting, largely but not entirely among the working classes. Middlesbrough had become a sizeable, predominantly working-class town shaped by the heavy industries which were its lifeblood, characterized by cyclical depressions which limited the stability and security of social life, and dominated by commercial leisure forms which placed a premium on short-term, immediate excitement. Throughout the century Middlesbrough was more socially homogeneous than most other industrial towns and had a relatively limited range of male occupations, usually physically demanding, with few jobs for women beyond domestic service. *Family* incomes were therefore lower, with significant fluctuation of income across the family life-cycle. Wages for highly skilled workers were relatively high but unreliable. It was men who earned and who largely determined leisure spending, working hard and often playing hard as well. Lack of financial security meant that betting provided a rare means of gaining a large sum, so it was no surprise that Middlesbrough evidence about the prevalence of betting and gaming was heavily drawn on by the Anti-Gambling League in the early twentieth century.

Middlesbrough nevertheless consistently presented itself as a town aspiring to the values of the respectable middle and working classes. This was because the town's new middle class, active in local politics, was predominantly Nonconformist, and there was a strong temperance lobby. The local weekly press, and later the local daily papers, our chief source for leisure studies, reflected the town's reputation as a centre of Nonconformist Liberalism, by overemphasizing more respectable leisure practices, and providing less evidence of less respectable, private or women's leisure.

This notion of respectability, although debated by some historians, provides us with a way of organizing the available material on Middlesbrough leisure. The first section examines some of the key aspects of respectable leisure as they emerge through the period, beginning with the 'improving' leisure forms for the workforce of the early period, and concluding with the later rise of more middle-class amateur sports. The second section looks at those leisure forms, often commercial, such as the music-hall or theatre, used by a whole range of groups for different purposes, and therefore not easily locatable as fully respectable. The third section examines those perhaps more 'sinful' pleasures, given less weight in the sources, but nevertheless an important part of the lives of some inhabitants throughout the period.

I

For the mainly male, migrant population of the early town, the public house provided a welcome that lodgings lacked, and the first temperance groups were organized as a respectable response to this, although the chronology of their development is unclear. The Middlesbrough Temperance Society was probably formed in 1834 and in 1837 the first 'Temperance festival' was held.[7] A series of revival meetings took place in the late 1840s, claiming large numbers of converts, and the Cleveland Temperance League was formed in 1855. Lectures were often full to capacity. Organized entertainments were often extremely popular, especially among the young, although warmth, free food and entertainment attracted some possibly not warmed by the fires of temperance. Indeed, temperance had little permanent success. In 1859 the Middlesbrough Temperance Society was still expressing concern that 'the intellectual, moral and religious elevation of the people has not been in proportion to the material progress of the town' because of counteracting influences, especially 'the drinking habits of the people'.[8]

The movement strengthened with the growth of organized religion. St Hilda's, the first of the Church of England churches, was built in 1838, and Nonconformist groups with places of worship soon included Baptists, Congregationalists, Unitarians, and Wesleyans. The Primitive Methodists had a chapel by 1841. A Quaker meeting house was erected in 1849 although active members were few. The 1851 religious census reported fifty worshippers in the morning and only thirty-one in the afternoon. The early industrialists, Middlesbrough Owners and others of the dominant elite supported 'rational' and 'respectable' uses of leisure time, as did the Church and Nonconformist groups generally. Their actions can be variously interpreted as a conscious exercise in social control to train and educate a new workforce; as an imposition of the Protestant ethic; or simply as benevolent paternalism. Their involvement was, however, very marked in this early period. The committee of the first Middlesbrough Mechanics' Institute (1840) contained many of their number including Wilson, Bolckow, Taylor, Bell and Gilkes. The institute had school rooms and reading rooms with periodicals, books and newspapers, but its membership was still less than 200 in 1858. A determined attempt to canvass the town and the different ironworks boosted membership to nearly 500, and a new building was erected at a cost of over £2,000. Local works gave generously according to their size and importance. But working men were less generous, to the puzzlement of the press, which demanded 'why is it that [working men] do not associate in support of one institution for the general elevation of the class to whom they belong?'[9] Membership reached a thousand by 1860, when it offered a series of winter lectures. Snowden & Hopkins went further by providing a reading room at their works, while St John's Church Young Men's Society had classes in English Grammar, Latin, History, Mathematics and German claimedly for the mutual improvement of the well-being, happiness, and temporal and spiritual prosperity of its forty members. Another early organization for workers, The Tees-side Iron Works Mutual Improvement Company, had free accommodation, and the employers gave it their support, yet in 1859 it had only ninety members using its reading room. Other organized activities in the town included Sunday schools and the usual variety of social, church and chapel activities. What seems clear is that such leisure opportunities were organized in a 'top down' fashion, with those providing them believing that they knew best what should be offered to the workers. None were particularly well supported, although in total a significant minority of workers were involved.

Other employer-organized leisure activities for workers included music. Isaac Wilson's pottery works had a works brass band by 1851. The Snowden & Hopkins band played regularly at Middlesbrough's first park, Jowsey Park near the docks, which was laid out with paths and trees. The Tees-side Iron Works brass band was described by the *Middlesbrough Weekly News* in January 1859 as having 'attained a degree of excellence unsurpassed by any of the bands in our neighbourhood'.[10] Employers and churches also began organizing rail trips, often annually as a subsidized treat with an emphasis on improvement. The railway to Stockton was initially used more for the transport of goods, so it was the building of the Redcar Railway in 1846 that provided an impetus for the earliest employer-organized seaside trips. Historical sites and scenic areas were also viewed as appropriate. In July 1859, for example, a Grand Trip went to Raby Castle from Middlesbrough although at the high cost of 2s 6d including tea. In 1860 the Independent Chapel congregation arranged a trip to the 'beauties, attractions and delightful retreats' of Middleton-one-Row with tea in the woods, but its fare of 2s limited its appeal. Most such sponsored trips were arranged for weekdays, which restricted attendance although numbers could still be quite large. In the same year nearly 1,400 people set off on a Tuesday morning for Scarborough for a Mechanics' Institute trip.

The beauties, attractions and delightful retreats of Middleton-one-Row to which the Independent Chapel organized an outing in 1860 (AJP)

The paternalistic desire of the ironmasters and other industrialists to shape leisure activities did not diminish during the prosperous 1860s and early 1870s. Indeed there was increased anxiety about the prevalence of pubs and prostitution. The Peases, Bolckow and Vaughan all played an active part in supporting temperance activities, and the heavily subsidized *Middlesbrough Temperance Visitor*, first published in 1870, enjoyed a limited circulation in the surrounding area. There were attempts to provide other educative alternatives. The 1871 opening of the Middlesbrough Reading Room and Free Library was a (late) Corporation response to the Free Libraries Act of 1850. It was done cheaply by taking over the Mechanics' Institute library, and presented as being for those of the working classes anxious to improve themselves educationally. Middlesbrough's first Working Men's Club opened in 1873 to provide 'rational and civilizing pleasures' for workmen.[11]

The park movement to provide open space for relaxation was another response of the city fathers to urbanization. The Middlesbrough Owners first offered land in 1863 but the cost of its development would have had to come from the rates and the Corporation was initially reluctant. It changed its mind after Bolckow offered to purchase a 92-acre site near Linthorpe. The words of the Archbishop of York at the Albert Park's opening in 1868 show it too was perceived as a rational alternative to less respectable pleasures, a place of innocent and healthful recreation, which would diminish intemperance by drawing men to purer pleasures. Facilities offered were not necessarily those likely to appeal to the intemperate. They included croquet and bowling, a maze, cricket ground, site for an outdoor gymnasium, and an unenclosed Exhibition Ground with grandstand. Demand for middle-class suburban dwellings nearby escalated; the commercially astute Bolckow had land there ready to meet it.

Societies organized by and for the cultural elite were slowly emerging. The Literary and Philosophical Society was founded (initially as the Athenaeum) in 1863 to promote art, science and literature. Many provincial cities had such societies from the early nineteenth century, but both its late development in Middlesbrough and its early poor accommodation reflected relative lack of interest in it by some of the ironmasters. Membership was predominantly male. However, it grew steadily and had some 200 members by 1871. Exclusiveness and shared interests bound together the Cleveland Club, formed in 1868 for gentlemen in the iron industry, and the Erimus Club formed in 1873 with some 300 middle-class members. Subscriptions were three and five guineas respectively. Other societies, such as the Orpheus Music Club, or Middlesbrough Horticultural Society, had an emphasis on expertise and competition, also found in other respectable activities such as the amateur brass band contests which flourished through the 1860s and 1870s. The first contest was held on Monday 27 August 1860, following agitation by the *Middlesbrough Weekly News* which believed in 'the good moral influences brought about by such exhibitions of skill'. Prizes for the eight

A place of innocent and healthful recreation: a busy Albert Park early in the twentieth century (MCL)

bands which first competed were, however, monetary rather than symbolic, although the winning conductor received a silver cup. On the same day a floral and horticultural show was held, with exhibitors from Darlington, Stokesley and elsewhere, bringing the country to the town, a perennial theme, perhaps also caught by the exhibition of the Cleveland Agricultural Society the same month. Significant numbers also participated in music making. The Middlesbrough Philharmonic Society had had its first series of subscription concerts in 1871, while the Middlesbrough Choral Society held its first subscription concert in 1869.

Cricket was the first organized team game to develop in Middlesbrough. It was seen as a respectable cross-class activity, although there were potential dangers even here, and the club formed in 1847 by artisan members of the Mechanics' Institute attempted to maintain its respectability by a rule book forbidding alcoholic drinks, swearing and any form of gambling. Far from being commercial in its approach, it had a fee-paying membership of some sixty individuals. At least one employer, Isaac Wilson's pottery, also had a side prior to 1851. There were two other cricket teams by the early 1850s, and in 1854–5 they amalgamated to form Middlesbrough Cricket Club, playing firstly on Albert Road, than at Swatters' Carr on Linthorpe Road. By 1858 the elected officers included Hopkins, Wilson, Ord, and others of the ruling elite, although playing membership was predominantly middle class, including tradesmen or senior employees from the iron companies. During the 1860s cricket success was used in a paternalistic way to boost the town's status. Middlesbrough's club captain, the ironmaster Thomas Vaughan, along with Hopkins and the builder Robert Todd, were instrumental in importing good players from outside the town to strengthen the team, either as professionals, through the offer of jobs, or by the paying of rail fares and lost time. However, high subscription fees and the running of three teams plus a junior side by 1865 still indicated a mainly middle-class playing membership. A commercial approach to achieving success during the 1860s and early 1870s, when cricket had limited attraction as a Middlesbrough working-class spectator sport, and crowds would only come to see top players and teams, saw the visits of All England XIs, an Aboriginal side and county teams. Competitive first team matches were irregular, usually fewer than ten per annum, and further revenue was raised for team building by leasing the ground for other activities. Blondin performed in front of some 5,000 spectators there in May 1862. Following the selling of the cricket ground for building purposes in 1874, a new ground was leased on Linthorpe Road, surrounded by a high wall, and with a £1,000 pavilion, all of which suggested an increased emphasis on commercial success and regional status by the committee, since other teams were now appearing, mostly playing on Albert Park.

More middle-class and amateur individualistic sports were also emerging. The increasing emphasis on 'respectable' amateurism and the resulting exclusion of working-class participants was most evident in rowing, which had formerly attracted widespread working-class betting on big money matches between professional scullers from the Tyne and Thames, who received a great deal of adulation, thanks to press coverage. The more middle-class rowers could not hope to compete with professionals often brought up and working full time on the river, and the 1860s saw the increasing growth of amateur clubs. In 1864 the Tees Amateur Boating Club was formed, based in Stockton, but with some Middlesbrough members. The Tees Rowing Club was formed the following year, and the Middlesbrough Amateur Boating Club in 1868, with its headquarters at Newport. Social exclusivity was reinforced by annual subscriptions of up to a guinea, plus an entrance fee, and the fact that members rowed in a uniform with a club badge.

In the last decades of the century, the move out of town to the suburbs and beyond by the ironmasters and other members of the old town elite led to a lessening of paternalistic influence and an increased stress on commercialized leisure. Less was now channelled into charity work, although the 1890s were to see some resurgence with the Middlesbrough Settlement (1892), the Middlesbrough Charity Organization Society (1893) and the Middlesbrough Fresh Air Fund (1896). Leisure was expanding, with a multitude of influences and cross-currents and an increasing acceptance of some working-class leisure patterns, although not of drink. Drunkenness received adverse publicity through the courts. Positive publicity for temperance came through the movement's ability to manage press support. The Temperance Hall was still the main centre for meetings, with free 'entertainments' and talks, mothers' meetings, flower shows, and the taking of pledges. Shopkeepers and businessmen, such as Amos Hinton, were key supporters. Child membership (the Young Abstainers' Union or the various Bands of Hope), as a result of adult pressure and the prospect of free entertainment, picnics and outings, was quite high. Membership of adult groups, such as the St John's Temperance Guild

Respectable entertainment: a United Presbyterian concert programme (CA)

or St Paul's Church of England Temperance Society, was relatively low. St Paul's had around forty mainly middle-class members in the 1880s, including teachers and bank staff.

Other respectable middle- and working-class recreations included home-based activity, religion, music in the form of choral societies or brass bands, the Mechanics' Institute, employer-provided leisure institutions, and sport. The Linthorpe Reading Room and Institute, established in October 1876, with 'substantial help' from Bolckow and others had just 105 members in 1877, of which only twenty-nine had paid an annual subscription.[12] The Middlesbrough Free Library moved to enlarged premises on the corner of the Municipal Buildings in Albert Road in 1887, with strong support from Alderman Thomas Bell and other council figures. The churches and chapels continued to play a key role in respectable leisure for both sexes and for all ages. They were not just for worship, but placed great emphasis on the social side and on music. Music-making was enjoyed by most sections of the Victorian population, and even working-class homes would often have a piano. Performances by a whole range of church and other groups could be found throughout Middlesbrough in schools, the Lit. and Phil. Hall, the Temperance Hall, or Oddfellows' Hall. There was a temporary joint committee of the Middlesbrough Choral and Philharmonic Societies in 1879, when they produced Handel's *Messiah* at the Temperance Hall in aid of the distress fund. Because of the depression of trade and distress in the town, the Choral Society committee was finding it difficult to produce concerts with professional soloists and full bands, and in November 1879 it was briefly forced to dispense with professional support altogether. The societies finally combined for the season 1882/3 as the Middlesbrough Musical Union, using its Elm Street practice rooms for soirées and winter concerts. Middlesbrough Amateur Vocal Society was formed in the 1885/6 season, signalling its independence from professional support. Brass band performances were a spectator attraction in the 1870s, but temporarily lost some popularity in the 1880s, before being revived in 1894.

Nationally, as press coverage reveals, the last quarter of the nineteenth century was characterized by a series of booms in middle-class sport. By the late 1880s the Middlesbrough weekly *Northern Review* covered rugby, cricket and association football and new sports such as cycling, tennis and golf. Several key strands now run through the further development of organized sport in Middlesbrough. These include the formation of clubs, a clear link between the fluctuations of the town's trade cycle and the actual numbers of players and spectators, and the reproduction of class divisions in the distinction between amateurs and professionals. What also comes across clearly is that the middle-class minority who wished to espouse amateur, respectable values could only do so where there was little working-class spectatorship, or where working-class participants could be excluded. Soccer provides an instructive case study of this, since it was at least initially relatively respectable and middle-class, but enjoyed growing working-class participation, unlike rugby, which emerged first in the early 1870s, with two or three friendly games per season being played in Albert Park. By 1878 there were three rugby football teams in the Cleveland region, of which Teesside Wanderers were the best organized. But thereafter there was little further growth in participation and little spectator interest.

Association football came later to the north-east. The first club, naming itself after the town, was not formed until 1876. By the end of 1878 there were five, including Middlesbrough Pupil Teachers, Lambton and St John's. Linthorpe was formed in the 1879/80 season, and North Ormesby in 1880, both with former members of the Middlesbrough Club involved. Early players were predominantly young, unmarried, recently arrived, and mostly drawn from the professions and commercial middle classes. Although few teams played regularly, their over-use of Albert Park, mainly on Saturday afternoons, caused complaints, and in 1879 the council banned football there. After 1880, however, there was a sudden surge in enthusiasm for the game. By the 1882/3 season there were no fewer than sixty-nine reported clubs in the Teesside region. Most played friendly matches, although Middlesbrough joined the powerful Sheffield Association, and took part (unsuccessfully) in its cup competitions from 1879/80 to 1883/4, generating larger local crowds of around 1,000 for key home games. The club played a key role in forming the

A middle-class, amateur sport: Middlesbrough Rugby Club players in 1896 (CA)

Cleveland Association in 1881, to create a cup competition, and entered the national FA Cup competition from 1883/4.

From 1884 to 1886 the numbers of Middlesbrough teams expanded only slowly, due to slumps in the iron trade and shipbuilding. The first signs were, however, emerging of a growing working-class presence as both participants and spectators, thanks in part to cup rivalry. Regular Cleveland Cup finals between Middlesbrough and close rivals Redcar generated much press and public interest, as did Middlesbrough's limited FA Cup success during this period, although Middlesbrough's later poor cup performances in comparison to their north-eastern rivals began early when Redcar beat them en route to the 1885/6 FA Cup quarter finals. From 1886, with an upturn in the trade cycle and a further expansion of the Saturday half-holiday, the game entered a new phase. It was now predominantly played and watched by the working classes, and club numbers expanded rapidly. Although their names are an uncertain guide, in the later 1880s many seem to have been occupational (e.g. Middlesbrough Post Office, Middlesbrough Vulcan Shipyard Juniors) or public house teams (e.g. Middlesbrough Royal Oaks), although the volunteer forces (e.g. Middlesbrough Rifle Volunteers), sports clubs (e.g. Erimus Quoit

Club), local areas (e.g. Middlesbrough North End) and church teams (e.g. Middlesbrough St John's) also contributed a quota.

While football expanded cricket contracted. By now the earlier ruling elite was losing some of its power over the club, and an increasingly well-organized middle-class group was asserting its strength. Many local members had been excluded from first team play by outsiders chosen by a committee now very distant from its membership. At the 1876 AGM the middle-class membership seized power. It demanded a move away from commercialism and regional success towards a firmer amateur base, with players to be from, rather than representing, the town. As elsewhere, the single 'professional' then appointed was a bowler. Paternalistic financial and other support was withdrawn, and financial survival was helped only to a limited extent by visits, from 1880, by the exciting but expensive Australian tourists, which drew crowds of up to 4,000 from the surrounding area.

The railway network now linking Middlesbrough to the rest of Cleveland gave an impetus in 1885 to two of the then standard developments in team sports: the forming of a local association, the Cleveland and Teesside Cricket Association, and the establishment of a cup competition, the Cleveland Cup, in which Middlesbrough participated. Although Middlesbrough met Redcar in the 1887 final at the Linthorpe Road ground, subsequent crowd interest was still modest. The railways provided teams with transport, not extra spectators. Middlesbrough joined the North Yorkshire League in 1893 but even a successful start to the season and a match against joint leaders Redcar in June 1894 only attracted 1,000 spectators.[13] The club was unsuccessful in the league against players from much smaller towns, who seemed better able to recruit good players. Press reports of matches in the *North-Eastern Daily Gazette* up to 1910 are sparse; attendance numbers are not quoted, and the rare AGM reports indicate that little revenue was raised through the gate from the 1890s. Cricket in Middlesbrough had become an amateur, predominantly middle-class sport in a predominantly working-class town. There was a relatively small pool of potential middle-class players, while the opposition to commercialism in a predominantly commercial culture meant that the gate money revenue for employing working-class professionals was very limited. Unsurprisingly this reinforced lack of success. Middlesbrough struggled even more in the new century and was forced to dispense with its single professional. Talented local amateurs were unwilling to play for the club because of poor results, and it was temporarily disbanded in 1911, a victim of its amateur approach.

In many individualized sports amateurism was overtly about whether or how to exclude the working class from participation, either through rules, or through the cost of participation. A significant number of sports were thus coming to be dominated by the middle classes, with their increasing time, space and income, voluntarism, and breadth and depth of social involvement.

A struggling club: Middlesbrough cricketers in the 1890s (CA)

Middlesbrough Bicycle Club was formed in spring 1877 with seventeen members. The season normally started at Easter, when members would assemble in their smart uniforms in Linthorpe Road before processing on their first trip. In 1882, for example, they rode first to Redcar where they dined, then by way of Stokesley to Broughton. Several other Middlesbrough amateur clubs were formed in the 1880s and in 1887 a bicycle track was even proposed for Albert Park. The period was characterized by clubability, since clubs provided both exclusivity and protection in social terms, but sales of bicycles were higher than club membership, and Young's cycle storage and showroom in Bright Street offered storage at a moderate rent and with free access, for cyclists who did not have a convenient place to keep their machines.

The even more select sport of golf was relatively slow to develop in the Cleveland area. Links courses developed first, and, following an abortive attempt to establish a small course at Coatham by Scottish enthusiasts, Seaton Carew became the first Cleveland course. Dr McCuaig became its first captain in 1882, and other Middlesbrough men were active in its early development.[14] By now tennis was not only a private lawn game but also had

Members of the Middlesbrough Crescent Cycle Club at the end of the century (CA)

formalized inter-town competitions held on summer Saturdays. An annual lawn tennis tournament in Albert Park was dominated by lawyers, doctors and other professions.[15]

Swimming, on the other hand, was slow to come under amateur influence and was dominated by professionals until *c.* 1875. But the hegemonic efforts of amateur swimmers led to the elaboration of an amateur code and the formation of the Amateur Swimming Association in 1886. In the same year the Middlesbrough Amateur Swimming Club was formed to encourage its members in the 'wholesome and healthy exercise of swimming', with a Monday practice night at the Middlesbrough baths. The club held club championships, private handicaps, monthly competitions, an annual gala and the usual club dinner. Although membership was never high the sport was taken seriously, and in 1912 the Middlesbrough swimmer Jack Hadfield won medals at the Stockholm Olympics.

Amateur sports organizations with a mainly middle-class membership had all the panoply of status and local press coverage but in reality were often unable to manage totally without professional support and skill. Middlesbrough cricket club needed its predominantly bowling professionals; Seaton golf club had a teaching professional; Middlesbrough swimming club had its professional instructor. Skilled professionals attracted interest. When 'Professor' James Finney, the 'champion swimmer of the world', appeared at Middlesbrough's Oxford Palace in January 1887, he gave a swimming demonstration and comic show in the Middlesbrough baths in front of privileged members of the town council, members of the medical profession and others of their circle. This blend of spectacle and performance caused 'a good many present . . . to join the club'.[16]

II

Such respectable pleasures as self-improvement through education, temperance, music making or amateur sport were the interests of small but influential minorities. A second group of leisure pursuits was commercially run, and was perceived and used by different social groups in different ways. These included entertainment of all kinds, tourism and commercial sport. Middlesbrough came into being for commercial reasons, and some aspects of commercial leisure occupied a prominent place from very early on. Live entertainment illustrates this well, with the theatre and music-hall becoming increasingly important from the 1860s. Indeed, some owners or lessees of halls used them as a vehicle for social mobility, council membership and wealth, while over the period there was major growth in audience size, especially but not solely in terms of lower-middle- and working-class attendance. Middlesbrough saw initial growth in the 1860s in the number of halls, their capacity, the sophistication of their amenities, the extension of programmes and added staff, including more professionalized performers. In Middlesbrough, as elsewhere, what Bailey described as 'publican entrepreneurs' initially predominated,[17] while from the last decade of the nineteenth century developments included the de-luxe hall or theatre, segregation of audiences, distancing of performers, a move from regional to national entertainment circuits, increased capitalization and the introduction of limited companies.

Early Middlesbrough lacked venues, although limited dramatic entertainment was performed in a temporary theatre set up in the yard of the Steam Packet Hotel in Stockton Street, and in a small theatre in Commercial Street. More populist entertainment was catered for through the still strong tradition of travelling theatre, with artists like Billy Purvis setting up their booths. By the 1850s Middlesbrough was also large enough to be on the itinerary for travelling circuses, such as Bell's Mammoth Circus, Sinclair's Panorama, or Ginnett's Hippodrome Circus, while Sanger's Circus visited Middlesbrough five times between 1850 and 1860. More regular winter theatre performances were first introduced by the former travelling showman James Hunter, who leased the small Royal Alhambra Theatre on the Corporation Landing in 1859 and presented three-act plays. Oddfellows' Hall was built for friendly society meetings, but its members soon realized that it had commercial possibilities and leased it out for entertainment. During 1860 it had entertainments ranging from the Christie Minstrels, and the African Opera Troupe, to a classical evening concert starring Mr Garner, who had 'the honour of singing before her majesty at Buckingham Palace', with seats at prices ranging from 2s 6d for front seats, to 6d for the gallery.[18] Such high prices suggest the audience would have been composed of the middle classes, skilled workers, clerks and foremen; their wives and younger children (at half price); or young unmarried males.

The earliest surviving theatre bill for Middlesbrough is of 1845 (CA)

The respectable theatre was well patronized by the richer and more powerful. By contrast the music-hall was to have a more mixed reputation. The earliest provincial ones developed in the 1830s and 1840s, often originating in the song taverns attached to inns, and charging admission, although usually in the form of drink purchase checks. But the 1860s was the key period of music-hall and theatre expansion regionally and nationally.[19] Middlesbrough's first hall, the Canterbury Music Hall, based in Joseph Hutchinson's Canterbury Hotel, a beerhouse in Feversham Street, first sought a spirit licence in 1860 when it was 'used as a singing saloon for some time past'.[20] Hutchinson was not from the dominant elite. He was also attempting to introduce a less respectable form of entertainment, so was opposed by many of the more paternalistic employers. Indeed, he finally acquired a spirit licence in August 1861 only on condition he discontinued the singing saloon. Like other early halls the Canterbury was not purpose-built but its success allowed Hutchinson to erect the Oxford Music Hall in Feversham Street in 1867 at a cost of £6,000–£7,000. The brick and stone building had boxes, pit and gallery (but still no stalls), and could accommodate up to 1,800 people. Hutchinson was now a councillor, and his successful application for a spirit licence carefully presented the hall as a good cultural influence.[21]

The mid-1860s also saw changes in the theatre. James Hunter moved from leasing the Royal Alhambra Theatre to owning and managing the newly created Theatre Royal in Durham Street. He suffered ill-health by 1868 and sold out to Frank Hall, a music-hall comic. Hall survived only some three months, facing competition from another important entrepreneur in the history of Middlesbrough entertainment, John Imeson, who owned a boot and shoe business in Sussex Street and was also the victualler of the Prince of Wales vaults in Albert Street.[22] Imeson began the building of the Royal Albert Theatre in Albert Street in 1866. It had two front entrances, boxes, stalls, pit and gallery, could accommodate some 2,000 people, and cost about £10,000. It was initially leased to the actor-manager W. Rousby, who left in late 1868. Imeson then temporarily acted as joint manager with James Hunter, the former owner of the Theatre Royal, and after this closed down during the 1869–70 season, Imeson renamed his theatre the Theatre Royal. It experienced a series of actor-managers, or husband-wife acting teams, who usually put together stock companies and new effects with a staple

Popular entertainment in early Middlesbrough was provided by touring companies such as minstrel groups (CA)

diet of pantomime, comedies and melodramas in three acts, or travelling opera companies, through a basic October to May season. Teesside's economic boom of the late 1860s and early 1870s led Imeson into expansion. In 1871 he built the Albert Hall and arcade in Sussex Street, with a shop and warehouse in the basement, and an assembly room above. Building cost some £1,200. By now a successful businessman and town councillor, Imeson also took over the Oxford Music Hall, presenting 'star performers' and 'the best vocal and acrobatic talent'.[23]

As the entertainment industry became more organized on a national basis individual entertainment entrepreneurs needed more skill and luck to survive. The Oxford 'Palace of Varieties' managed to cope with the slump of the later 1870s only thanks to careful financial management on Imeson's part, and in the mid-1880s the publican, racehorse owner and town councillor Richard Weighell took it over. He presented some of the most popular variety artistes in the profession, with weekly changes of company. Even in 1896 it was claiming to be 'the only variety music hall of any class in Middlesbrough'.[24] On Weighell's death, however, it struggled, and his wife and trustees sold the hall in 1898. By 1901 it was being used as a warehouse.

More working-class Cannon Street got its own hall when another local owner, George Hearse, the beerseller landlord of the Palmerston Hotel, built

Actor-manager W. Rousby portrayed as King Lear by Dominie *in 1875 (MCL)*

The Prince of Wales Palace Music Hall in the mid-1870s at a cost of some £8,000. It was successful from the late 1870s, and Hearse subsequently became an alderman, and a prominent wine and spirit merchant, but by the 1890s the lack of press reportage suggests it was in difficulties. One reason for these struggles was competition with a new hall organized and financed largely from metropolitan sources. The Middlesbrough Empire was erected in 1889 by former barman J.L. Graydon, the manager of the London Middlesex Music Hall, and drew heavily on metropolitan performers rather than those from the northern region. In 1895, now known as Alvo's Empire, it was advertising the 'greatest company of London star artistes ever brought to Middlesbrough',[25] and generally attracted good crowds during the boom years.

The Theatre Royal, run by Imeson's sons from the mid-1880s, continued its policy of touring companies, melodramas, farcical comedies, musical comedy, opera, and pantomime. Here again, many of these were from the London West End. By 1890 it was facing competition from one result of civic pride, the new town hall, which like the Temperance Hall was being leased out for concerts and performances of opera by organizations such as the St Cecilia Musical Society. To counter this the Middlesbrough Theatre Company was formed to bring in new capital, with the Imeson brothers as managing directors.

Even the circuses were growing larger in their scale of operations. Captain Transfield's American circus (whose performances were supposedly 'upheld by the clergy of every denomination'[26]), Fossett's Circus and Holtum's Circus, all with international performers, appeared at Corporation Road in the 1880s, with tickets ranging from 3d (gallery) to 2s (dress circle). Sanger's dramatic and hippodromic company, which visited Middlesbrough in 1895, included horses, elephants, camels and dromedaries, African lions and a menagerie, field artillery and ambulance wagons for a 'gigantic military spectacular drama', sixty-six wagons, and a large company of artistes.[27] Admission prices were very high, however, from 6d to 10s 6d.

The new century was characterized by larger buildings and associated increased

A day at the seaside: a crowded esplanade at Redcar in 1908 (MCL)

capitalization. The Empire Palace of Varieties became a limited company to cover the costs of its rebuilding and refurbishment between 1897 and 1899, after which top artistes like Marie Lloyd appeared there. The Middlesbrough Grand Opera House Company Limited opened an opera house on the corner of Southfield Road in 1904 at a cost of £38,000 and the Hippodrome Theatre of Varieties (£23,000) opened in 1906 in Wilson Street. Both struggled, although Imeson's takeover of the Opera House in 1909 added better management.

Another commercial leisure industry, tourism, was slower to develop. Although Redcar was to be among the top resorts of the interwar period, in the 1860s all the Teesside resorts lagged well behind resorts elsewhere as the middle-class seaside holiday market was expanding. On Teesside, when Sunday was usually the one day free from work for those of the working class who could have afforded the fare, tripper numbers were also then relatively low, because the railway company was reluctant to run Sunday services to Redcar, in case they interfered with religious observance. Even a prolonged press campaign to improve the service had only limited success. This contrasts with the resorts of the north-west, where not only trips, but working-class visits of four to seven days during wakes weeks were common by the 1870s. The select resorts of Saltburn or Coatham attracted higher proportions of wealthier, long-stay visitors than the more popular resorts of Redcar and Seaton Carew during the early 1870s but the former resorts were hit hard by the economic slumps which followed and thereafter grew only slowly. Rising real incomes among the working classes led to some increase in tripper numbers at Redcar and Seaton Carew during times of boom, mainly but not exclusively at weekends. Largest numbers of trippers were at Whitsuntide, when there was the added attraction of Redcar races, although first the Sunday School Unions and later the railway companies themselves also organized cheap trips during the Stockton race week.

Football also became increasingly commercial at the top level and by 1886 reputation and commercialism were increasingly driving Middlesbrough. In the 1886/7 season the first team played thirty-two games, including 'friendlies' against Hibernians, Aston Villa, Blackburn Rovers, Bolton Wanderers, Sheffield, Third Lanark and the Corinthians. Crowds were still not large, around 2,000 at more important games, and receipts in the 1886/7 season were £871, much of which was spent paying guarantees to attract these top teams. Other north-eastern teams began importing Scottish professionals but initially Middlesbrough held out, in part because in the 1887/8 season they still had the highest gate receipts (£1,026) in the north-east. But by 1889/90 the formation of the Football League had driven Middlesbrough to join the Northern League, the members of which almost all employed semi-professionals. The Middlesbrough committee was dominated by middle-class ex-players who still publicly espoused amateur values, as did much of the club membership (those paying an annual subscription roughly equivalent to a season ticket). At Middlesbrough's 1889 AGM a move by some members to introduce payment, win bonuses and expenses was defeated by 'a large majority',[28] but its amateur team, despite being partly composed of imported artisan players, who were found work, was outclassed over September and October. In November industrialists and workers from the Cleveland Dockyard were prominent in the formation of a new professional club, Middlesbrough Ironopolis, using the Paradise Ground off Linthorpe Road, and playing regular friendlies against top teams. This move pushed Middlesbrough into importing paid players too at the end of November. Doubts as to whether 'the Middlesbrough public will support two clubs to the extent of carrying on two first class teams'[29] initially proved incorrect. Both clubs did well in 1891/2. After an abortive attempt at amalgamation in 1892, when Middlesbrough was offered (and refused) the opportunity of joining the Second Division of the Football League, Ironopolis joined in 1893/4. Middlesbrough felt the pinch, with 1892/3 gate receipts of only £1,414, and reverted to amateurism. Ironopolis struggled in the League, and with poor results, poor crowds and poorer gate receipts was forced to fold. Middlesbrough recovered quickly. Nominally amateur, the club was successful in the powerful Northern League against professional teams, and won the Amateur Cup in 1894/5 and 1897/8, before reverting again to overt professionalism and joining the Football League's Second Division in 1899/1900 as a limited liability company, by which time it had become a major working-class attraction on Saturdays.

III

A third group of less respectable leisure pursuits emerged early and continued through the period. The public house was a key feature, and even as the first Middlesbrough streets were being erected, Middlesbrough Farm House appears to have been in the process of conversion into a hotel and brewery, and the first public house, the Ship Inn, was being built. Early Middlesbrough was characterized by overcrowded houses, and shortages of accommodation. The workforce was predominantly North Yorkshire born, predominantly male, and between the ages of fifteen and forty-five. This meant that the town had many of the elements of the American frontier towns, with public houses and prostitutes both experiencing brisk business, thanks in large part to a gender imbalance in the population, and a general absence of other amenities. Public house expansion was rapid. The 1841 census recorded four brewers, fifteen innkeepers, eighteen publicans and two spirit merchants living in the town, and by 1859 the Temperance Society estimated that there were 'about eighty public houses and beer-shops in Middlesbrough', which together with 'gin palaces and Singing Saloons' had exercised an 'unhallowed influence'.[30] High levels of drunkenness led to regular fights. Although men were the main offenders, drunkenness affected both sexes. There were 226 female drunkenness offences prosecuted between 1859 and 1864.[31] Prostitution was also seen as a 'social evil' by the press, and led to subscriptions to open a penitentiary in Albert Road in 1859 to reclaim the 'fallen'.[32] This was a prime example of double standards, since prostitution remained near the top of commercial recreations for men. The street was prostitutes' main locale, although the police superintendent's annual returns identify some beerhouses and public houses as brothels and houses of ill fame.

Most firms worked long hours and time to enjoy leisure was extremely limited. Sunday was for many the only free day. But there were few facilities open that day. It is therefore unsurprising that there were regular complaints about 'loungers' occupying the streets, involved in pitch and toss schools, dog fighting, drinking and obstructing those more respectable groups out for a walk or going to church. There was some social zoning to this. The old town centre was the focal point but much took place near the ironworks, and the river bank and the Sailors' Trod, South Street, Nile Street, and Marton Road were all regularly mentioned. Saturday, Sunday and Monday nights were those most characterized by heavy drinking and the *Middlesbrough Weekly News* in August 1859 was complaining that Middlesbrough streets were 'the scenes of drunkenness and fighting almost every Sabbath'.[33]

The drunkenness was unsurprising. Middlesbrough was a town where in many jobs heat and fumes necessitated liquid intake. Visiting sailors were unlikely to be teetotal. Policing of both these leisure forms was stepped up and there were attempts by magistrates to limit activity. The increase of unlicensed beerhouses from 30 in 1861 to 126 in early 1868 shows how publicans attempted to get round the law; the fact that one in four was prosecuted in 1867 shows how far some magistrates saw them as contributing to 'increase in immorality and crime'.[34] From the 1870s the attempts to limit the widespread availability of alcohol began to meet with success. The number of beerhouses had fallen to forty-seven by 1877. The numbers of public houses (sixty-nine in late 1867, seventy-four in 1887) grew only slowly. Drunkenness prosecutions are unreliable, but were mostly between 600 and 700 a year throughout the 1880s, proportionately lower than previously.

For the working classes, with little free time, except on summer evenings and Sundays, many activities had a link with gambling – betting on pitch and toss, on horses or greyhounds, or on pedestrianism. Many individualized and early team sports such as pugilism and professional rowing were also associated with betting and initially held very irregularly. Commercial recreation grounds were soon developed to meet this need. Pedestrianism was the first major attraction in the north-east and 5,000 were attracted to the Victoria Grounds (the main enclosed commercial recreation ground) to see the 'championship of the north' between the experienced local man J. Rowan and a younger Gateshead runner for a £50 stake in March 1859. As elsewhere, publicans were often involved, and the Cleveland Running Ground, 'lately opened' in 1860 near Linthorpe and hence outside the control of the Middlesbrough Owners, was where men reputedly went to drink first and run afterwards, or run first and drink afterwards. Wrestling in the Cumberland and Westmorland style was also popular, and organized occasionally by local innkeepers as an attraction to gain custom. Anxieties about the effects of these led to haphazard and ineffective attempts to control them.

The recreation grounds soon also began to present greyhound and whippet racing as well as pedestrianism. By the 1880s the two main commercial venues were the Hyde Park New Ash running grounds and the Victoria Recreation running ground, although these may be merely changes of nomenclature and not new venues. Both charged 'gate' money, and organized matches, races and handicaps on Saturdays for money prizes. Although contests were usually in heats to spin out the entertainment and betting, entries could be large. In 1882, for example, at the former a novice pedestrian race over 110 yards attracted fifty-seven entries; at the latter a dog race attracted 250 entries for the £12 prize. At both venues total prize money was limited, and usually ranged between £5 and £15 per meeting, while crowds were predominantly male.

Professional sports, often associated with betting, now attracted large crowds. The largest crowd during this period in Middlesbrough was for what proved to be an ill-fated attempt to revive professional rowing in the town. While the Tees was rarely a racing venue, it had produced some competent professionals, mainly competing elsewhere. In 1882 the landlord of the Shakespeare Hotel sponsored the Newcastle-born rower Robert Boyd to train in Middlesbrough. Boyd (b. 1852) had held the English championship, but had more recently unsuccessfully competed for the world championship with the Canadian, Edward Hanlan. Some 12,000 spectators watched Boyd give a rowing demonstration at Newport in February. According to the *Cleveland News* Boyd 'strove to get a match rowed in our midst' quite deliberately 'in order to gain the river Tees a name' and hoped to see other matches in the future.[35] In July 1882 a match of £200 a side was arranged with Laycock, the Australian champion. The course was from Newport ironworks to the Middlesbrough dock entrance, and the race attracted excursional trips from London, Sheffield, Hull, Edinburgh and Newcastle, as well as surrounding towns and villages. Such major events always led to absenteeism; factory discipline never absolutely ruled. Many of the works were suspended for the afternoon if not the whole of the day. Boyd, however, was overmatched, being defeated by twelve lengths, in front of a crowd 'estimated at 80–100,000'.[36] Boyd continued to live at the Shakespeare Hotel until his death in 1886. His funeral attracted a huge crowd of all classes, and an unusually long cortege in a significant demonstration of popular sympathy for a sporting hero. After this, amateur rowing held supreme.

The limited power of the middle class and respectable Nonconformist groups to control popular sport spectatorship is even more in evidence when horse racing is examined. Horse racing was a cross-class sport and attractive both in terms of attendance and in terms of betting. Many men saved up for annual trips to Redcar races at Whit, and Stockton races in August. Whit was a traditional holiday but August was not. When Stockton races were first revived in 1853 they were of middling status and initially most Middlesbrough industries did not shut down. But by the 1860s Stockton was the third most important meeting in the north after York and Doncaster, with top horses and jockeys attracted by high prize money. Increasingly thereafter, absenteeism at the major works forced more Middlesbrough companies to shut down during the meeting.

In the 1860s and early 1870s increased real wages for some workers under boom conditions also led to more widespread betting specifically on horse racing above and beyond annual August attendance at the nearby Stockton track. Horse-racing information was becoming widely available outside the inner world of the turf, thanks to the emergence of the specialized sporting press and their 'turf correspondents' at the major training areas and meetings, who could send information rapidly via the new electric telegraph service. Betting clubs (the Albert was a recognized betting club by 1880; a membership of 200 paid 10*s* 6*d* annually), and street betting on horse races became very popular and were found on a range of Middlesbrough sites, as was pitch and toss. For street betting accepted bases included Sussex Street, an area in Snowden Road known as the betting ground and the Marshes. Police tended to ignore it unless there were disturbances, while some magistrates' responses show increasing toleration. The music licence for the cricket field was granted in 1887 even though 'there had been several complaints that gambling was freely indulged in on the cricket field'.[37] Some members of the town council were involved in horse racing and betting themselves. Alderman Weighell was a racehorse owner, while Frank Cook, another councillor, was sued by one bookmaker for the 'balance of a bet made on . . . the race for the Manchester Cup in 1882'.[38] Between the 1870s and 1890s police prosecuted intermittently using byelaws against obstruction of the pavement. Middle-class fears that betting was becoming ever more prevalent, with working-class women and children also involved, can be found in a variety of sources, not least Lady Bell's 1907 account in *At the Works* of its extent in Port Clarence. Middlesbrough Watch Committee's minutes show further strengthening of the byelaws in 1896. By 1900 they were calling attention to 'the fact that gambling is greatly on the increase and expressing the hope that magistrates will levy heavy fines'.[39]

IV

Middlesbrough leisure and sport in the years leading up to the First World War was becoming recognizably modern in many of its elements. Although economic conditions still affected demand for commercial entertainment, it was increasingly highly capitalized, and new leisure forms were arriving. Thomas Thompson opened Middlesbrough's first cinema in 1908. It struggled initially, but its popularity grew. In late 1911 a second cinema, the Grand Electric Theatre opened, and in 1914 the Pavilion, both in Newport Road. There had been a short-lived skating rink in the 1870s, and in 1910 the Olympia skating rink opened in Oxford Road.

Middlesbrough's economic and social structure had limited the directions leisure could take and it was dominated by working-class, predominantly less respectable leisure forms. Leisure had become segregated in terms of space, time, gender and class; institutionalized through state and local licensing and policing; and increasingly specialized and differentiated. In sport, minority middle-class amateur sports coexisted alongside the more popular professional soccer and the sports associated with betting. Rising real incomes and free time had put both within the reach of wider numbers. By 1898, for example, Middlesbrough had at least twenty-two cycling clubs, some with women sections, while in 1908 Middlesbrough's first golf club opened on a 60-acre site at Devil's Bridge.

But looking back over the period, what is most striking is the way a predominantly working-class town, ruled by a business and commercial elite, adopted leisure patterns that were predominantly commercial or less respectable in their thrust, although in a context of ever wider choice. Leisure spending was still limited by income. Indeed, in 1909 the chief constable could report noticeably less drunkenness in the town on those Saturdays when Middlesbrough were playing at home than when they played away. Expenditure on drink was falling as a percentage of total spending on leisure. Better education now meant a more literate population, more able to benefit from Middlesbrough's library and reading rooms. Yet much of this population was also perhaps keen to read about the fortunes of football teams or race horses. In part leisure was a diversion from the harsh reality of work, but it was also a key source of emotional and intellectual satisfaction, a way of giving meaning to life.

Finally it is worth returning to another point made by Asa Briggs. Briggs emphasizes that all cities were different in terms of economic and social structure, or provincial 'cultures'. Middlesbrough had its own unique features and chronological variations from the general pattern of leisure development as outlined by leisure historians, not least due to its relatively late development, and its atypical economic and social structure, linked to the heavy industries which sustained it. It had significant similarities with Barrow-in-Furness, also a Victorian new town, reliant on heavy industries, with a predominantly working-class population where there was likewise an emphasis on heavy gambling, the public house, and street life although alongside more emphasis on rugby than association football.[40]

NOTES

1. *Middlesbrough Weekly News*, 8 July 1864; W.E. Gladstone on his visit to Middlesbrough in October 1862, quoted by Asa Briggs, above, p. 6.
2. Pioneers include A.P. Donajgrodzki (ed.), *Social Control in Nineteenth Century Britain* (1978) and H. Cunningham, *Leisure in the Industrial Revolution* (1980).
3. J.K. Walton and J. Walvin (eds.), *Leisure in Britain, 1780–1939* (Manchester, 1983).
4. H.E. Meller, *Leisure and the Changing City* (London, 1976), preface.
5. W. Lillie, *The History of Middlesbrough* (Middlesbrough, 1968).
6. Briggs, above, pp. 14–15, 25.
7. *Middlesbrough Daily Exchange*, 28 October 1887.
8. *Middlesbrough Weekly News*, 3 September 1859. Brian Harrison has argued that temperance was strongest in areas of heavy drinking. See B. Harrison, 'Pubs', in H.J. Dyos and M. Wolff, *The Victorian City*, Vol I (1973), p. 162.
9. *Middlesbrough Weekly News*, 20 January 1859.
10. *Middlesbrough Weekly News*, 1 January 1859.
11. White's *Directory of the North Riding* (Sheffield, 1867), p. 554.
12. *Middlesbrough Weekly News*, 16 November 1877.
13. *Northern Echo*, 18 June 1894.

14. *Cleveland News*, 5 August 1882.
15. *Cleveland News*, 2 October 1886.
16. *Daily Exchange*, 20 January 1887.
17. P. Bailey, *Music Hall; The Business of Pleasure* (Open University, 1986), p. ix.
18. *Middlesbrough Weekly News*, 25 August 1860.
19. In Newcastle, although Balmra's music-hall opened in 1848, the Victoria (1857), Grainger's Hotel (1860) and the Tyne Concert Hall (1861) are of this period. See K. Barker, 'The Performing Arts in Newcastle upon Tyne', in Walton and Walvin, *Leisure in Britain*, p. 63.
20. *Middlesbrough Weekly News*, 25 August 1860.
21. *Middlesbrough Weekly News*, 30 August 1867.
22. White's *Directory*.
23. *Handbook and Directory of Middlesbrough etc* (Middlesbrough, 1871).
24. *North-Eastern Daily Gazette*, 24 October 1896.
25. *North-Eastern Daily Gazette*, 1 June 1895.
26. Circus bill of 1883, held in Cleveland Archives, U/PAT (2) 18 vol. 3.
27. *North-Eastern Daily Gazette*, 1 June 1895.
28. *Newcastle Daily Chronicle*, 15 May 1889.
29. *Northern Review*, 30 November 1889.
30. *Middlesbrough Weekly News*, 4 August 1860.
31. N. Moorsom, 'The Demon Drink and Social Attitudes in Mid-Victorian Middlesbrough' (unpublished MA thesis, Teesside Polytechnic, 1985), p. 38.
32. *Middlesbrough Weekly News*, 13 August 1859.
33. Ibid.
34. *Middlesbrough and Stockton Gazette*, 13 August 1868.
35. *Cleveland News*, 8 July 1882.
36. *Redcar Gazette*, 10 July 1882.
37. *Daily Exchange*, 24 August 1887.
38. *Daily Exchange*, 4 July 1887.
39. Cleveland Archives, Middlesbrough Watch Committee Minutes, 29 November 1900.
40. B. Trescatheric, *Sport and Leisure in Victorian Barrow* (Barrow-in-Furness, 1983).

CHAPTER 7

HOUSING THE COMMUNITY, 1830–1914

Linda Polley

Housing the citizens of Middlesbrough has always demanded considerable civic attention and a large proportion of the town plan. The relative novelty of the town's existence, the speed with which it materialized and grew, and the very close relationship of industry and community, all contributed to the rate and direction of expansion and to different types of development. From 1840, when the town was only ten years old, the housing stock of Middlesbrough began its phenomenal increase, fanning out southward from the original plan in an ever-widening triangle.

The provision of housing was generally seen throughout the Victorian era as being the responsibility of capitalist enterprise, and the great majority of houses were constructed by the speculative builder with the aim of selling or letting at a profit. As Asa Briggs has so rightly pointed out, Middlesbrough itself started life as speculative development, a wholly new town created by Joseph Pease and his Quaker associates to attract workers and investors and to rival the established ports nearby. The astuteness of their endeavour is fully recorded in successive plans and maps of the town, each one charting a larger and more complex urban community and providing some explanation of how and why the town developed in the way it did.

Initially they show how quickly the original layout was outgrown and how rapidly the town was forced to extend southwards. Town plans also indicate increasing social stratification reflected in the differing size, style, type and location of houses: the closely packed 'little brown houses' built as near to the works as possible, the larger terraced and semi-detached houses for the financially and socially better-off, and finally the spacious detached villa residences in leafy suburbs for the most affluent inhabitants of the town. The planning of nineteenth-century middle-class speculative housing shows a gradual move towards curved and sweeping avenues, increased garden space and tree-lined streets. For the estates of poorer houses, the only consideration was to cover the ground with as many and as quickly as possible. Market forces dictated building standards and space provision, resulting in housing plans shaped by economics rather than aesthetics or even convenience. Speculative developers built what and where they believed the market required, their success or failure dependent on being able to anticipate the quantitative and qualitative demands of the town's burgeoning population.

The unfettered speculation of the early nineteenth century was also encouraged by the paucity of building rules or regulations. Before the 1860s very few provincial towns felt it necessary to exert more than limited powers over construction or development, and only in the second half of the century did a *laissez-faire* hostility to government intervention give way to gradual acceptance of the need for statutory control. Even then, belated recognition of the connection between disease and squalid housing resulted in reactive legislation, responsive to situations only as they became critical. Speculation continued to produce most British housing right up to the outbreak of war in 1914, and despite a local economic 'slump' during the 1870s and early 1880s, Middlesbrough's experience was no exception.

During the first decade of Middlesbrough's existence, Richard Otley's plan for the Owners of the Middlesbrough Estate was firmly established 'on the ground', and the town experienced its first big population increase, from 154 inhabitants at the 1831 census to 5,463 in 1841. The Otley plan of 1830 was a straightforward symmetrical grid with church and market in its central town square, the geometric approach intending to ' . . . produce some uniformity and respectability in the houses to be built.'[1] The 123 building plots were spacious, the twelve streets were wide, and quite specific deeds of covenant attached to the conveyances ensured that some of the founders' civic intentions were realized, if only temporarily.

The piecemeal approach to early building revealed in a view of the town in 1832 (MCL)

Building started almost immediately. A contemporary illustration, 'Middlesbrough in 1832' shows a number of the original houses, some also serving as business premises. The houses are shown built in groups and individually, in a variety of shapes, sizes and types. This piecemeal approach to development, inherent in speculation open to all-comers, certainly encouraged uniformity, but at the same time discouraged the Middlesbrough Owners' intended regularity right from the outset.

This view, across the drainage ditch that ran parallel to Stockton Street, focuses on what appears to be either a terrace of identical houses or a row of shops with accommodation above. Commercial Street is to the extreme left,

Typical 'builders vernacular' – 31 Commercial Street (CA)

Dacre Street with three houses faces the Ship Inn, and the wider West Street is to the right of the central terrace. On the far right is a row of houses on Richmond Street probably built by one developer (or builder) for resale or let. Number 31 Commercial Street is fairly typical. This very plain, classically proportioned 'builders vernacular' style owes a lot to local brick building traditions, local materials and perhaps even local expectations in this untried environment. The same house type was repeatedly erected in the new town in a variety of sizes, in rows and in ones and twos, providing domestic and commercial accommodation for families of differing size and status.[2]

By 1840, three more streets had been added to Otley's plan: King Street, halfway between North and Stockton Streets; George Street running north-west from Stockton Street to the town's boundary; and Graham Street between Feversham and East Streets. These new thoroughfares were much narrower and an intimation of worse to come. By 1845 most of the original plots had been built upon and more new streets added in a triangle to the south and another square to the south-east.

Henry Street, built off South Street sometime between 1845 and 1851 illustrates how quickly that muddy 'village' of 1832 changed into a much more urban and overcrowded environment. It also shows how inbuilt differences in similar house types provide alternatives in quality of provision and ultimately the cost of rent. The 'front' half of Newcastle Row was at the bottom end of Henry Street. Newcastle Row was a double terrace of thirty-six very small houses placed literally back to back (each with three shared walls) and three tunnels through a long and narrow

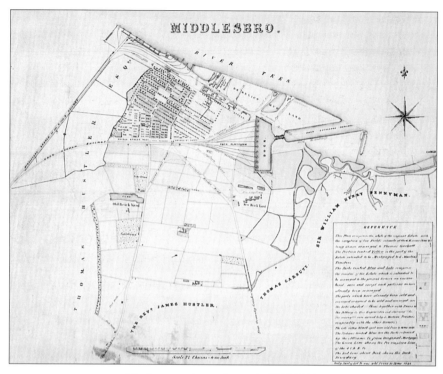

The first expansion, under way by 1845 (CA)

An overcrowded environment: back-to-backs at the bottom end of Henry Street (CA)

communal yard. The houses at the top of Henry Street, beyond the narrowing of the road after the bend, are slightly larger with their own individual back yard and privy. The differentiation between the 'bottom' and 'top' ends of the street is not immediately apparent from the façades, although they do appear to be the work of different builders or developers. These houses are all still in the unadorned style of much early nineteenth-century working-class housing, and the new town also included some larger although not much more sophisticated versions.

Juxtapositioning of residential, commercial and industrial premises in Back Commercial Street (CA)

The close juxtaposition of buildings dictated by the compact town plan meant that residential, commercial and industrial premises were located side by side in a profusion of sizes. It also meant that a wide variety of residential accommodation was built in close proximity, and as well as the narrow infilled closes, the ordnance survey of 1853 indicates a number of larger houses on the periphery. On the corner of Gosford and Cleveland Streets for example, John Gilbert Holmes, one of the town's first shipbuilders, bought two of the original plots in 1831 and constructed a large house with elaborate gardens to the rear. Immediately opposite on Cleveland Street, Henry Bolckow and John Vaughan lived from about 1840 in the two large corner houses which were built in 1835. These also had a very large and elaborate shared garden. To the south along Queens Terrace an impressive row (originally Victoria Terrace) was built in 1850 to house a number of newly established professionals. The relatively close proximity of inhabitants of diverse occupation, earnings and social standing was notable but inevitably short-lived.

Middlesbrough remained confined to the area north of the railway line until the middle of the 1850s. John Vaughan's discovery of iron ore in the Cleveland Hills in 1850 initiated a second, much more intense phase of industrial prosperity for Middlesbrough, and encouraged economic growth of such scale and magnitude that the town was hard pressed to keep pace. The rapid development of the 1850s and 60s was in the hands of numerous small builders and a few architects, with plots of land acquired and developed in an unstructured and unregulated way.

The first building 'south of the border' took place along both sides of the new Albert Road in a southerly direction to its junction with the equally new Corporation Road and east as far as Marton Road. Running parallel to Linthorpe Road were Linthorpe Mews, Dundas Street, Dundas Mews, Albert Road, Albert Mews, Richardson Street and Gurney Street. Zetland Road, Brunswick and Wilson Streets were at right angles to the north and Fry Street, Mount Street and Short Street filled in the awkward triangle eastwards to Marton Road. Throughout the 1850s a number of builders and developers constructed housing here for the influx of workers and their families, interspersed with the occasional shop, pub or workshop.

Most of these houses were extremely small, with one room about 15 feet square downstairs and one of similar dimensions above, with a small pantry and coal store at the back of the house. Ashpits and privies were located across a back yard about the same size as the downstairs room. Plans for two terraces of eight houses to be built back to back between Linthorpe Mews and Dundas Street, were drawn up for Joseph Sharp in 1856. The downstairs room measures 15 feet 5 inches by 12 feet 2 inches; one small window in the pantry, and the back door placed directly opposite the front, no doubt meant very dark, cramped and draughty living quarters. There is no space between the two rows of back yards, which share a back wall, and tunnels between pairs of houses on Linthorpe Mews allow access to ashpits and the back yards of Dundas Street, but reduce further the size of each Linthorpe Mews ground floor. Similar plans for cottages off Wilson Street, submitted for approval by Henry Doughty in 1856, show the same pinched dimensions and minimal living space with a communal back court rather than individual yards. Architecturally, there is not much difference in appearance, although generally speaking the mews houses were slightly smaller than those on the streets. The door treatment differs somewhat in each developer's scheme, but there was little room for artistic licence, nor was there demand for anything other than the maximum number of cheap houses on any given plot. Economic limitations, the use of local materials and the reliance on 'pattern books' for building plans explain the seemingly unified appearance of these early Middlesbrough streets.

Predictably, houses built along Albert Road were larger. As a main thoroughfare to and from the railway station, it 'earned' the right to larger plots, a number of commercial premises and less intensive residential development. Typically the smaller streets were 'hidden' behind the wider main thoroughfares, a common occurrence in Victorian cities and towns. A byproduct of the grid plan, this layout also allowed the developer to offer at least two different house sizes, the large number of smaller ones helping to finance the bigger, more spaciously sited examples.

In the early 1850s Middlesbrough was still a compact, albeit increasingly dense, settlement which extended only slightly beyond its original layout, and was surrounded by undeveloped countryside. Although it was a thriving town with obvious urban possibilities, it had already developed a number of urban problems. The town's Royal Charter of Incorporation, signed in 1853, outlined procedures for the administration and supervision of the borough. The immediate priorities of the newly formed town council were reflected in their appointment of four committees: finance; streets and lighting; watch and police; and sanitation. In 1853, the estimated population of Middlesbrough had risen to 9,332 (compared to 5,463 in 1841) and the evidence points to severe and unhealthy overcrowding in much of the developed area north of the railway line. The uniform and respectable environment originally intended was almost immediately compromised by the choice of the 'convenient' but low-lying riverside site. Damp was always one of the greatest problems of the town, and as the iron industry developed, smoke and noise became the other two main pollutants. 'No one would have chosen the site if their first consideration had been people rather than coal.'[3]

There were no proper building controls in the town until after 1858; infill building into the original grid plan happened almost immediately, and extra narrow streets and courtyards continued to be added. In some cases, the building of rows of cottages along both sides of what had initially been quite large plots, created a back-to-back arrangement of houses with dark, airless courts between. Durham Place was one such street, built before 1853 behind the Golden Lion Public House on Durham Street. A communal pump was located at one end of the court and the bricked-across end gives onto St Hilda's graveyard beyond. One arched doorway was the only access through to the narrow back row.

These conditions were obviously a breeding ground for all types of disease and pestilence, and Middlesbrough withstood three separate attacks of cholera – in 1849, 1852/3 and 1854/5. The last, most virulent visitation, started, according to the *Darlington & Stockton Times*, in houses in Stockton Street. Given the fact that the western boundary of the Stockton Street plots (and the towns) was a stell, or open drainage ditch, with increasing demands being made upon it, this is hardly surprising.

Throughout this period, and indeed throughout the century, housing development in Middlesbrough continued to be driven mainly by the need for speed of provision. Quality was repeatedly sacrificed to the call for quantity, particularly where low-cost working-class houses were concerned. As elsewhere, the regulation of building was seen as a health and sanitation issue and the Public Health Act of 1848 was not adopted in Middlesbrough until 1855. Like several other provincial Victorian towns, Middlesbrough had voluntarily adopted limited powers to regulate building under a number of private Improvement Acts, but at this stage building regulation was more often than not defined as a curb on public nuisance rather than a guide to standards of construction. The Middlesbrough Improvement Act of 1841/2 devolved management of all streets to newly appointed Commissioners, including '. . . Erections, or Buildings, Materials, Implements and other things . . .'. It dealt specifically with the numbering of houses and the naming of streets, obliged private individuals to keep their drains in working order, required all external doors to open inwards, decreed that '. . . ruinous or dangerous houses . . .'[4] were to be taken down, and declared that houses were not to be thatched. None of these regulations were much concerned with the quality of life lived within.

A Private Act was brought before Parliament in 1855 to 'Apply the Public Health Act 1848 to the District of Middlesbrough'. It was this bill that required all plans for new buildings to be deposited with the Surveyor of the Local Board of Health for approval and permission to build. But as the body's main concern was with drainage and sewage disposal, this meant that many of the houses built in Middlesbrough in the 1850s and 60s were still cheaply and hastily erected, although an individual back yard gradually became the norm. These priorites are also reflected in the quality of the plans submitted. Those few which remain from the 1850s were no doubt drawn by the builder or developer, are extremely sketchy and contain the very minimum of information.

The Middlesbrough Extension and Improvement Act of 1856 seemed to promise action, empowering the Local Government Board to

> . . . regulate and improve all public and private streets, roads, lanes . . . to regulate the structure of Walls of New Buildings in reference to stability and the prevention of fires, to regulate the space to be provided in connexion with buildings to secure a free circulation of air and the ventilation of buildings, and to regulate generally the construction, erection levels, position, maintenance, cleansing, repairs, and alterations of all houses, warehouses, manufactories, and other buildings, sewers, drains, necessaries, ashpits, cesspools, receptacles for sewage, dust, soil, and slaughterhouses within the district.[5]

However, this Act merely empowered local government rather than assigned any obligation, and although well intentioned was somewhat lacking in motivational force.

More positive action was taken under the Local Government Act of 1858 which supplied each local authority with a model 'Form of Byelaws' and encouraged many, including Middlesbrough, to adopt a slightly more rigorous approach to building regulations. But these byelaws were still not compulsory, in theory to allow for variation in local practice. This may also help to explain the length of time it took for the model byelaws to reach local statute books. Middlesbrough's relatively limited byelaws were not drawn up until October 1867 and conferred in 1868, ten years after the passing of the Act.

It was not really until the 1875 Public Health Act that local authorities began to create byelaws which systematically regulated standards of construction and development. The resulting 'byelaw housing', built to local authority requirements, is therefore characterized by identifiable specifications in each locality, and was much criticized at the time for its monotonous sameness and the fact that many builders 'built down' to minimum standards. Another contemporary argument against byelaw housing was that it raised the cost of building and therefore the cost of rents. The uniform monotony of the byelaw streets was a result of building houses to specified standards in large quantity; standardization led to least expense and inevitable repetition. In fact, aesthetic values were sacrificed for construction and services, and the houses were repetitive, but they did provide a very gradual improvement in working-class housing conditions. It is perhaps worth mentioning, however, that the uniformity and standardization of earlier byelaw-free speculative development in Middlesbrough rendered this particular criticism locally irrelevant.

Much of Middlesbrough's row or terraced housing was constructed under local byelaws during the 1880s and 90s and exhibits the solid uniformity of the type, much more impressive in the aggregate than when considered alone. Remaining examples can be seen on Pearl, Emerald, Ruby and Amber Streets, built in 1888; in Baker and Bedford Streets built in the early 1890s; and in King Edward Square, built in the first decade of the twentieth century.

Despite the fact that no employers in Middlesbrough built housing specifically for their workers during the early nineteenth century, the Owners of the Middlesbrough Estate controlled the location and cost of house building purely by being in sole possession. Selling parcels of land as and when it suited them meant they could control the direction, quantity and to some extent even the quality of urban extension from the very beginning. During the 1860s, however, Thomas Hustler also took advantage of the continuing growth of the town and sold land lying beyond the north-eastern boundary of the Middlesbrough Estate for housing and industrial development. The Stockton and Middlesbrough Turnpike Road had been laid out in 1857 and made a free public highway, Newport Road, in 1866. The building of 'training walls' by the Tees Conservancy Commission from 1859 had improved navigation and provided wharfage and building land for, among others, Bernard Samuelson's Newport Ironworks in 1864, Richard Hill & Co. in 1868 and Fox, Head's Newport Rolling Mills. This opening up of the Tees Navigation and extension of the Ironmasters' District created a further demand for housing and a new industrial community was built north of Newport Road and along Cannon Street. Development of fairly uniform workers' accommodation started at the north-eastern ends of both roads which were intersected at right angles by streets built up in a rather ad hoc way. By 1870 the houses stretched as far south-west as Milton Street with a

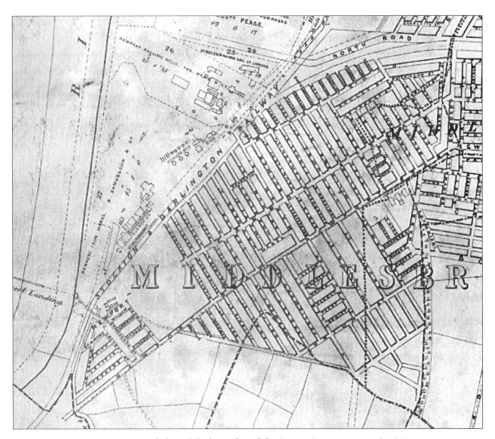

Construction in dribs and drabs. a plan of the Cannon Street area, 1874 (CA)

few outlying terraces off Samuelson Street close to Newport Landing. By the
early 1880s the Cannon Street development had nearly doubled the area of
Middlesbrough, constituting a closely-knit and almost self-contained
community. The housing there continued to be constructed in dribs and
drabs by builders working on a relatively small scale, building a few houses
or a row at a time in order to raise the finance for their next endeavour.
There are very few photographs of the Cannon Street area except those taken
during demolition in the 1960s, but enough evidence remains to indicate
that builders had continued to erect a tried and tested minimal housing
type.

During the early 1860s, terraces of larger houses were built on the south
side of Newport Road, which were intended for the families of professional
men, engineers and the more successful builders. Later on and further down

the housing scale, the area between Newport Road and Union Street was developed as terraced housing, this time for the lower middle classes, the tradesmen and shopkeepers. Many of these houses in Fleetham, Church and Milton Streets were owner occupied, and had long back yards used as either gardens, or more often as workshop space.

At the same time the Middlesbrough Estate land was being developed further, to the west of Albert and Linthorpe Roads in the 1860s, and south of Corporation and Grange Roads in the 1870s. This separate ownership and development is instantly discernible on any map of the town in the rather awkward coming together of the Middlesbrough Owners east–west pattern of roads and streets, and the diagonal grid of Newport and Cannon Wards.

By 1871 the population of Middlesbrough had risen to nearly 40,000. As the town expanded physically it continued to develop socially and culturally, evolving a more complex infrastructure of shops, services and public amenities. During the 1860s and 70s Middlesbrough acquired and administered all the trappings of a thriving urban environment: larger gas and water works, hospitals, an Exchange, numerous churches and more numerous chapels, daily and weekly newspapers, a police force, a fire brigade, a workhouse, a grammar school. During this time the town also began to edge along its two main thoroughfares, Linthorpe and Marton Roads. Linthorpe Road was encouraged to further growth by its earlier role as the only road south. Its arterial importance was increased by the accumulative positioning of first the cemetery, then Southfield Villas from 1853, Albert Park in 1866, Linthorpe from the 1870s, and was consolidated by all the infill building in between. Although Linthorpe Road was initially a residential street, many of its houses were converted to shops as early as the 1860s, and this road gradually became an important commercial venue for increasingly prestigious retail premises.

Marton Road's early development was at its busy northern end, but during the 1860s it became increasingly popular with builders and developers, and various sizes and types of houses were erected there. At the same time, the middle-class suburban development at Grove Hill and Linthorpe Village consolidated the importance of both roads and created a need for even further southern extension of the borough boundary.

Migration of the more wealthy and influential started fairly early on. Some, like Henry Bolckow and John Vaughan, moved to large country houses in outlying villages, but for those who could not aspire to that level of grandeur and expense, the southern reaches of the town seemed to offer a practical and healthy distance from which to commute. A new house in the suburbs promised improved standards of health, an absence of urban stress, and an elevation of self-esteem through associations with the landed gentry. The withdrawal of the middle classes to what was then the outskirts of town, followed by the subsequent urban encroachment of these suburbs, exhibits a recognizable pattern. By the end of the century Middlesbrough boasted four residential suburbs: Southfield Villas from 1853, North Park Road from 1866, Grove Hill from the 1860s and Linthorpe from the 1870s.[6]

Southfield Villas and North Park Road had limited room for expansion and as the first, less remote suburban developments, they were soon engulfed as the town extended southwards. Grove Hill on the other hand maintained an exclusivity in keeping with its accommodation for Middlesbrough's elite. The development of Linthorpe Village tells a slightly different story. The motivations of both builders and buyers were similar, but development and building was much more diverse, making this perhaps a more accessible suburb. This was partly due to chronology; Linthorpe was started much later, when the suburban ethos was beginning to filter down to the lower middle classes. Linthorpe is an Edwardian suburb rather than a Victorian one, and exhibits all the architectural quality of that period.

Laid out in the 1870s, Linthorpe initially fell victim to a downturn in the local economy which had a temporary effect on building and the housing market. J. Albery writes of newly built houses in Middlesbrough empty and boarded up in the 1870s, unable to be sold or let.[7] By 1880 a number of individual villas had been built along Linthorpe Crescent, but there were still many vacant plots. Linthorpe's building boom had to wait until the early twentieth century when a variety of developers, builders and businessmen took advantage of an increase in the demand for what were termed 'Medium Class' semi-detached and terraced houses.

One of the first people to take advantage of the idea of Linthorpe as a desirable place to live, a lucrative investment and even perhaps a vehicle for self-promotion, was Theophilius Phillips. Phillips had been mayor of Middlesbrough in 1895 and a town councillor from 1884–7 (North West Ward) and from 1889–1904 (South and Linthorpe Ward). In 1879 Phillips had one of the earliest new villas built for him on Linthorpe Crescent by a local architect, Roger Lofthouse. During the 1880s and 1890s, The Crescent and The Avenue were further developed with architect-designed detached and semi-detached villa residences, built either speculatively or, like Phillips' house, for occupancy by the client. Generally speaking those on The Crescent were for client occupation and those on The Avenue built for sale or re-let.[8]

During the 1890s, another Middlesbrough architect, Arthur Newsome, was working on houses in The Crescent and The Avenue, but also on two new adjacent streets: Limes Road and Poplars Road. Phillips must have liked what he saw of Newsome's work, because in 1899 proposed plans for 'Phillipsville Estate', south of Orchard Road, were submitted for approval by Phillips as developer with Newsome as his architect. The Estate was initially three streets, planned as a cross: Phillips Avenue intersecting Claude Avenue and bounded on the south by Westwood Avenue. Mayberry Grove was later added to connect Westwood and Claude Avenues.

Phillips and Newsome built a number of houses there quite quickly, and the

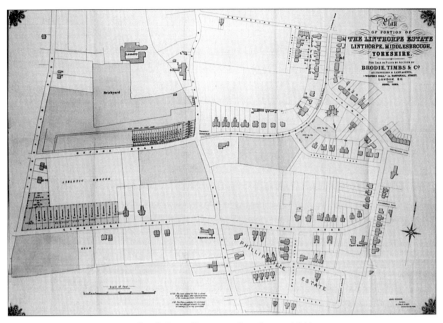

The Phillipsville Estate Plan of 1905 (CA)

quality (still discernible today) implies they were a good and profitable investment. It also indicates that by the turn of the century Linthorpe had established itself as a rather desirable suburb with obvious opportunities for speculation. One of its main selling points was the suburb's location at the terminus of the tram line. In 1905 and 1907, a company of London auctioneers, Brodie and Timbs, offered for sale by auction a large number of building plots on Oxford, Roman, Cambridge and Thornfield Roads, advertising them as offering ' . . . Capitalists, Builders and others an opportunity of obtaining excellent building plots which cannot fail to prove highly remunerative in a very short space of time'. Minimum building values were stipulated for the variously sized plots, obviously with a view to maintaining a certain neighbourhood 'tone'. All those plots were developed fairly quickly, again mostly in pairs of detached and semi-detached Medium Class houses.

Even today, a stroll through Linthorpe reveals the quality and Edwardian character of most of its houses, and a wealth of architectural features can be identified which have retained their domestic appeal. The initial impression is one of red bricks, moulded terracotta decoration and elaborate, usually white, painted woodwork. These bricks are smoother than the mottled and unfinished examples found in earlier large houses in the town, and the contrasting woodwork ranges from sash windows through a variety of canopies and balconies to elaborate barge boarding on gable ends. Further investigation reveals mock half-timbering on roughcast walls, decoratively hung tiles and, along Oxford Road, uniform iron railings on first floor balconies. All of these elements are found in varying degrees of elaboration and are all an intrinsic part of the competitive commercial context in which they were built.

The development of Linthorpe was just one aspect of an Edwardian building boom in Middlesbrough, a boom which produced a wide variety of housing of all types and sizes. This second burst of Middlesbrough's architectural extension, during the 1890s, 1900s and 1910s, was the product of a revitalized local economy, an increased number of prospective home owners or tenants and continually improved building byelaws.

The house-buying public was changing in its make-up and aspirations. Originally the prerogative of the wealthy upper middle class, a modified suburban lifestyle soon came within the grasp of the emerging lower middle class, the 'black-coated army' of clerks, managers, commercial travellers and small businessmen, who having 'got on' monetarily entered into the process of 'going up' socially. The table illustrates the relationship of income to housing status and levels of rent. Each of these income groups was catered for by architects and builders in Middlesbrough during this time.

Relationship of Income to Housing Status and Levels of Rent, 1890–1914

Occupation	Income (p.a.)	Size of House	Cost of House to Build	Rent (p.a.)	Servants
lawyers/ merchants/ top civil servants	£1,000– £3,000	15 rooms	£1,000– £3,000	£100	5
lawyers/ doctors/ top clerks	£500– £700	n/a	£1,000	£100	n/a
lower paid pros/ higher clerks	£350	7–8 rooms	£500	£40– £60	1–2
lower clerks/ shopkeepers	£200		£200–£300	£25– £45	1
lower clerks	£100– £150	5–6 rooms	£120–£200	£12– £30	Live out help

By 1901 Middlesbrough's Building Byelaws had become extremely comprehensive, much more detailed and quite specific. They ran to seventy-eight pages of closely typed instructions concerning standards of size, strength, distance apart, dimension, height, thickness and even definitions for everything from ashpits to baths, beams, chimneys, concrete, drains, floors and flues, gutters, handrails, lavatories, overflows, party walls, rafters, roofs, string courses, timber, ventilation, walls, water closets, windows, woodwork and yards. Plans submitted for approval reflect the more detailed demands placed on development. In almost all cases they were drawn by an architect or surveyor and reflect the increased skills required by professional status, sophisticated architectural designs rather than construction plans.

By that time building too had become a much more sophisticated and skilful process, aided in its development by specialization within the industry, advanced materials and construction technologies and the increased statutory regulation. Edwardian houses were being built to a higher standard, much faster, and were providing wider choices of size and style. Local areas that had been left empty by Victorian development were soon covered with a wide spectrum of decently built and differently promoted urban 'villages'. From the very small examples on Angle Street, up through the similar but larger houses in the Ayresome Park area, to impressive terraces on Southfield and Claireville Roads, Middlesbrough builders were busy supplying quite a healthy demand.

Speculative building for the Edwardian lower-middle class: Angle Street (CA)

Angle Street is a good example of the speculative developer and architect creating a cohesively structured urban environment together. The small but compactly designed houses were the work of a local architect called Forrester for the developer W.H. Whitfield, and were planned and built in groups of ten or twenty over a period of about five years. Their ground-floor bay window, a unique selling point in such a small house, marks them out from the earlier flat-fronted byelaw-houses and indicates that they were probably aimed at the better-off working-class tenant or owner. The almost continuous cycle of planning, building and selling or letting indicates a successful product, and the continuity of design, materials and construction guaranteed a unified whole on completion. The wide street still marks this development out as a cut above its Victorian counterparts.

Slightly further up the social scale, the Ayresome Park area had been earmarked for housing development, at least on paper, as early as 1875. In that year, a 'Plan of Freehold Building Land' was drawn up by Charles Fisher Jnr, Architect & Surveyor of 6 Vaughan Street, Middlesbrough, for the landowner, his father, also Charles Fisher, of Sandhutton, near Thirsk. This plan of the land for sale on the 'Ayresome Grange Estate' shows and names Parliament Road and Ayresome Street, but the intersecting streets in between bear little resemblance to what was eventually built in either name or position. T.M. Smith's 1882 map of Middlesbrough shows a bigger grid pattern of streets adjacent to the old cemetery, to the south of what is now Parliament Road. Development here too was no doubt hindered by the depression of the 1870s and only started in earnest in the first decade of the twentieth century.

Roger Lofthouse, probably the most successful nineteenth-century Middlesbrough-based architect, was extremely busy in the town during the first decade of the new century, working for speculative builders and developers as well as for private clients. Between 1904 and 1906 he provided designs for five builders or developers on Aire Street alone, presumably providing the same plan for them all. An advertisement of 1908 in the *Erimus Advertiser*, a free local newspaper, gives an indication of the size and value of some of the Ayresome Park houses at that time, which was directly related to site location and service provision. These were smaller than the Medium Class homes being built in Linthorpe, and consequently very much in demand.

Development along the western end of Southfield Road started in 1853 when it was still about a mile and a half from the centre of town, but the town soon caught up and overtook this secluded suburb. The houses here are in a variety of shapes and sizes, again with the larger ones fronting the main roads with narrower streets and smaller houses fitted in behind. Generally speaking, the houses get smaller as the road travels eastwards. Very similar houses in size and style were built at Clairville Road with similar decorative railings. By 1914 Middlesbrough could boast a very wide choice of houses to any prospective tenant with enough income to meet his or her requirements.

Housing for the upwardly mobile in Edwardian Ayresome Park (CA)

Meanwhile, back in the older parts of the town, these choices were just not on offer. At the turn of the century, when Florence Bell was researching and writing *At the Works*, published in 1907, a large number of the town's inhabitants were living in rapidly deteriorating slum conditions. Houses were now eighty years old, and they were neglected, ill-equipped, insanitary and crumbling. Many houses originally designed and built for single families had degenerated by the end of the century into multiple occupancy. The Boer War had focused attention on a general lack of fitness in the average recruit which was believed to be directly attributable to social standing and indirectly to housing conditions. Legislation was seen to be failing and building byelaws still applied only to newly built houses. In Middlesbrough, as elsewhere, the housing 'problem' began to take shape as a public issue.

In September of 1900, Dr Charles Dingle, Medical Officer of Health, submitted to the Sanitary Committee a report concerning a number of streets near the Nile Street area in St Hilda's ward. After harrowing statistics regarding living conditions, deaths and diseases (for example, density per acre 429 persons – average for borough 34.35; death rates for this area 30.09 per 1,000 – rest of borough 20.46) he concludes:

169

I find from my inspection of this area there is a very large portion of it in such a condition from bad arrangement of houses, bad sanitary accommodation, and bad repair, that I would advise its being dealt with under Part I of the Housing of the Working Classes Act 1890, as . . . an unhealthy area. . . .

He goes on to quote Part I section 4 of the Act to the effect that ' . . . an improvement scheme should be made in respect of such an area'.[9]

Four years later, after repeated attempts to cajole property owners into making improvements, a special meeting of the town council recorded that the houses in the Nile Street area were ' . . . declared an unhealthy area . . .' and stated that it was

. . . desirable that an Improvement Scheme should be made in respect of the said area, and for that purpose the Borough Engineer be instructed to forthwith prepare plans, specifications and estimates for a Scheme showing the houses and the land to be taken, the rearrangement and reconstruction of the Streets . . . the number of houses proposed to be erected in lieu thereof for the accommodation of persons who may have to remove.[10]

Housing for the downwardly mobile: Nile Street, condemned in 1900 by Dr Dingle, but still standing thirty years later (MCL)

Yet despite this registered concern nothing was done and the area was still causing problems during the 1930s.

Another national response to industrial urban squalor was the Garden City movement, developed by Ebenezer Howard and taken up by a number of enlightened and philanthropic industrialists. The North of England Housing Reform Conference held in Newcastle in April 1902 was attended by seven representatives from Middlesbrough Town Council at the behest of the General Purposes Committee. One of the speakers was John H. Barlow, Secretary of the Bournville Village Trust. 'Mr Barlow will be able to show, from his knowledge of the Bournville experiment, the value of the work which Local Authorities can do by acting along the lines suggested in the resolution.'[11]

The conference was an attempt to persuade local authority members to adopt Garden City principles in providing 'artistic self-contained cottages' for their overcrowded and unhealthy poor. It was proposed that local byelaws should be altered to render impossible the building of long unbroken rows of houses with doors opening '. . . direct upon the common pavement . . .', and with cramped back yards. The conference also encouraged local authorities '. . . to acquire land under compulsion . . .' which it could then use '. . . municipally or lease under the Act of 1900 . . . for the purposes of building houses for the people'.[12]

A response by those attending was read into the council minutes, but was very non-committal. Perhaps the councillors from Middlesbrough felt somewhat on the defensive as the house type the conference castigated so roundly was exactly what had been consistently provided for Middlesbrough's working men and women. But inevitably the ideas emanating from the Garden City and Housing Reform Movement did eventually have some effect on Middlesbrough's 'movers and shakers'.

What resulted nationally from the growing demand for more comprehensive legislation was the Town Planning Act of 1909, the last attempt to make local authorities responsible for housing without the incentive of a direct subsidy. The implication was that these poor urban conditions would continue to be replicated unless 'intelligent anticipation', i.e. planning, became the norm for local authorities. If nothing else, the economic dimension must have appealed; forward planning was promoted as a way of saving money whereas reactive ad hoc legislation by its very nature often proved to be costly.

A *North-Eastern Daily Gazette* article of 1912, headlined 'Great Scheme Submitted by Borough Engineer',[13] tells the story of Middlesbrough's response to the Town Planning Act of 1909. The newspaper reported on an outline planning scheme that painted (with very broad brush-strokes) what the council would like to be able to achieve and the piece is full of Garden City allusions. The scheme was to cover 810 acres in seven separate areas. It promised ' . . . wide radial artery main roads . . . the limitation of the number of houses per acre to eight or less for the better class houses . . . and not more than 18 or 20 for others.' Residential roads were to be ' . . . laid out in the form of crescents and rectangles and Mr Burgess foreshadows the laying out of plantations and public walks. . . .'

The six areas were named as Longlands, Belle Vue, Grove Hill, Park Side, North Acklam, and South Acklam. A new road was planned to link all these together ' . . . 60 feet wide . . . in three sections . . .' east–west from Acklam Road to Marton Road. The plan promised compulsory indoor WCs and no back streets, low density development with open spaces to be left, particularly on main roads, ' . . . small plantations to adjoin main artery roads as protection from dust where . . . motor and other mechanical traction is undertaken . . .', and residential roads in '. . . crescents and rectangles to suit the varying conditions of the land'.[14]

Almost simultaneously, the Middlesbrough Corporation Act of 1913 extended the borough boundary to include North Ormesby, and the small part of Marton which surrounded the Corporation's asylum. Reading between the lines one can see local councillors beginning to warm to this new notion of 'town planning', but Middlesbrough's plans, like all others, were overtaken by events. The outbreak of war a year later meant that grandiose town planning schemes would have to wait for the duration. Between 4 August and 7 September 1914, 5,000 Middlesbrough men enlisted and soon restrictions would be placed upon 'unnecessary' building by the Ministry of Munitions. Any domestic building done during the following five years was to house the influx of munitions workers, and perhaps that's part of a different story.

NOTES

1. Owners of the Middlesbrough Estate *Deed of Covenant* 1831, Cleveland County Archive.
2. A small brickyard at Linthorpe had been acquired with the Middlesbrough Estate which was initially let out by the Owners on a yearly agreement. In 1839 a new brickyard with new 'Yester' brickmaking machinery, was set up just off what was then Cleveland Bridge Road, later Marton Road, to deal with the increasing demand for easily accessible building material.
3. C. & R. Bell, *City Fathers* (1969), p. 137.
4. Cleveland County Archive, Middlesbrough Improvement Act of 1841/2.
5. *Darlington & Stockton Times*, November 1855.
6. For a detailed account of Middlesbrough's Victorian suburban expansion, see L. Polley *The Other Middlesbrough, a Study of Three Nineteenth Century Suburbs* (University of Teesside, 1993).
7. J. Albery, 'Housing', in Max Lock, the *Middlesbrough Survey and Plan* (Middlesbrough Corporation, 1946).
8. This was definitely a growth period for the area: population figures for Linthorpe in 1861 show 702 inhabitants, for 1871 10,551 inhabitants, 1881 18,736 inhabitants and 1891 25,341 inhabitants. G.A. North, *Teesside's Economic Heritage* (County Council of Cleveland, 1975), pp. 155, 163.
9. Cleveland County Archive, Dr C. Dingle, 'Report of the Medical Officer of Health', Sanitary Committee Minutes, September 1900.
10. Cleveland County Archive, Council Minutes, 1904.
11. Cleveland County Archive, Circular advertising 'North of England Housing Reform Conference', 1902.
12. Ibid.
13. Cleveland County Archive, undated newspaper cutting in scrapbook compiled from 1912 by Cecil Gorman (Borough Engineer).
14. Cleveland County Archive, Cecil Gorman Scrapbook.

CHAPTER 8

'CITY BEAUTIFUL': PLANNING THE FUTURE IN MID-TWENTIETH-CENTURY MIDDLESBROUGH

J. W. Leonard

There are many ways of taking stock of Middlesbrough in the mid-twentieth century. Statistics abound; there is a mass of visual material at hand locally; but above all there is the *Middlesbrough Survey and Plan*, completed in 1945. This volume was produced by a team of well-motivated young architects, planners and social scientists, largely female, under the leadership and guidance of Max Lock, himself well under forty, and, like most of the members of his team, having strong Quaker leanings. Besides the *Survey and Plan* itself there are related contemporaneous publications by members and associates of the team and a wealth of press coverage, local and national, of this phase of the town's development, especially after the acceptance of the published plan. Similarly there are council minutes and census reports. And finally I have been fortunate also to have met Max Lock and some of his team a few years ago.

There is no better way of understanding the town both physically and socially at the end of the Second World War than by making use of the wealth of detailed material that came from the forty or so members of the Lock team. The value of the picture of local conditions that comes from Lock's work is based on a number of factors: the youthful vigour of his team, their expertise, their commitment and the help and cooperation they received from both local and national government sources. In a very obvious way, and many would think sadly so, the reports that the team submitted along with much related research material stay fresh and of value to the historian at the end of the century while the object of their enquiry really came to nothing. By making use of the work of this team one is paying homage to the heroic effort of Lock and his colleagues; an effort fired by the Home Front enthusiasms of the later war years.

The official presentation of the material that embraced Lock's work took place in 1946, making this particular year a focal point for developments before and afterwards. During the interwar years the town had suffered from high unemployment with all its attendant ills, whereas the actual experience of the war was less destructive than that known by many other urban centres.

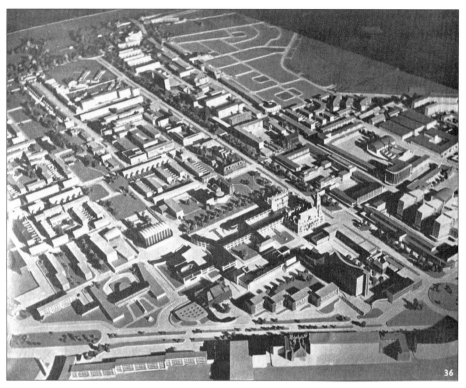

Rational rearrangement: Max Lock's vision for the future of Middlesbrough (MCL)

However, it was from the circumstances of the war that Max Lock and his team received their commission. On 17 January 1946, therefore, Middlesbrough Council took a momentous step in its history. It accepted the *Middlesbrough Survey and Plan* as the blueprint for its future urban development.

The Max Lock Plan, as it is often styled, called for sweeping changes in housing, town layout, social facilities, transport, and many other related aspects in the life of the people of Middlesbrough.

The plan embraced three phases of time: five, fifteen and thirty years from the point of the policy's inception. These phases covered redevelopment, lower density housing, rearrangement of the shopping areas, new suburban housing estates, and wedges of open space connecting these suburbs with the town centre. A green buffer zone was to be created between the housing areas in the town centre and the adjacent industrial zones. In this economic respect, the basic staples, iron and steel, were to be augmented. Sub-regional locations were accordingly proposed in order to sustain a wider industrial base than had traditionally been associated with the later years of the 'infant Hercules'. These changes in their turn necessitated transport developments, and accordingly new road links were proposed in order to supplement the rail and water links already available.

The somewhat jumbled mix of roads then existing was to be reorganized into four categories. Through traffic was to use an east–west axis of arterial parkways, while industrial traffic was to be given an improved road that was to run south of the railway line. Main town traffic was to use subsidiary radial roads, and what was termed strictly local traffic was consigned to its own by-roads.

However, the most obvious problem that faced the town at mid-century was that of bad housing. This itself could be related to two causes: the longer-term one was the initial speed of industrial growth with its vast labour requirements, and the more immediate one was the poverty coming from interwar unemployment. In regard to the first cause many fatalistic accounts have been written such as that of Lady Bell in her book, *At the Works*; but some more recent surveys have attempted a more analytic approach.

Under the plan, housing was to be cleared and redeveloped in the three phases already mentioned. The then current high densities of the town centre and its northern fringe could be up to 140 persons to the acre. These were to be reduced to a maximum of fifty for the replanned central area, up to forty for the inner suburbs, while the outer suburbs were to enjoy densities of no more than thirty. Housing layout was to be related to discernible neighbourhood patterns; open space was to be created on a more equitable basis than was then the case, and alongside these improvements were to come compatible changes in health and well-being: new health services to be provided, and the system of education to be restructured and updated.

Turning once more to bricks and mortar, the team proposed that the town's shops were to be reorganized into four main groupings: the chief centres, their sub centres, local centres, and the strictly local centres. Allied to this sweeping rearrangement the town centre was to be replanned with the town hall as the focal point. Moreover in these years immediately following mid-century there was to be provision for both cultural and entertainment centres, as well as zones for business, marketing, and warehousing; also planned was the provision of clubs, swimming-baths, and car-parking.

The introduction to the plan was written by Ruth Glass, head of the sociology unit of the Lock team. Although written really for her own report on the structure of the Middlesbrough neighbourhoods, this introduction was considered by Lock to be suitable as a preface for the entire field of investigation. He based this conclusion on the fact that Glass's emphasis on the human background was really the element against which all aspects of the survey were considered. This particular emphasis gives us a vivid and analytic picture of what the town looked and felt like at this point.

She saw Middlesbrough as typifying a town that originated and expanded in the nineteenth century, which fact accounted for both its defects and assets. Its reputation was based on the single-minded power of the iron and steel industry, the sheer speed of its growth, its grid-iron street layout, and its alleged ugliness. Not for it the castle or cathedral nucleus, but the coke-ovens and blastfurnaces. Its lords of the manor were its ironmasters.

Consequently the town scenery was defaced by industrial structures, and its sky unnaturally lit by industrial flame or obscured by industrial smoke. She saw this same industry as cutting the town off from its river, whose bed it muddied, and whose banks it littered with industrial debris and vast slag heaps. Such is borne out by the artist John Piper who, visiting Middlesbrough at this time, painted the slag heaps, considering them to be the most impressive sight in the whole town. Glass summed up this complex situation with a quotation from Lady Bell in order to stress that the town was still a 'place in which every sense is violently assailed all day long by some manifestation of the making of metal'. In this sense she saw the town at mid-century as being stuck in the early 1900s.

Nevertheless she also saw such phenomena as assets, although not in terms of things rustic or antique. She considered that what the town lacked in diversity and tradition it made up in a vigorous kind of beauty based on its very bleakness and impetuosity. Thus battles had been fought there, and were still being fought against the hardships and dangers of work, against the running down of raw materials, and against the market hazards of the town's staple industries. Considering this daily mundane struggle, she saw the evidence of courage and success all around her. However, there was another side to the coin.

Rapid growth may have had its heroic side but the human cost could be too high. The expansion of the built-up area away from the river kept pace with the decay of the older town to the north. This northern extremity was confined by the river, the Ironmasters' District to the west, and the docks to the east. Expansion could only be southwards, and unfortunately this took the form of sprawl. Consequently strict social divisions, albeit of a limited breadth, emerged: northerners and southerners, poorer and better off, successes and failures. It was this stark juxtaposition of evident extremes within these local confines that gave Glass the key to the town's basic contemporary problem; and her analysis of this fact, accompanied by imaginative fieldwork, gave, in their turn, rise to far-reaching recommendations.

The manifestations of this crucial mid-century problem went something like this. The better-off families moved out of the older town, and the more prosperous the family the farther they moved. As a result the poor were left in their rows of tight little streets on either side of the railway track. This area of housing around the northern end of Linthorpe Road was built originally in the second half of the nineteenth century, and, given the sort of mobility just mentioned, or maybe the lack of it, it continued to deteriorate until by the end of the Second World War only wholesale reconstruction could provide a remedy. Meanwhile suburbia continued to expand, seemingly oblivious to this northern blight. One can see a novelist's attempt to come to terms with this sort of insensitivity in Orwell's *Keep the Aspidistra Flying*, written ten years earlier, when Gordon Comstock goads Ravelston into the broody contemplation: 'But what of the real poor? What of the unemployed in Middlesbrough, seven in a room on twenty-five bob a week? When there are people living like that, how dare one walk the world with pound notes and cheque-books in one's pocket?'

Similarly industry became polarized. It became dispersed, and, in places, obsolete. Such obsolescence followed the exhaustion of the Cleveland ironstone mines, the shift from iron to steel production, and the effects of the interwar depression. Whereas at the start of the twentieth century the Ironmasters' District was wholly intact, now, halfway through the century, there were derelict and gaping spaces between going concerns; such deformities were also to be seen in the dock area. Conversely new industry had been erected beyond the boundaries of the county borough. New steel plant appeared on both sides of the Tees down-river of the town, and, coming out of the needs of the First World War, a new basic industry emerged: the ICI works at Billingham, on the north bank of the river. Some small-scale clothing and service workshops were also established, but these were of far less significance.

Glass considered that this widespread dispersal of both housing and industry had divided Middlesbrough, and, in place of the former rigid and confined divisions of the town there was now a feeling of shapelessness. This really encompassed three things: the sharp spatial divisions between the poor and the better off, the vastly uneven provision of public amenities between these spatial divisions, and the lack of a central focal point to pull them together. We have noted that the town's industry could be said to possess a kind of vigorous beauty, its housing on the other hand had a kind of awful symmetry.

From north to south, really along the full length of Linthorpe Road, there were four distinct residential belts that stretched across the town in an east–west orientation. The very poor lived in the most northerly belt, being the unskilled from the steel works and the labourers from the docks. Only nine years ago Griselda Rowntree looked back at her early impressions of St Hilda's ward, this most northerly belt, from the time of the survey. She was one of the young assistants to Ruth Glass at the time, and recalls that the area 'seemed to be inhabited by life-worn pensioners, tired and bedraggled housewives and their swarming children. There were fly-blown shops at each street corner, many of them boarded up.'[1]

Next came the semi-skilled and artisans of mixed trades. Naturally their income and skills exceeded those extreme northerners, and they tended to be grouped in an area which moved southwards from Corporation Road to Southfield Road. The next group lived in an area that surrounded Albert Park. Here we are clearly moving up-market, but with serious qualifications. Many of these houses in this third belt had originally been occupied by prosperous nineteenth-century families and their servants. When this group made the inevitable move southwards, the vacated premises underwent radical changes in occupational densities, or sometimes their functions changed. Sub-division of the houses often occurred to be then used by several families or sometimes let as furnished lodgings. Functional changes came when the houses were converted into offices, club premises, or even accommodation for small businesses. Thus by mid-century this third belt comprised a wide range of social groups and functions. Not in fact dissimilar to the current situation.

The last wide belt that made up the southern limit of the town housed the middle classes. Here the range of Middlesbrough's social bands came, geographically and qualitatively, to an end: the upper classes had long since fled and taken to their distant manor houses where their lives were even farther removed from the town than their residences; where, if the Pease family evidence for the 1930s is at all typical, no doubt, in the words of Louis MacNeice's contemporary satirical verse, 'Bagpipe Music', 'their halls were lined with tiger rugs and their walls with heads of bison'.

These southern suburbs tended to be of interwar construction, and they catered for the town's minor executives, professionals and rich tradespeople. However, on either side of this area were municipal estates: Whinney Banks to the west and Grove Hill to the east. These local authority developments detracted from the clearcut socio-geographical distinctions that have so far been described.

If in this year of 1946 one were to have walked from north to south along (say) Linthorpe Road, there would have been apparent a succession of definite residential districts, showing clear individual physical and social characteristics. Comparative prosperity increased as one moved southwards, with the extremes at the two ends; that is, from slums to suburban villas. Glass herself saw this axis as a kind of melting-pot for those who had just left the slums, and those whose journey had taken them only partially southwards.

This discrete nature of the town's districts was made more acute by the uneven spread of amenity provision. The main public amenities were in the north; the breathing spaces were in the south. Northern amenities included the railway and bus stations, the major churches, the main shops, clubs, pubs, cinemas, theatres and restaurants. The town hall and general post office were similarly situated. These various institutions comprised for the most part the necessary urban equipment for the later nineteenth and early twentieth centuries. Not only were these facilities grouped at one end of the town but much of it was, by this mid-point in the century, outmoded. The south on the other hand was rich in space having little more than low density housing, some shops and a few schools.

Thus the mid-century town was split: the older town to the north of Albert Park and the modern town to the south. Yet by normal standards the old town was not really old: in his pioneer study of the Victorian city, Asa Briggs dubbed it the New Community. It had, however, aged before its time; it had grown old through excessive wear and tear. Designed for the most part as a working-class area, it was now crowded and ugly. Yet here also were the locations for work, trade, transport, administration and entertainment; here also was the warmth of the town in the enforced sociability of this northern population.

The modern town, as we have seen, presented the converse. Here was spaciousness but Glass also detected social barrenness: the main effect of this low density housing being to divide people; to give them private space and to create impediments to many social contacts. These suburbans had escaped from the dirt and noise of the older town, and were enjoying rural infiltrations. Many of their streets were pleasantly tree-lined, and their houses possessed gardens, yet apart from the necessary schools and a few usefully situated shops, they had few urban amenities. Their wards were frigid, shapeless and disjointed. In this sense they exhibited the negative suburban qualities that had been condemned by Lewis Mumford in his book *The Culture of Cities*, and were to be even more forcibly criticized in his later study *The City in History*. While remaining dependent on the old town they never fused with it; at this stage of their development they had not matured beyond their initial status as merely suburban.

Yet this lack of merger perplexed Glass. After all, demographic and urban growth had been very rapid and continuous. Suburbia seemed to be rather out of place in such a town. One is here reminded of the first academic judgement along such lines when sixty years earlier E.G. Ravenstein had classified the town alongside such industrial centres as St Helens, West Bromwich and West Ham. In his article, 'On the Laws of Migration', this researcher categorized all of these towns as being quite un-English in their heavy, masculine character. However, one can still ask why, by this mid-point in the century, this particular example of suburbia did not merge with the rest of the town. The answer remains the same: the strict social divisions that have already been noted, giving rise to a variety of incompatibilities.

As we have seen, the northern decay and the southern expansion were like two sides of the same coin, but the give-and-take between the two was almost entirely one-sided. The southerners had to frequent the old town in order to have access to a whole range of amenities while the open spaces of the south attracted few northerners; of those who did travel to suburbia it was simply to pass through en route to the Cleveland Hills or the nearby small towns or villages. The north gave but did not receive, thus the basic division was further widened.

While it might be thought that the two southern municipal estates at this time would facilitate greater north–south contacts, the reverse was true. Although all the southern districts were of low density housing, enough differences prevailed to maintain this north–south type of division: differences between suburbia proper and municipal houses and their tenants.

There were expected contacts between the municipal suburbans and the northerners for they were from the same family groups: some simply had moved while others had remained. There were social visits each way, but private suburbia continued to remain aloof. This aloofness formed a kind of wedge between the two municipal estates, and so the contact between the two was severely restricted, and the old town had to remain their common point of contact.

Even the private enclave experienced aspects of disjointedness. Apart from the evident predilection for privacy, these southerners were an incomplete class: many of their social equals, and almost all of their social superiors had moved much farther away. The kind of assurance that this remaining middle class could get from proximity with its captains of industry was not forthcoming: the owners of the town's industries and their upper-management had long been absentees.

This last example illustrated the need for an urban centre in order to pull the various parts together. Industry was no longer serving this function. It had become too large-scale, too impersonalized, and, following the interwar experience, too uncertain. The pursuits of the population had become more varied than earlier in the century with the onset of the new leisure outlets that were part of interwar modernity, and the enforced economic inactivity of that same period had turned people's minds in new directions. Middlesbrough was by now becoming an administrative and service area for the south Tees-side region, but the current institutions could not as yet challenge the might of industry; consequently the town lacked the necessary cohesive power to pull the disparate social parts together.

In other words, there was a central area that had been developed over ninety years and so contained most of the town's public amenities and, as such, constituted the main meeting point, but not the town's centre of gravity. All of the suburbans, private and municipal, had to make quite a long journey to get to this northern area, so consequently there was a movement of some central institutions, shops and services southwards in order to cater for a more effective demand than was normally found in the north. Thus a kind of T-shaped pattern evolved whereby the downward stroke, along Linthorpe Road, was diminishing the significance of the cross-stroke, the original central area.

As a result of this southwards pull, the central area had become part of the northern periphery. Its former status had gone, and its precarious situation added further to the town's imbalance. Glass nevertheless saw the town's ills as relatively minor ones: social and geographical segementation, and an unequal distribution of amenities. Her basic solutions were to recondition the old town, to diversify industry and so create a fuller complement of social classes, and to develop the too scarce social and cultural interests of the town, and so replace the monotony of the place with a better balance between work and leisure.

She characterized this point in the town's development by suggesting that although no longer a child, Middlesbrough had not yet caught up with its growth. Its incongruities derived from its adolescent character so the need was to facilitate its transition to adulthood. This would be achieved by joining together the disparate parts by better transportation: suburbia to the old town, and suburb to suburb; and by social engineering: the redevelopment of the blighted areas whereby the geographical and social balance of the town would be restored.

Alongside these changes there would have to be positive steps towards a more equitable distribution of public amenities. Such steps implied major changes at the centre; she suggested that this part of the town would either have to be enhanced or moved southwards. It is difficult to believe that Ruth Glass was serious when she suggested moving the centre. Years later, Lock himself emphasized the impracticality of such an idea. Really she was making the point that the centre would have to be re-equipped in many ways and so rendered appropriate for the second half of the twentieth century. Finally a real appreciation of the complementary functions of the suburban and the central would mark for the town the achievement of its maturity.

Let us return to the most basic inequality of the town at this time: the huge difference between north and south. Not that such conditions were peculiar to mid-twentieth-century Middlesbrough; many industrial centres exhibited such inequalities, especially before the pre-war slums clearance drives were resumed in the 1950s. But Middlesbrough did seem to be one of the worst cases; members of the Lock team had seen bad housing before but never so much in such a restricted area, and moreover where the contrasts with much better housing were so inescapably apparent.

Lock chose to highlight the plight of those living in the most northerly wards. He felt that his readers needed some convincing, and he concurrently made a case that blight removal warranted as much consideration as the rectification of blitz damage. He reminded his readers that the then current town planning Acts now recognized that blight was the chief problem of the average English industrial town. He clearly implied that blight on the scale shown by Middlesbrough ought to have equal claims on national finances as those of the many blitzed areas elsewhere in the country. In fact the 1944

Town and Country Planning Act excluded loan charges for a limited period in the case of blitz damage while blighted areas had to rely on the less generous terms laid down by earlier legislation.

He considered that almost all elements of the life of the town at this time showed some aspect of blight be they industry, transport, housing, education, public health, retail trading, sport, recreation or culture. Building decay was bad enough but the extreme inequality of standards was even worse. He compared the lot of that large minority, one third, of the population who were living in the blighted areas with the rest of the population who were better housed.

He explained that to inhabit the older part of the town was to experience inequality of standards no matter what area of life one otherwise attained. Of course if one had the means of upward mobility but chose not to travel along that Linthorpe Road conduit, then one was unusual but, that aside, Lock presented the worst scenario. To live there, he stressed, was to have one's personal resources taxed to the utmost.

You were deprived whether you lived in Cannon, Newport, St Hilda's or Vulcan wards. You returned home from work to a house with no bath. Most likely the house was not big enough to accommodate a bath, having little more ground area than a suburban outhouse. We have already seen the comparative number of people to the acre, and in terms of houses this meant that ten suburban houses occupied the space that was taken by fifty in the old town. While in the town as a whole 48 per cent of houses had baths, only 10 per cent were so lucky in the northern wards; even the higher Middlesbrough proportion compares badly with the national figure of 66 per cent at this time.

This lack of space was an all-pervasive circumstance. There were no gardens, hardly room in fact to get a pram indoors, and the only place to take it outside was on the street pavement. This third of the citizens enjoyed almost none of the town's open space. One thing always leads to another, and this problem of congestion led to problems of dirt, which, in their turn, gave rise to health problems. Five to nine times as much dust, soot and dirt fell there compared to the suburbs. In bulk terms this meant that the area received from 250 to 450 tons per square mile per annum. It went without saying that it was as difficult to keep oneself clean as to keep one's things clean, and, not surprisingly, the people of the area experienced twice the rate of infectious and chest diseases and infant mortality compared with their fellow citizens. These sorts of differences have a kind of Victorian ring about them, and in these respects the town at mid-century seems to have been about two generations behind many other parts of the country.

A more detailed look at this congestion can be had from a short article by Louise Morgan in *Good Housekeeping* which she wrote only two months after Lock submitted his masterplan to the council. In walking round this blighted third of Middlesbrough she saw entire families squatting on the pavements because there was nowhere else to go, and it was very difficult to manoeuvre chairs through the narrow front doors of their houses. One kitchen she saw measured only 3 feet by 2 feet 6 inches; even the housewife had trouble squeezing herself into the place and, as Morgan comments, the fitments were minimal and microscopic. In this particular house, she notes that the family of five fed, washed, and lived their domestic waking lives. Outside there was not a touch of green in the whole district, and even the long-distance view was blocked by gasometers.

This actual location can almost certainly be seen in a number of photographs that appear alongside the maps, sketches, tables and text of the published survey and plan. The most revealing of these photographs shows a sailor, apparently on leave, telling a friend that 'This part's no place to bring one's pals back to.'[2] Here also one sees the adults squatting on the pavement, the gasometer, and wartime evidence such as Victory V signs on the walls and a blast-proof shelter in the middle background. This publication, however, shows no interiors but some shocking examples can be seen in Peter Cook, *Remember . . . Middlesbrough: a Contemporary History* (n.d. *c.* 1980) published ironically at a time when the Lock plan would have reached final maturity.

Lock's solution to this most basic of the town's ills was twofold: first industrial, whereby industry was given appropriate locations, underwent achievable diversification, and was provided with the necessary transport links; then urban, whereby not only was blight to be removed but also the causes of blight such as the conflicts over land use. Thus he proposed to retain the industrial basis of the town in a newly appropriate form and, at the same time, to deal with those problems that Ruth Glass and her assistants had uncovered. This twin-track approach was to be tackled quickly and comprehensively; there was to be no more of those pre-war piecemeal approaches. He looked both backwards and forwards over a generation or so, and emphasized method rather than the ideal of great sweeping urban and industrial changes. He saw that the changes that had taken place from the end of the First World War until this mid-point of the century were no more than he was asking for down to 1975. For him it was simply a matter of planning, and here he echoes much contemporary thinking which had been influenced by the successful organization of the war effort.

A special issue of the *Architect's Journal* in August 1945 brings out the potential similarities of change on either side of this mid-century position. Three stages of housing change were proposed: by 1950, 4,700 new houses were to be provided, by 1960 this provision would reach 13,000 and by 1975, 19,700 would have been built. Lock saw his plan as realistic when compared with the 1,200 houses that had been constructed between 1920 and 1940.

No place to bring one's pals back to: a Middlesbrough interior in the mid-1950s (MCL)

Lock's plan was soon modified and considerably watered down. One is often struck by the wide difference between the insider view of the subsequent changes to the town and that of outsiders. In 1953 William Lillie, the then Borough Librarian, commemorated the centenary of incorporation in a history of the town. In his consideration of the seven years since the end of the war he remarked that the Corporation had built over 4,000 houses and that in the same time over 500 had been constructed by private builders. This was, he reflected, a notable achievement considering the restrictions in regard to materials and labour and the need for government approval. Nine years later, the Leeds historian, Eric Sigsworth, assessed Middlesbrough's slum clearance performance from the time of the Lock Plan until 1960. Of course, while Lillie was looking at new housing, Sigsworth was considering old housing. He noted, however, that by 1960 10,050 houses were to have been cleared under the plan when work would have been due to start on a further 12,150 demolitions. The whole was to be completed by 1975. The modified plan of 1951 had, however, decided that only 500 houses per annum were to be demolished between 1951 and 1956, when the annual rate would drop to 400, and Sigsworth showed how much the shortfall was compared with Lock's plan. However, the actual achievement was even worse. He noted that

184

between 1951 and 1956, only eighty-four houses were demolished, and from 1956 to the end of 1961 only a further 1,052 had gone. In reality, Lillie was highlighting continued suburban growth which was further exacerbating the inequitable situation outlined by Glass, while Sigsworth drew attention to the slow progress on the inner core problem stressed by Lock.

This kind of tension can be seen in so many of the published assessments of the town from the early 1920s to the present day. These irreconcilable approaches were very evident at mid-century and insiders missed no opportunity to right what they saw as past insults to the image of the town. Almost always there was a refutation of some comments made by Douglas Goldring in the mid-1920s when, during two weeks' stay in the town, he confessed to being still dazed and incredulous when he subsequently came to record his impression in his travel book *Gone Abroad*. It was probably his description of the living areas of central Middlesbrough as 'acres of pig-styes used for housing men and women' that most upset the feelings of the town's defenders. On the theme of dreadful beauty, which Glass was to echo twenty years later, Goldring said that apart from the awesome industrial pollution the only thing of beauty in the town was the Transporter Bridge. Even here he had the later support of Pevsner who, forty years later, said that without doubt this construction was the most impressive building in the town. More generally he added that the big-townish appearance of central Middlesbrough went only skin-deep, and that everywhere, looking out of the few main streets, were the interminable rows of two-storeyed cottages. Thus he concluded that outside the centre 'hardly anything called for a perambulation'. It is worth bearing in mind that these observations in the relevant *Buildings of England* series were made twenty years after the council had accepted the Max Lock plan.

Yet in many respects the interwar period had seen the creation of the modernity that, given the long hiccup of the war years, was responsible for so much of the pleasanter and lighter side of life that was being taken more and more for granted by the mid-century. One principal, almost essential, element of this mood is the fact of low density suburbia which, in the case of Middlesbrough, was almost entirely a product of these interwar years. However, even here, a few years before Lock and his colleagues came to the town, there were local criticisms.

Somewhat in the style of Clough Williams-Ellis, Marion Coates-Hansen, a long-standing Labour councillor, for instance, criticized the layout of the mid-thirties private housing estates. At a meeting of the Planning Committee on 18 December 1934 she drew attention to the similarity between the straight lines of the streets and those of New York. She complained that every design was almost the same, and so consequently there was a perpetuation of the same type of house. Yet the chairman defended the town's housing schemes and compared them favourably to those in any other part of the country. For him it

Dead monotony? Whinney Banks estate newly built in 1934 (MCL)

was the dead monotony of the Corporation estate which exhibited the sorts of characteristics of which Mrs Coates-Hansen spoke.

Two months later the Housing Committee debated the phenomenon of well-off tenants living on those municipal estates. One councillor cited instances of a Board of Trade official, a cinema manager, a bank clerk, school teachers, an insurance superintendent, excise officers, and others tenanting subsidized houses. The borough treasurer agreed that such tenants existed but showed that this situation was related to rental policy. He reminded the meeting that at one time the council had been very glad to obtain this sort of tenant, and no doubt would be glad of them again. If such tenants were to be excluded through a change of policy, then the cost would have to be borne by the committee: these particular tenants were occupying the most expensive of all the council houses.

The rental policy to which the treasurer referred had to follow government prescription for certain classes of house. The rents in this instance could not be afforded by the labouring classes. To change this, the council had fought unsuccessfully for rent reductions, and, had they prevailed, would have admitted low earners to these particular houses. Even so the treasurer had instructed the housing managers not to let houses to anyone with an income over £3 per week or, exceptionally, £3 10*s*. It was suggested in the committee that blastfurnacemen and steelworkers had been told that their earnings were above the wage limit for municipal houses, but it was affirmed that salaried people, such as the ones cited, were the only potential tenants capable of paying the rents of the particular houses that they were occupying.

In similar vein the chairman assured the committee that, following allegations of car ownership by municipal tenants, there were no longer any private cars on any of the municipal estates. Mrs Coates-Hansen added that salaried tenants ought to be paying the full economic rent, which prompted the treasurer to explain that the estates had been built under different housing Acts, and so concessions could be granted in some cases but not in others.

It can be seen from these brief exchanges that in spite of assertions of monotony, municipal, suburban residence was desirable, be the tenant salaried or low waged. The fact, however, that there were areas of well-paid council tenants somewhat detracts from the symmetry of Glass's analysis.

At the same time as these discussions on the architectural style of municipal estates or the wherewithal of their tenants were taking place, calls for planning and criticisms of non-planning came up periodically. For example, on 28 November 1934 Alderman Weatherhead suggested that a special meeting of the Planning Committee be called in order to formulate a policy on town planning. He described the current methods of building on the outskirts of the town as higgledy-piggledy.

This was in response to the committee's consideration of the large number of plans for housing development. The members had approved a scheme to build houses near Green Lane at prices ranging from £600 to £900. Such houses, not surprisingly at mid-thirties prices, were considered to conform better to the amenities of the neighbourhood than some earlier plans. Also sanctioned was a plan for an estate of eighty-six houses off Tollesby Road, and a plan for five houses and shops at the junction of Mandale Road and Acklam Road. Rejected, however, was a plan to utilize 20 acres of land off Acklam Road for the provision of 282 houses costing from £380 to £500. The withholding of approval was on account of the proposed density of 13.8 to the acre: the fixed maximum of the committee was twelve. Nevertheless, turned down also was a proposal to build 134 houses at a density of ten to the acre off Acklam Road. Here the committee's objection was taken on the grounds that the length of the proposed road contravened the existing byelaws.

Alderman Weatherhead feared that if the acceptances continued at their present rate then there would be nothing left of Middlesbrough to which anyone could apply a town plan. The chairman reminded the meeting that they were only newly formed, and that this particular committee had not yet had a real opportunity to get into its stride. He added the cliché that 'Rome was not built in a day', to which Mrs Coates-Hansen replied 'that all the same, Middlesbrough could be spoiled in six weeks'.[3]

Just over eight months later these same members were seen by the local evening press to be 'history makers'; this was in regard to town planning. That afternoon's meeting had resulted in the submission to the Ministry of Health of a zoned plan for the town. They saw this plan as the 'city beautiful' which was to arise to the south of the town. This new Middlesbrough was going to be a place of trees and pleasant lawns, wide roads and shady walks. Shops were to be erected only where they were zoned. All building was to be according to plan. The chairman, himself a builder, noted that this was the end of the higgledy-piggledy building.

He congratulated Geoffrey Knowles, the Planning Surveyor, on completing the job; and he thanked also those who had constituted his town planning committees, adding that the Middlesbrough of the future would become a veritable garden city. Knowles told reporters that the Quaker pioneers had given the town a splendid start with wide roads and fine streets, but that their ideas had not been adhered to so carefully. He considered that the modern city fathers were now seeing to it that the roads of the future should be similarly spacious. Moreover, unlike the original settlement, these modern roads would be tree-lined and provided with grass margins.

In spite of the surveyor's skating over the early history of Middlesbrough, and exaggerating current trends, the rhetoric and apparent popularity of planning is plain to see. In this case the final result was the provision of the wide suburban road that leads from the east of Linthorpe due southwards to Marton as well as the section of ring-road that goes from Acklam to just north of Marton. Nevertheless it is interesting to note that the language of town planning had been so acceptable in the town eight years before the appointment of Lock.

If the enjoyment of low density housing was a principal element of modernity, another was the collection of changes that came to the town centre, as happened in most centres, in this interwar period. Such changes could be as noticeable in Middlesbrough as in certain other provincial towns. For example, writing on modern Leeds, Michael Meadowcroft considered that in 1919 this 'city was on the brink of great changes in civic enterprise and social acceptance'.[4]

Often modernization was to be seen in enterprises such as offices, banks, shops, pubs, schools, hospitals and libraries, where sometimes the influences of the Modern Movement were flaunted alongside the more traditional styles such as classical or neo-Georgian. New enterprises also appeared, such as large branches of national or at least regional departmental stores, bus stations, dance halls and most pervasive, purpose-built cinemas. These latter were often as impressive in their architectural styles and interior arrangements as the films they showed. These modern developments were usually contained within new or greatly updated road systems such as ring-roads, wide radial roads, automatically controlled intersections, pedestrian safety measures, etc. These large-scale changes implied some demolitions which, in turn, often led to new building developments.

What was coming into being was a new phase of urban uniformity that constituted a further development of those aspects of sameness that Asa Briggs had noted. He saw the individuality of his Victorian cities being

The influence of Modernism in Middlesbrough: the Regent Cinema, Newport Road (MCL)

undermined by such factors as byelaw housing, tramway systems, the emergence of the motor car, chain stores and branded goods.

As we have seen, Lock gave special attention to that third of the Middlesbrough population who lived in the northern wards, and even here he saw a few compensations in their lives compared with those of southerners. Apart from the warm human contacts that he detected among the inhabitants of the older parts of town he saw other advantages that sprang from their central situation. These were mainly the shops: close at hand, around the corner, and plenty of them; and their proximity to the many cinemas within the town centre. He was writing of course at a time when cinema attendances reached their peak in that pre-TV age.

This aspect of Lock's observations, and those aspects of modern living which were anyway emerging in the town centre are illustrated by the two editions of *Middlesbrough: Pictorial & Industrial*, edited by a local fine art printer, Harold Hood, in 1926 and 1934. Through this revealing publication one can see some of the changes that were considered worthy of comment in the two decades prior to the Second World War. Hood's first edition was unashamedly a booster effort for the economic fortunes of the town and its general image: the editor in fact exhorts his fellow townsmen to buy copies as presents for friends and relatives in England

Shimmering streets at the entrance to a Kinema: The Elite Cinema in 1934 (MCL)

and abroad, and businessmen to present them to clients and customers. After a short introduction by Sir Hugh Bell, Hood presents his case for a re-evaluation of the town based on the visual evidence in the book. His assessments of the town's churches and cinemas are similar: a few well designed but most of them ugly. The majority of the cinemas he saw as little more than architectural accidents, and even in those that were acceptably designed, he found fault with their interiors, where 'no interest was shown in either appearance or ventilation'. This he put down to the apathy of management and the indifference of the audiences. He had praise, however, for the atmospherics of industrial pollution, and even for the effect of rain on pavement and buildings, where, he said, beauty was to be seen in the 'shimmering streets and the entrances to theatre or kinema'.[5] His photographs tended to be more conventional.

He showed docks, wharves, factories and works (inside and out), prominent buildings and some of their prestigious rooms, and some aerial views of main streets. Softer tones came from views of suburban Linthorpe with its late Victorian and Edwardian houses, and from views of the Cleveland Hills. Some leisure aspects came with a couple of purpose-built cinemas and some café interiors, yet apart from the cinemas, all of these could have illustrated a study of Victorian Middlesbrough.

However, some modernity came with the fifty or so advertisements for local firms and businesses. These presented a more contemporary feel with the thrust of their salesmanship and the boldness of their illustrations. Eight years later the book came out in a second edition, now published by the Corporation. This time Hood's introduction was cut down to a short apologia for the town followed by a long account of the town's progress in municipal housing and town planning. Whereas the first edition praised the individual efforts of the town's leading citizens, this time he condemned the unregulated developments of the private housing speculator, who, he said, should be brought under planning control for the general good.

This shift in emphasis was borne out by some of his photographs. Examples were included of the estates at Grove Hill and Whinney Banks (the districts

Softer tones: Claude Avenue, Linthorpe, part of the Phillipsville Estate (MCL)

that for Ruth Glass hemmed in the private suburbia of Middlesbrough's southwards drift). Examples also appeared of Constantine College (grandfather of the University of Teesside) and other contemporary additions such as the new Tees Bridge at Newport and the ICI works at Billingham. But unfortunately for the historian the shift in emphasis from the private to the municipal sponsor meant that no advertisements were carried in the later edition.

Such then was the appearance of the acceptable parts of the town in the immediate pre-war years. In spite of the booster values behind both editions of Hood's book, they graphically show the town that presented itself to Lock's team in 1945; that is, apart from the whole of the blighted area and war damage. Middlesbrough never suffered the intensive bombing that might have been expected because of its concentration of heavy industry. On the other hand, while the war brought the albeit slow and piecemeal process of modernization to a halt, it also brought full employment and a rise in living standards for many.

A hope for the future? Constantine College in 1934 (MCL)

Of major importance, too, was a new-found confidence in the town in the shaping of its own destiny. The immediate manifestation of this was the appointment of Max Lock, which revealed a determination to make a new and objective assessment of Middlesbrough's heritage and what was required to equip it for that brighter future which, it was believed, the post-war years would bring. As we have seen the Max Lock team presented a fuller and more substantial picture of the town than ever before. From this mass of evidence and its related material we can clearly see where Middlesbrough stood at mid-century, if not, as the team idealistically envisaged, date a new beginning for the town. Fifty years later it is indeed very different, but it is by no stretch of the imagination Lock's town.

NOTES

1. From an interview given at the Dorman Museum, Middlesbrough, 3 April 1987.
2. *Middlesbrough Survey and Plan*, p. 16.
3. *Northern Echo*, 19 December 1934.
4. M. Meadowcroft, 'The Years of Political Transition', in D. Fraser (ed.), *The History of Modern Leeds* (1980).
5. H. Hood, *Middlesbrough: Pictorial and Industrial* (1st edn, Middlesbrough, 1926), introduction, no pagination.

SOURCES AND FURTHER READING

1. The Growth of a New Community

There is a most valuable nineteenth-century account of Middlesbrough in H.G. Reid (ed.), *Middlesbrough and its Jubilee* (1881). See also for early accounts *Middlesbrough, its History, Environs and Trade* (1899) and T. Bulmer's *History, Topography and Directory of North Yorkshire*, Part I (1890). Lady Bell's *At the Works: A Study of a Manufacturing Town* (1907) is a classic description of what late-nineteenth- and early twentieth-century Middlesbrough was like. It should be compared with Ruth Glass's *The Social Background of a Plan, A Study of Middlesbrough* (1948).

In Middlesbrough Public Library there is a useful manuscript history of the town – the Tweddell manuscript. There is also a lively *Record of the Proceedings* at the opening of the town hall in 1889. The newspapers, however, provide the only account of most of the critical and interesting episodes in the life of the growing community.

The steel history and its economic vicissitudes are discussed in D.L. Burn, *An Economic History of Steelmaking* (1950).

Cowen, whose views on Middlesbrough and on Victorian cities in general have been quoted, is the subject of a book by E.M. Jones, *The Life and Speeches of Joseph Cowen, M.P.* (1885). Its motto is taken from Emerson – 'Eloquence is a Triumph of Pure Power'. Lowthian Bell's *Principles of the Manufacture of Iron and Steel* (1884) and his memorandum on 'The Iron Trade' which he offered to the Royal Commission on the Depression of Trade in 1886 are important documents.

Mr D.C. Hearn has collected much valuable material relating to Middlesbrough's ironmasters and their social and political affiliations which he hopes to be able to put together in published form.

It is interesting to compare Barrow-in-Furness and Middlesbrough. See S. Pollard, 'Town Planning in the Nineteenth Century: The Beginnings of Modern Barrow-in-Furness' in the *Transactions of the Lancashire and Cheshire Antiquarian Society* (1952–3); J.D. Marshall, *Barrow-in-Furness* (1959); and F. Barnes, *Barrow-in-Furness and District* (1957). See also P.H. White, 'Some Aspects of Urban Development by Colliery Companies' in the *Manchester School* (1953).

2. 'Jacky' and the Jubilee

Local and national newspapers provide the most interesting and detailed evidence of the Middlesbrough Jubilee. At the local level, there are three principal papers which each provide a distinctive angle on the event. The *North-Eastern Daily Gazette* contains the most information, particularly in its coverage of the planning process. However, it needs to be remembered that Hugh Gilzean Reid was its proprietor, and this paper therefore tends to offer the 'official' version of things. Another Middlesbrough paper, the *Daily Exchange*, is also very comprehensive in its coverage, but acts as an important corrective to the *Gazette*. There were two levels to their rivalry; they competed for readers in a circulation battle, but also locked horns over politics, with the *Gazette* offering a Liberal line and the *Exchange* a Tory one. The third local paper, the *Northern Echo*, was a Darlington-based newspaper, Liberal in its sympathies, but sufficiently detached from the internal politics of Middlesbrough to provide a more objective viewpoint; its coverage of the event is very full indeed, and is particularly strong in its handling of the historical record. Other local papers such as the *Stockton Journal* and *Darlington and Stockton Times* contain much less material, but none the less carry some useful nuggets. At the national level, the *Illustrated London News* and *The Graphic* are particularly valuable for their visual evidence, but also have accompanying text. *The Times* and *The Pall Mall Gazette* also cover the Middlesbrough Jubilee in their editorials.

Several local publications from this period are also valuable. William Hall Burnett's *Cleveland Worthies* (1886) and John S. Jeans' *Pioneers of the Cleveland Iron Trade* (1875) are two good examples of the 'Smilesean' genre; Jeans' coverage of the 'Stockton and Darlington Railway' Jubilee – *Jubilee Memorial of the Railway System – A History of the Stockton and Darlington Railway* (1875) – is also worth consulting. Reid's own published record of the Jubilee, *Middlesbrough and its Jubilee* (1881), contains edited versions of most of the articles and editorials from the *Gazette*, but is worth looking at in its own right as a conscious attempt to present a more permanent historical record. Other local histories from the period include William Fallows' *A History of Old Middlesbrough* (1861) which, as its title suggests, deals almost exclusively with the pre-industrial settlement and John Walker Ord's *History and Antiquities of Cleveland* (1846) which combines historical record and contemporary comment, setting early Middlesbrough in a wider Cleveland context. J.C. Atkinson's *The History of Cleveland* (1874) is a more scholarly historical record of the area, but is less lively and interesting in its treatment of the contemporary scene. Landor Praed's *History of the Rise and Progress of Middlesbrough* (1863) is one of the earliest attempts to construct an historical record of the new industrial community, and while it jumbles its material in a very confusing and fragmentary fashion, it none the less contains some interesting primary source material. Isaac Lowthian Bell's *Notes of a Visit to Coal and Ironmines and Ironworks in the United States* (1875) may not sound very relevant but contains some fascinating comparisons between the Cleveland iron trade and its rivals in the USA, besides providing an interesting insight into local responses to emerging competition abroad.

The early history of Middlesbrough is covered in several more recent studies. A useful overview can be gained from I. Bullock's 'The Origins of Economic Growth on Teesside, 1851–81', *Northern History*, 9 (1974), 79–95. The politics of the new town are described in D.W. Hadfield's, 'Political and Social Attitudes in Middlesbrough, 1853–1889, with Special Reference to the Role of the Middlesbrough Ironmasters' (unpublished PhD thesis, Teesside Polytechnic, 1981). Derek Harding's recent study of Hugh Gilzean Reid, 'Sir Hugh Gilzean Reid and the Daily Gazette' in *Cleveland History*, 64 (1994) provides a valuable insight into one of the town's early leaders, and is just one of many articles relating to various aspects of Middlesbrough's history which appear in different numbers of this local history journal (previously called *The Cleveland and Teesside Local History Society Bulletin*). The best study of the industrial history of the iron and steel industry can be found in C. Hempstead (ed.), *Cleveland Iron and Steel: Background and Nineteenth Century History* (British Steel Corporation, 1979). G.A. North's *Teesside's Economic Heritage* (Cleveland County Council, 1975) is also a useful source for the wider industrial and commercial picture. A much earlier work, W.W. Tomlinson's *North-Eastern Railway* (1915) contains substantial sections on Middlesbrough and Cleveland, and manages to marry a wealth of evidence with some very sharp accompanying analysis. William Lillie's *The History of Middlesbrough* (1953) is a mine of information, but offers little in the way of critical interpretation. Similarly, R. Gott's, *Henry Bolckow: Founder of Teesside* (1968) pulls together some interesting material on one of Middlesbrough's 'founding fathers', but adopts a rather 'official' line in its uncritical assessment of the man. Norman Moorsom has been the most prolific of recent local historians, producing a number of general accounts, all of them very accessible to the general reader; they include *The Birth and Growth of Modern Middlesbrough* (1967); *The Stockton and Darlington Railway – the Foundation of Middlesbrough* (1975); *The Book of*

Middlesbrough (1986). A more specialized work is his *Middlesbrough's Jubilee and Centenary* (1978) which provides a chronological listing of the newspaper references relating to the planning of the 1881 Jubilee.

A number of published studies set Middlesbrough in its regional and national context. At the regional level there is Norman McCord's *North East England: The Region's Development, 1760–1960* (1979) and David Rowe's recent essay in Volume One of F.M.L. Thompson's *The Cambridge Social History of Britain, 1750–1950* (1990). At the national level, of course, there is Asa Brigg's pioneering essay, 'Middlesbrough: the Growth of a New Community' (above ch. 1), which might be augmented by H.J. Dyos and M. Wolff (eds.), *The Victorian City: Images and Reality*, Vols. 1 & 2 (1973) and the more recent volume edited by R.J. Morris and R. Rodger, *The Victorian City: A Reader in British Urban History, 1820–1914* (1993). Indeed, the latter not only compares Middlesbrough's growth with other Victorian urban centres, but also includes an introductory essay which sets Briggs's work in its historiographical context, showing how an appreciation of the Victorian city by both historians and planners was very much influenced by his lead.

3. The Infant Hercules and the Augean Stables

Despite the spectacular history of the town, there is very little readily accessible literature available on its economic and social history. Asa Briggs, 'Middlesbrough' is the essential starting point. North, *Teesside's Economic Heritage*, provides a general survey of economic change in the region while Hempstead, ed., *Cleveland Iron and Steel* is a valuable collection of essays which contains some fascinating detail on technological developments. Other aspects of the town's economic history are less well served. There is a short article on the development of Hinton's before the First World War, D. Taylor, 'The Jamaican Banana: or how to be a successful businessman in nineteenth century Middlesbrough', *Bulletin of the Cleveland and Teesside Local History Society* (1982) based largely on papers in the possession of the author. See also above pp. 00.

In writing on the social history of the town I am greatly indebted to a variety of historians whose hard work in researching the question of working-class living standards underpins much of what I have written. The following deserve particular mention. For the late nineteenth and early twentieth centuries, A.A. Hall, 'Working-Class Living Standards in Middlesbrough and Teesside, 1879–1914', unpublished PhD thesis, Teesside Polytechnic, 1979 (the main argument is summarized in A.A. Hall, 'Wages, Earnings and Real Earnings in Teesside: a reassessment of the ameliorist interpretation of living standards in Britain, 1870–1914', *International Review of Social History*, 26, 1981), and for the interwar years, K. Nicholas, *The Social Effects of Unemployment on Teesside, 1919–39* (Manchester, 1986). There is a wealth of material, deposited in the Cleveland County Archive, in such sources as the Ranger Report and the annual reports of the Medical Officer of Health that has yet to be fully utilized.

4. The Frontier Revisited

Friendly societies continue to be strangely neglected by historians, the only detailed regional studies being D.R.J. Neave, 'Friendly Societies in the Rural East Riding, 1830–1912', unpublished PhD thesis, University of Hull, 1985, and J.J. Turner, 'Friendly Societies in South Durham and North Yorkshire, *c.* 1790–1914' (unpublished PhD thesis, University of Teesside, 1992). The standard textbooks on society history remain those by P.H.J.H. Gosden, *The Friendly Societies in England 1815–75* (1961) and *Self-Help: Voluntary Associations in Nineteenth-Century Britain* (1973). An important earlier contribution is W.H. Beveridge, *Voluntary Action* (1948).

For contemporary sources the reader should consult the *Annual Reports of the Registrar of Friendly Societies* (from 1855), published as bound British Parliamentary Papers, and M. Baernreither, *English Associations of Working Men* (1889).

Records of societies in Middlesbrough and the Teesside area can be found at Cleveland County Archives Department in Middlesbrough and (rules and membership returns of registered societies) at the Public Record Office in Kew. The Robert Wood Collection at the Gray Art Gallery and Museum in Hartlepool contains a large collection of printed rule books for local clubs in the region. The only surviving source for the activities of (most) small local societies – especially annual clubs – are local newspapers. The printed records and society histories of the large Affiliated Orders like the Oddfellows (Manchester Unity) and the Ancient Order of Foresters (Southampton) contain much local material.

5. The Evolution of a Political Culture

The main works, several already cited in preceding chapters, are as follows:

Briggs, A., 'Middlesbrough'

Cass, S.J., 'Labour in Middlesbrough, 1900–1914' (unpublished MA dissertation, Teesside Polytechnic, 1982)

Chase, M., 'The Implantation of Working-Class Organisation on Teesside, 1830–1874', *Het Tijdschrift voor Sociale Geschiedenis*, 18, No. 2/3 (July 1992); 'Chartism, 1838–1858: Responses in Two Teesside Towns', *Northern History*, 24, (1988); 'Dangerous People? The Teesside Irish in the 19th Century', *North East Labour History Bulletin*, 28 (1994)

Gott, R., *Henry Bolckow, Founder of Teesside* (Middlesbrough, 1968)

Hadfield, D.W., 'Political and Social Attitudes in Middlesbrough'

Harding, D., 'Sir Hugh Gilzean Reid and the *Daily Gazette*'

Lillie, W., *History of Middlesbrough*

Nicholson, T., 'A Few Choice Spirits', *Working Class Radicals in Cleveland, 1870–75* (Teesside Paper in North-Eastern History, No. 3, 1993)

Pugh, A., *Men of Steel, By One of Them* (1951)

Purdue, A., 'George Lansbury and the Middlesbrough Election of 1906', *International Review of Social History*, 18, Part Three (1973)

Reid, H.G., *Middlesbrough and its Jubilee*

Saville, J. & Bellamy, J. (eds.), *Dictionary of Labour Biography*, vol III (John Kane), vol IV (Alfred Edwards) and vol IX (Alice Schofield-Coates)

Shippey, M., 'Women in Cleveland Politics, c. 1894–1919' (unpublished MA thesis, Teesside Polytechnic, 1990)

Tomlin, D.M. & Williams, M., *Who Was Who in 19th Century Cleveland* (Redcar, 1987)

Ward, D. & Lewis, R., 'Culture, Politics and Assimilation; The Welsh on Teesside, c. 1850–1940', *Welsh History Review*, 17 (December, 1995)

6. Leisure and Sport

Middlesbrough's industrial history has been of such interest to historians that its leisure has received scant coverage, and the quality of the available published material is variable. Much writing produced locally has lacked the broader insights that an awareness of the national pattern would bring. In writing this chapter the author has therefore had to draw heavily on local newspapers, the use of which is both arduous and time consuming. Of Middlesbrough Central Reference Library's collection, the *North-Eastern Daily Gazette* is perhaps the most useful in that it provided general coverage of sport and other leisure for almost the entire period. Other newspapers found useful for the earlier period included the *Middlesbrough Weekly News and Cleveland Advertiser*, and the *Middlesbrough Daily Exchange*. The *Northern Review*, covering the period from 1886 to 1894 was useful for sport and entertainment. Lady Bell's *At the Works* reflects an upper-class understanding of how working-class employees at her husband's Port Clarence works spent their money on leisure pursuits. Her analysis of the importance of betting is particularly interesting.

Among secondary works the following have proved useful:

Baker, R., *A History of Middlesbrough Cricket Club, vol 1, 1855–1911* (Middlesbrough, 1989)

Lillie, W., *History of Middlesbrough* provides an overview of leisure and sport

Marshall, K., *Middlesbrough's Good Old Days; The Music Hall Theatres* (Redcar, 1988)

Moorsom, N., 'The Demon Drink and Social Attitudes in Mid Victorian Middlesbrough' (unpublished MA thesis, Teesside Polytechnic, 1985)

Saunders, J.W., *Cinema in Middlesbrough* (Middlesbrough 1991)

Taylor, D. *'A Well-Chosen, Effective Body of Men': the Middlesbrough Police Force, 1841–1914* (Teesside Paper in North-Eastern History, No. 6, 1995) discusses the control of public behaviour

Woodhouse, R., *Celebrations; The Empire Theatre Middlesbrough, 1897–1987* (Middlesbrough 1987).

Cleveland History, formerly *The Cleveland and Teesside Historical Society Bulletin*, reflects the growing interest in leisure studies over the last thirty years. Articles include R. Humphreys, 'Spending Leisure Time on Teesside in the Mid-Nineteenth Century', *Bulletin*, 24; S. Metcalf, 'Albert Park; A Place for the Recreation of the People', *Bulletin*, 38; D.W. Pattenden, 'Horticulture in Mid-Nineteenth Century Middlesbrough', *Bulletin*, 40; W.B. Saunders, 'The Golden Age of Continuing Education in Middlesbrough', *Bulletin*, 45; J.J. Turner, 'The People's Winter Gardens in Middlesbrough', *Bulletin, 46;* J.J. Turner, 'The Growth and Development of Friendly Societies in Cleveland and Teesside, 1835–1914', *Bulletin,* 48; R. Baker, 'The Formative Years of Middlesbrough Cricket Club', *Bulletin,* 54; R. Goodall, 'Cycling Clubs of North Yorkshire and South Durham 1876–1914', *Bulletin,* 57; T. Coxon, 'Music Hall Posters', *Bulletin*, 65.

7. Housing the Community

The attraction of research for the history of housing and town development must lie in the use it makes of such a wide range of source material. Historical evidence can be found in national and municipal legislation and records, in newspapers and journals, in contemporary comment, in private and public maps and plans, in photographs and paintings, in diaries and letters, in architects' and builders' records, in advertisements and, last but not least, in the remnants on the ground. The fascination is in tracking them all down and placing seemingly disparate documents side by side to re-create the larger picture. Middlesbrough is very well served with a number of archival collections and the following are a selection of those used for this study:

plans deposited for Planning Consent from 1855

records of the Engineers Department: plans and maps, private and municipal

records of the Clerks Department: local legislation, building byelaws, Improvement and Extension Acts

local municipal papers: council minutes and miscellaneous publications

national legislation: e.g. Housing and Town Planning Act

photographs

OS maps from 1853

newspapers and journals, local and national and also ephemera like promotional leaflet for Housing Conference.

Contemporary local commentary like that of Florence Bell in *At the Works* and reportage like Harold Hood's *Middlesbrough: Pictorial and Industrial* (1926) can also be very useful.

More general reading for the history of housing includes:

Helena Barrett & John Phillips, *Suburban Style, The British Home 1840–1960* (1987)

Colin & Rose Bell, *City Fathers, The Early History of Town Planning in Britain* (1969)

John Burnett, *A Social History of Housing, 1815–1985* (1986)

J.H. Harvey, *Sources for the History of Houses* (1974)

Helen Long, *The Edwardian House: the Middle Class House in Britain 1880–1914* (Manchester, 1993)

Stefan Muthesius, *The English Terraced House* (New Haven, 1982)

8. Mid-Twentieth-Century Middlesbrough

There are copies of the *Middlesbrough Survey and Plan* in Middlesbrough Reference Library along with supplementary studies such as Ruth Glass, *The Social Background of a Plan* (1948) and Denis Chapman, *A Social Survey of Middlesbrough* (1945). There are also council minutes and appropriate press coverage of the events dealt with in this chapter. The Economic Development and Property Department, Middlesbrough Borough Council should hold material related to the three-day visit paid by Lock and other members of the team to Middlesbrough in 1987. Details of the event can be found in Derek Gunby, *Planning History Bulletin*, 9, 2 (1987). A number of relevant undergraduate and postgraduate dissertations can be consulted in the University of Teesside Library.

Some idea of the range of material relating to the *Survey and Plan* can be had from J.W. Leonard, 'A People's Plan', in P. Swan and D. Foster (eds.), *Essays in Regional and Local History* (1992). For the subsequent fate of the plan see Valerie Cunningham, 'Middlesbrough's Housing Plans and Achievements, 1945–51' (unpublished BA dissertation, Teesside Polytechnic, 1983) and David Walsh, 'Planning for Peace: the Middlesbrough Experience' (unpublished BA dissertation, Teesside Polytechnic, 1987). The optimistic, 'insider' view of later developments is to be found in W. Lillie, *Middlesbrough*; the pessimistic 'outsider' in E. Sigsworth, 'Homes Unfit for Heroes', *Yorkshire Post*, 5 July 1962.

The negligible impact of bombing during the Second World War is explored by Alan Robinson and Tony Scott in *Middlesbrough at War: the Home Front* (1985) and Geoff Bailey, 'Preparing for the Blitz' (unpublished MA thesis, Teesside Polytechnic, 1987).

House and Fullerton, *Teesside at Mid-Century* (1965) and North, *Economic Heritage*, provide full statistical details. Both of these works place Middlesbrough in a Teesside context; a trend increasingly common from the early part of the century culminating in the formation of the short-lived Teesside County Borough in 1968.

INDEX

Numbers in *italic* denote illustrations

INDEX